EDITIONS SR

Volume 21

The Call of Conscience

French Protestant Responses to the Algerian War, 1954-1962

Geoffrey Adams

Published for the Canadian Corporation for Studies in Religion / Corporation Canadienne des Sciences Religieuses by Wilfrid Laurier University Press

1998

This book has been published with the help of a grant from the Humanities and Social Sciences Federation of Canada, using funds provided by the Social Sciences and Humanities Research Council of Canada.

We acknowledge the financial support of the Government of Canada through the Book Publishing Industry Development Program for our publishing activities.

Canadian Cataloguing in Publication Data

Adams, Geoffrey, 1926-
   The call of conscience : French Protestant responses to the Algerian War, 1954-1962

(Editions SR ; 21)
Includes bibliographical references and index.
ISBN 0-88920-299-0

1. Protestants – France – Attitudes – History – 20th century. 2. Algeria – History – Revolution, 1954-1962 – Foreign public opinion. 3. Public opinion – France – History – 20th century. I. Canadian Corporation for Studies in Religion. II. Title. III. Series.

DT295.A55 1998   965'.046'0882044   C98-930428-0

© 1998 Canadian Corporation for Studies in Religion /
Corporation Canadienne des Sciences Religieuses

Cover design by Leslie Macredie using a photograph of
Maurice Causse, champion of Christian-Muslim fraternity
(Courtesy of Maurice Causse)

Printed in Canada

The Call of Conscience: French Protestant Responses to the Algerian War, 1954-1962 has been produced from a manuscript supplied in camera-ready form by the author.

Order from:
WILFRID LAURIER UNIVERSITY PRESS
Waterloo, Ontario, Canada   N2L 3C5

Lorsque l'on combat tout à la fois contre un peuple entier, et contre sa propre conscience, on ne peut pas gagner. . . .

– André Philip, *Le socialisme trahi* (1957)

Quand l'État démoralise la Nation, c'est dans la conscience des citoyens que s'est refugié la légalité.

– Paul Ricoeur, testifying at the trial of Pastor Etienne Mathiot (March 1958)

For Jack
and for all those who worked
for peace and reconciliation
during the Algerian War

CONTENTS

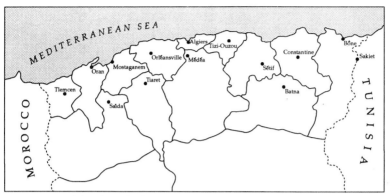

Algeria, with its administrative divisions (1962)

The Reformed Church in Algeria (1954)

KEY

■ C.I.M.A.D.E. Foyers
○ Distribution Centres

Source: Base map by Andre Lemiere, 1994.

CIMADE in Algeria
(Courtesy of André Lemière, Paris)

CHRONOLOGY OF EVENTS

1830
5 July   French capture of Algiers

1839   First Reformed Church in Algeria

1841-47   Marshal Bugeaud establishes French control of
                          Algeria

1848   Algeria, divided into three departments, becomes an
                          integral part of the second French Republic

1852-70   Napoleon III attempts to recognize the special
                          identity of Algeria; creation of the *Bureaux arabes*

1870
4 October   Algeria's settler minority gains representation in the
                          National Assembly in Paris; the territory gets its first
                          governor-general

1898   Algeria awarded its own legislative assembly, the
                          Délégations financières

1914-18   Algerians, subject to recruitment by lot in the French
                          army since 1912, serve during World War I

1919
4 February   Special status (with voting rights) for 5,000 Algerian
                          Muslims

1930   Colonial Exposition in Paris celebrates 100 years of
                          French presence in Algeria

1936   Blum-Viollette reforms fail to pass National
                          Assembly

1942
November   Allied landings in Algeria

1943
February   *Manifeste du peuple algérien* of Ferhat Abbas

1945
8 May   Sétif insurrection and repression

1946   *Union Démocratique du Manifeste Algérien*
                            (UDMA) of Ferhat Abbas; *Mouvement pour le*
                            Triomphe des Libertés Démocratiques of Messali
                            Hadj

1947
September   *Statut de l'Algérie*; *Délégations financières*
                            transformed into *Assemblée algérienne* based on
                            European and Muslim electoral colleges
1954
March   Creation of the *Comité Révolutionnaire pour l'Unité*
                            et l'Action (CRUA)
October   Creation of the *Front de Libération Nationale* (FLN)
                            and of the *Armée de Libération Nationale* (ALN)
1 November   Beginning of the insurrection

1955
25 January   Soustelle named governor-general of Algeria
5 February   Fall of the Mendès France government
25 February   Edgar Faure becomes premier
2 April   National Assembly votes state of emergency in
                            Algeria
20 August   Massacres of Europeans in the Constantine region
12 December   Elections in Algeria postponed

1956
2 January   Triumph of the *Front Républicain* in French
                            elections
1 February   Guy Mollet becomes premier
6 February   Mollet's disastrous visit to Algiers
9 February   Robert Lacoste named governor-general of Algeria
12 March   National Assembly votes special powers to deal with
                            Algerian situation
11 April   Call-up of French reservists
12 April   Dissolution of the Algerian Assembly

20 August	FLN resolves to pursue battle until independence won
22 October	French forces intercept plane carrying four key leaders of the FLN, including Ben Bella
November	Suez expedition and its abortion
15 November	Salan made commander-in-chief Algeria

1957

7 January	Massu given plenipotentiary police power in Algiers
February	Visit of Tania Metzel to Algeria
21 May	Fall of the Mollet government
June	Publication of André Philip's *Le socialisme trahi*
June-October	Battle of Algiers
11 June	Abduction and disappearance of teaching assistant Maurice Audin
12 June	Arrest and torture of leftist Henri Alleg
July	Trial of Maurice Causse for harbouring Chafika Meslem
5 November	Felix Gaillard becomes premier
December	Arrest of Pastor Etienne Mathiot for helping Si Ali escape across Swiss border

1958

31 January	Adoption of the *loi-cadre* defining "Algerian personality"
8 February	French bombardment of Sakhiet
27 March	Seizure of Henri Alleg's *La Question*
15 April	Fall of the Gaillard government
13 May	Insurrection of settlers and army men in Algiers. Formation of Committee of Public Safety to maintain French Algeria
14 May	Pierre Pflimlin voted in as premier
16 May	Muslim-European fraternization in Algiers
1 June	De Gaulle receives parliamentary mandate as premier
2 June	De Gaulle gets plenipotentiary power to deal with Algerian crisis
4-7 June	De Gaulle visits Algeria
19 September	Proclamation of Provisional Government of the Algerian Republic presided over by Ferhat Abbas
28 September	Referendum on constitution of Fifth Republic
3 October	De Gaulle announces Constantine Plan

23 October	De Gaulle proposes the "paix des braves"
23-30 October	Elections to National Assembly
10 December	Paul Delouvrier replaces Salan as Delegate General in Algeria

1959

April	Michel Rocard report on Algerian resettlement camps
16 September	De Gaulle endorses self-determination of Algeria
October	Jacques Beaumont submits report on resettlement camps to Boegner
December	Premier Debré opens first Algerian pipe-line

1960

24 January-1 February	Barricade Week in Algiers
5 February	Soustelle resigns from the ministry
3-5 March	De Gaulle visits mess-halls in Algeria, refers to "Algérie algérienne"
25-29 June	Abortive French-Algerian discussions at Melun
5 September	Publication of the *Manifeste des 121*
6 September-1 October	Trial of Jeanson network in Paris
27 October	Peace demonstrations in French cities
4 November	De Gaulle evokes possibility of an "Algerian Republic"
22 November	Louis Joxe put in charge of Algerian Affairs
9-13 December	De Gaulle visits Algeria. Muslim crowds demonstrate support for FLN; violent settler demonstrations.

1961

8 January	French voters approve self-determination for Algeria in referendum
30 March	French government and GPRA announce negotiations will begin at Evian 7 April
22-25 April	The Generals' Putsch
20 May	Negotiations begin at Evian. French army declares one month truce
13 June	Evian discussions suspended
10-28 July	Peace talks at Lugrin

27 August	Ben Youssef-Ben Khedda replaces Ferhat Abbas as president GPRA
17-18 October	Algerian demonstrations in Paris severely repressed
2 November	Hunger strike by Algerian prisoners in France

1962

11-18 February	French and GPRA delegates meet at Les Rousses
5 March	Second Evian conference opens
18 March	Evian accords signed
19 March	Cease-fire in Algeria
27 March	Provisional Government formed under Farès
8 April	French referendum on Evian accords
20 April	Salan, head of the OAS, arrested in Algiers
1 July	Algerian people choose independence
3 July	De Gaulle recognizes Algerian independence

ABBREVIATIONS

CIMADE	Comité Inter-Mouvements d'Entraide auprès des Evacués et Déportés
CN	*Cité nouvelle*
CPED	Centre Protestant d'Etudes et de Documentation
ERF	Eglise Réformée de France
FLN	Front de Libération Nationale
FPF	Fédération Protestante de France
GPRA	Gouvernement Provisoire de la République Algérienne
JOC	*Journal officiel de la République Française. Débats.* Assemblée nationale.
LAP	*L'Algérie protestante*
OAS	Organisation Armée Secrète
OURS	Office Universitaire de Recherche Socialiste
PSU	Parti Socialiste Unifié
RCS	*Revue du Christianisme social*
REF	*Réforme*
SEM	*Le Semeur*
SFIO	Section Française de l'Internationale Ouvrière
TFJ	*Tant qu'il fait jour*

ACKNOWLEDGEMENTS

A generation after it ended, the Algerian war (1954-62) has produced a substantial body of writing, some of it polemical, some of it journalistic, much of it sober and reflective.[1] The present work explores the responses to the war by members of the French Protestant community on both sides of the Mediterranean.

Research for this study was based in part on an examination of the existing literature, including primary sources such as newspapers, parliamentary records and memoirs. Much additional information was gleaned from conversations as well as correspondence with individual Protestants who had been actively engaged in the conflict. Many of these men and women opposed the war and the government which sanctioned it as well as the military men who directed it. Some of them openly supported those working for the liberation of Algeria from French control. A few championed the cause of French Algeria till the end.

The writer is in great debt to those Protestants on both sides of the conflict who agreed to discuss their role in the Algerian drama. Their hospitality, their courtesy and patience in responding to an outsider's battery of questions about what was always a painful experience and at times had all the grim tension of an undeclared civil war, and their candour in revealing what had often been kept private for thirty-odd years, are deeply appreciated. Whatever the intrinsic merits of the text that follows, it is surely enriched by their testimony.

Professor André Encrevé, a leading authority on modern French history, offered invaluable counsel early on in this research project, providing a helpful list of persons to contact and warning against a number of pitfalls which the writer hopes to have avoided. Pastor Michel Leplay, editor of the Protestant weekly *Réforme*, suggested a series of highly productive leads and, with the utmost tact, expressed reservations about a number of the author's original assumptions. Mme Cane and her colleagues at the *Centre Protestant d'Études et de Documentation* extended a generous welcome and unearthed a treasure of unprinted and printed material. Frédéric Cépède of the *Office Universitaire de Recherche Socialiste* introduced the writer to the rich resources of the Office's library and pointed to critical materials dealing with the internal battles over Algeria within Socialist ranks. Michel Rocard gave generous access to unpublished texts which he had produced during these intra-party debates.

Mlle Madeleine Barot, co-founder of the *Comité Inter-Mouvements d'Entraide auprès des Deportés et Réfugiés* responded generously to a Canadian professor's interest in exploring the role played by CIMADE during the war and opened doors which would otherwise have remained closed.

Fortunately for the writer, André Lemière was putting his archivist's skills to work on the immense documentary resources of CIMADE just as this research was getting under way. His generosity in undertaking a preliminary editing of papers dealing with Algeria helped sharpen the focus of this study.

Pastor Jacques Beaumont, secretary-general of CIMADE during the Algerian crisis, now living in New York, agreed to two lengthy interviews during which he responded to a variety of questions with patience and good humour while offering a reflective vision of the work of the Protestant relief organization.

Jean Carbonare, one of Beaumont's key lieutenants during the war, was all too modest in discussing his work for peace and reconciliation and his efforts to maintain a personal link with the new Algeria after the war. Mlle Mireille Desrez talked with passionate enthusiasm about her struggle as a CIMADE team-worker to improve the physical and psychological conditions of Muslim women and children whose lives were violently disrupted by the war.

Professor Bernard Picinbono of the University of Paris-Orsay, scion of a prominent settler family, recounted his conversion from support for the European minority to the espousal of peace and economic development in an independent Algeria. Professor Bernard Roussel of the Sorbonne recalled the extraordinarily difficult responsibilities he assumed as a young Reformed pastor in Algeria during the last years of the war. Doctors Patrick and Monique Schlötterer, who lived out much of their youth in Algeria in the midst of the conflict, talked with a mixture of nostalgia and bitterness about lost opportunities for French-Algerian and Muslim-Christian amity.

Maurice Causse, an uncompromising champion of open dialogue between Protestants and Muslims, agreed to enter into what became (for the writer at least) a richly rewarding correspondence, followed by lengthy conversations in France about his experience as a Christian activist during the Battle of Algiers. Thanks to Professor Causse, the author was introduced to the family of his friend François Hauchecorne, now deceased, who was chief librarian at the *Bibliothèque Nationale* in Algiers during the war years. Bertrand and Sylvie Hauchecorne offered the hospitality of their villa near Orléans to the author, including privileged access to their father's papers.

Pastor Jacques Maury, president of CIMADE, offered his candid personal reflections on the moral dilemma facing Protestants during the war when he was secretary-general of the leading Protestant university student organization. Pastor Tania Metzel recalled the anguish she felt as a chaplain during three visits to Algeria during the conflict. Pastor Pierre Cochet of Passy, who as a student had been an eloquent and enthusiastic champion of the maintenance of French Algeria, managed to recall the tensions engendered within the Protestant community with a mixture of passion and ironic detachment.

Eric Westphal, retired after a long and distinguished career as a civil servant, recalled memories of two anguishing and at times highly dangerous years spent in Algeria as advisor to Delegate-General Paul Delouvrier.

As research progressed and the text took shape, colleagues at Concordia University in Montreal offered both encouragement and critical comment. My friends Reford and Natalie MacDougall, whose support had sustained an earlier study on eighteenth-century toleration, generously renewed their confidence. My friend Dr. Gerald Lancaster scanned successive drafts with the critically clinical eye that only a trained scientist can bring and made a number of valuable suggestions about both form and content; his advice and support were invaluable at all stages of the manuscript's development. Elizabeth Gardham took on the often thankless task of transforming crude typescript to finished text and offered unfailing encouragement when spirits flagged. Erik Dessureault, a computer technician for the library, formatted the final version of the manuscript to conform to the publisher's requirements.

The thoughtful comments of friends and colleagues have allowed me to correct or remove factual errors or dubious exercises in analysis. Any lapses in judgment or flaws in recording the facts are of course entirely my own responsibility.

This book has been published with the help of a grant from the Humanities and Social Sciences Federation of Canada, using funds provided by the Social Sciences and Humanities Research Council of Canada.

The writer is in particular debt to the following: Professor Martin Rumscheidt of the Atlantic School of Theology in Halifax and Publications Officer of the Canadian Corporation for Studies in Religion, who conveyed invaluable counsel and substantial encouragement as the manuscript evolved; Dr. Michael J. Carley, Director of the Aid to Scholarly Publications Programme of the Humanities and Social Sciences Federation, who saw to it that the text was given a critical review; and Sandra Woolfrey, Director of the Wilfrid Laurier University Press, who signalled her interest in and support for the manuscript in its original form, thereby giving the writer a powerful incentive to proceed and leaving him with a very real sense of gratitude.

Albert Finet, editor of *Réforme* during the Algerian War
(Courtesy *Réforme*, Paris)

INTRODUCTION

Representing about two percent of the population since the Revolution which granted them their emancipation, France's Protestants have consistently played a disproportionate role in their nation's political, economic and cultural life. The middle years of the nineteenth century (1830-1880) were a kind of Golden Age in French Protestantism. François Guizot was the dominant political figure of the 1840s; his coreligionist Premier William Waddington headed a cabinet in 1879 which had a majority of Protestant ministers. The Neuflize, Schlumberger and Mallet banking houses had much to do with the financing of French industrial development during these years and laid the basis for what became known as the *Haute Société Protestante*. Intellectuals from Germaine de Staël to Hippolyte Taine helped promote admiration and even emulation of the Protestant culture of England and Germany. In the 1880s, three Protestants (Fernand Buisson, Félix Pecaut and Jules Steeg) successfully launched the system of free, compulsory, and secular education which became one of the cornerstones of republican culture and politics. Finally, Baron Haussmann gave Paris an urban architectural chic which lasted for more than a century.

This remarkable contribution has until recently been to a large extent ignored by French Protestant scholars. The tercentenary anniversary of the Revocation of the Edict of Nantes changed all this however, producing a minor flood of books about the Huguenots by a new generation of Protestant historians led by Jean Baubérot and André Encrevé.[1] A few years later, a colloquium was held in Paris to analyze (and celebrate) the Protestant involvement in the Resistance and in 1994 Professor Encrevé assessed the Protestant role in the Dreyfus Affair.[2]

The present work sets out to examine Protestant reactions to the undeclared war between France and Algeria (1954-1962). For the purposes of this study, Protestants (among whom members of the Reformed or Calvinist churches make up by far the largest group) are defined to include not only those who followed the obligations of their faith (*pratiquants*) as well as those who retained a basic belief without fulfilling these obligations (*croyants*) but also men and women of Protestant background who had drifted away from both practise and teaching but who remained conscious of (and proud of) their spiritual inheritance. This group, often referred to as *protestants d'origine*, might better be described as Protestants in the cultural or sociological sense, people who were still possessed of a set of values and convictions derived from a shared experience as a vigorous, self-conscious minority.[*]

---

[*]Also included in the category Protestant are members of the *Eglises libres*, a group of breakaway Reformed churches, Lutherans, as well as supporters of a variety of *petites Eglises* such as Darbyists and Methodists.

1

Students of modern French history use the term Protestant inclusively. Members of what were once among France's most powerful banking families (Hottinguer, Mirabaud, Schlumberger and Vernes, to name just a few) are taken to be Protestant, however tenuous their attachment to the faith. Anyone who belongs to the Monod dynasty is considered Protestant without a check on church attendance. And, following the Socialist electoral triumph in 1981, commentators pointed to the large number of Protestants (eight) in the ministry, including not only practising members of the Reformed communion (Georgina Dufoix, Pierre Joxe, Catherine Lalumière and Michel Rocard) but also Gaston Defferre who had long since been "détaché" from his childhood faith.[3]

Even from the purely theological point of view, it has always been difficult to define who is or is not a Protestant. Having started out as non-conformists and having made a personal reading of the Scriptures and/or the stirrings of individual consciences the basis of their revolt against Rome, Protestants have faced a grim dilemma ever since. How is it possible to ward off the antinomian tendencies which the Reformation let loose while at the same time framing a coherent and stable doctrine? During the Enlightenment, many French Protestants were drawn to Freemasonry and the concept of God as Supreme Architect. In the nineteenth century, some went even further, espousing what amounted to a Protestant version of free thought.[4]

At the time of the Algerian conflict, the faithful within the French Protestant community could be divided (albeit in somewhat oversimplified fashion) between *progressistes*, liberal in theological as well as in social and political matters, and *intégristes*, devoted to the traditional Calvinist creed and tending either towards political neutrality or towards right-wing opinions. During the late 1950s and throughout the 1960s, however, the "progressives" and their sympathizers held key positions in Protestant youth organizations (scouts, student unions and volunteer groups). As the war intensified, these elements assumed an increasingly dominant role in the decision making bodies of the *Eglise Réformée de France* (ERF) and the *Fédération Protestante de France* (FPF).[5]

During their reflections on the Algerian question, pastors as well as lay men and women were bound to be influenced by the prevailing trends in Protestant theology and social thought. For many, the dominant mentor was the Swiss theologian Karl Barth (1886-1968) who rejected the tendency of many nineteenth-century Protestants not only to dilute Calvin's stern teachings about human nature but to compound this spiritual lapse by endorsing the view that a utopian society could be created on earth. While in no way opposed to meliorist politics, Barth condemned as illusory any doctrine that aimed at reperfecting humankind and (for his readers at least) restored the traditional Protestant emphasis on Revelation as the sole means of salvation.

The other key influence on French Protestant activists at mid-century was that of *Christianisme social*, a small but determined group of pastors and lay people which had come together at the turn of the century to formulate a critical analysis of the existing capitalist system. Advocates of "Social Christianity" preached an end to economic exploitation and alienation. They were bound to see in the condition of the Muslim masses in Algeria a tragedy born of European capitalist greed.

Nowhere in these pages will it be argued that spiritual inspiration alone guided those French Protestants who took sides during the conflict. It is clear nevertheless that the overwhelming majority of pastors and lay people who became engaged in the debate over Algeria were motivated by a profound Christian faith.

For those of Protestant background, the question of motivation is less obvious. However, Jacques Soustelle, the governor general of the territory in the early phase of the war, who was strongly backed by leftist Protestant activists at that time, regularly referred to his huguenot origins as a source of both pride and inspiration. (A Protestant burial service was held following his death). And the historian Charles-André Julien showed his continuing affinity for the Protestant world in which he had grown up by showing up in the spring of 1955 to argue the case for de-colonization at the annual meeting of *Christianisme social*.

Such individual cases apart, it should be stressed that politically sensitive French Protestants, however loose their links to the church might be, had a long tradition of civic commitment based on a core of shared memories. They remembered the Revocation which had led so many of their coreligionists to flee France or to do battle in the Camisard revolt against Louis XIV; they recalled 1789 as the beginning of a decade which had seen their full civic and religious emancipation and which had made all but a few of them into dedicated republicans. They were proud of their role as propagators of the idea of *laïcité* and the promotion of a secular school system. They celebrated (perhaps somewhat exaggeratedly) their part in the Dreyfus Affair and in the founding of the *Ligue des Droits de l'Homme*. Finally and more immediately, they pointed with pride to their disproportionate role in the internal Resistance against Vichy and the Nazis and in support for de Gaulle's *La France Libre* in London and Algiers. Thus, whatever their relationship to the faith of their ancestors, Protestants saw themselves (and were seen by others, often with resentment) as having played and as still being destined to play a key role in French civic life.[6]

It would be foolhardy to make the case for a specific French Protestant mindset informed by traditional religious faith but not limited to persons still attending temple. However, two myths concerning the huguenot mentality pervade modern French history and offer a suggestive explanation of

Protestant attitudes, especially as these attitudes find expression in times of crisis. The first myth is rooted in an analysis of the behaviour-pattern of the upper strata of French Protestant society, often characterized as puritanical, somewhat cold and self-righteous, yet full of probity and thus admirably suited to public service, cosmopolitan (especially anglophile) and thus suspect to hard-line nationalists. Maurice Couve de Murville (who played a minor but not insignificant role in the Algerian drama) fits this stereotype remarkably well.

The other, radically different, myth is based on an examination of the long-term outlook and behaviour of huguenots in the rural south where memories of the Camisard revolt against Louis XIV remained vivid in the 1950s and where resistance to the central authority (whatever its ideological colouration), together with bitter resentment of Catholic clerical power, have created fertile ground for left-wing politics (and on occasion armed insurrection) in defence of freedom of conscience. This is the culture which shaped not only the outlook of Jacques Soustelle but that of many radical Protestant activists who fought to end the Algerian conflict.[7]

Whatever their spiritual or ideological perspective, these Protestants tried to answer a series of difficult moral questions between the outbreak of the rebellion on All Saints' Day (1 November) 1954 and the signing of the peace at Evian which ended the war on 18 March 1962.

To begin with, they asked themselves if the myth of assimilation which held that Algeria was an integral part of France (but which had meant in practice that only European settlers were treated as full-fledged citizens) should be translated into reality for the majority as well. Or, should integration be renounced in favour of recognizing the peculiar status of Algeria in association with the mother country. Even more radically, should Algeria become an independent nation? Should the status of the *colons* whose religious and cultural links tended to be Catholic, Protestant or Jewish be modified to allow for a more just and appropriate form of power-sharing? Should the Muslim masses be brought (with or without their consent) to enjoy the benefits of French civilization (more precisely the gains of the Revolution of 1789). This might come about through the promotion of literacy and general education, the separation of religion from secular affairs and the advancement of individual as opposed to communal or tribal rights.

Some questions were related to the rationale for the war. Were those who took up arms against France in 1954 motivated by the irrepressible or even noble impulse towards national liberation which swept through the Third World after 1945 and which might be seen as inspired in part by the Revolution of 1789? Or were they engaged in a terrorist conspiracy abetted by pan-arabists such as Egypt's Nasser and encouraged for their own hegemonic purposes by Washington, Moscow and Peking? Was France waging a "just war" in defense of her territorial integrity and her subjects' well-being? Were the techniques of counter-insurgency used by French troops in the field (many of which were inspired by the army's experience doing battle with Ho Chi Minh in Indochina), defensible or were they in violation of national as well as international law?

Some questions were peculiar to the French Socialist movement. Was the democratic Socialist tradition represented by Premier Guy Mollet and the leadership of the *Section Française de l'Internationale Ouvrière* (SFIO) subverted by the party's hard-line policy on Algeria as a dissident minority within the party including the Protestants André Philip and Robert Verdier maintained? Was the return to power of Charles de Gaulle following the insurrection of 13 May 1958 in Algiers a threat to republican institutions as Philip and others argued? Or was it a welcome opportunity to rehabilitate the regime and to transform an outmoded imperial-colonial relationship into one based on mutual respect and collaboration?

Other questions were of a more purely spiritual nature. Was Algeria's overwhelmingly Muslim population an appropriate mission target for Protestant evangelists, despite the tendency of the government to discourage (although not to prohibit) such proselytizing efforts and the clear indifference of the indigenous masses to such a missionary endeavour? Were the increasing numbers of Muslims living and working in France in need of special material as well as spiritual attention? Finally, what was the responsibility of the French Protestant community to the streams of *colons* (European settlers popularly known as *pieds-noirs*, a term many of them came to adopt with pride), and pro-French Muslims who fled from Algeria as independence became a reality and they sought "repatriation" to avoid the very real possibility of persecution, not to say slaughter?

Protestant reflections on these matters had a significant impact on two key areas of national politics: the campaign to legalize conscientious objection and the internal battle to reorient the Socialist Party. These results are duly noted. The central focus of this study, however, is on the ways in which men and women of Protestant faith and background wrestled with the moral issues brought to light by the Algerian conflict.

It would be absurd to contend that every French Protestant who tried to answer these questions was nobly motivated or that all the actions taken by Protestants during the seven-and-a-half-year conflict were inspired by moral imperatives alone. On the other hand, it is hard to deny that those Protestants who confronted the moral dilemmas posed by the insurrection of 1954 were convinced that what they said or did was in the best interest of all those implicated in the conflict on both sides of the Mediterranean.

The extensive literature devoted to the conflict in Algeria includes several works specifically dealing with the reaction of the intellectual community. Martin Evans, *The Memory of Resistance: French Opposition to the Algerian War* (New York: Berg, 1997) and James D. Le Sueur, "French Intellectuals and the Algerian War: Decolonization, Violence, and the Politics of Identity"(Ph.D. diss., University of Chicago, 1996) provide a close analysis of the growing opposition to the conflict in the French intellectual community at large. Jean-Pierre Rioux and Jean-François Sirinelli, *La guerre d'Algérie et les intellectuels français* (Paris: Editions Complexe, 1991) offer a chapter on the perspective of Catholic thinkers. André Nozière, *Algérie: Les chrétiens dans la guerre* (Paris: Editions Cana, 1979) deals (as the title suggests) with the views of Protestant as well as Catholic churches in Algeria, but not in France.

Primary sources reflecting the views of metropolitan French Protestants about Algeria abound. To begin with, French Protestant officialdom devoted a considerable amount of attention to developments in Algeria. Two years before the insurrection, the Algerian synod of the *Église Réformée de France* created a five-person *Comité d'Études Nord-Africaines* to study conditions in the Maghreb and to submit regular reports. In 1953, the *Fédération protestante de France*, the overarching organization which brings together almost all of France's many Protestant churches and sects, established an annual series of study-days designed to bring together representatives of the Protestant churches of the Maghreb and its own executive committee, the *Conseil national*. Finally, the *Église Réformée de France*, as well as other formally organized Protestant groups met, deliberated and passed resolutions affecting Algeria between 1954 and 1962.

Réforme, the leading Protestant weekly, is fundamentally liberal but opened its pages to a wide variety of viewpoints; *Cité nouvelle* and *Revue du Christianisme social* were militantly leftist; *Tant qu'il fait jour* was founded by conservative Protestant laymen and pastors in 1958 specifically to challenge what its staff saw to be the tendentiously liberal and anti-national outlook of *Réforme*; *Le Semeur*, the organ of Protestant student opinion, became increasingly sympathetic to Algerian nationalism as the conflict deepened. *L'Algérie protestante* was the bi-monthly journal of the territory's small Protestant community.

The *Journal officiel*, the official publication of the National Assembly, offers a full record of the parliamentary debates on Algeria, including the many interventions of Protestant deputies such as André Philip, Gaston Defferre and Francis Leenhardt. The typewritten minutes of the Socialist Party (*Section Française de l'Internationale Ouvrière* or SFIO) and its successor parties, SFIO *Autonome* and *Parti Socialiste Unifié (PSU)* reveal the intensity of the battle waged by Protestant dissidents to change the party's Algerian policy.

The archives of the *Comité Inter-Mouvements Auprès des Evacués*

(CIMADE) offer a direct insight into the efforts of individual Protestants to alleviate the suffering of Muslim as well as European victims of the war. A number of personal reflections dealing with the conflict have appeared in print. Finally, correspondence and interviews with those who experienced the conflict at first hand or who debated the maintenance of a French presence in Algeria have made clear (to the writer at least) that Protestant consciences were indeed engaged in what some historians have called France's most dramatic moral and ideological battle since the Dreyfus Affair.

Notes

1   Jean Baubérot, *Le Retour des Huguenots* (Paris: Cerf, 1985), and André Encrevé, *Les Protestants de France de 1800 à nos jours* (Paris: Stock, 1985).

2   "Les protestants français pendant la Deuxième Guerre mondiale," a colloquium held in Paris, 19-21 November 1992, and André Encrevé, "La petite musique huguenote," in P. Birnbaum (ed.), *La France de l'Affaire Dreyfus* (Paris: Gallimard, 1994), pp. 451-504.

3   V. Jauvert and M. Lenoir, "Le pouvoir des protestants," *Le nouvel Observateur*, 31 October 1991.

4   Writing in 1903, Pastor Jean Réville defined the strength (and unconsciously the weakness) of this perpetual theological flux when he wrote: "Liberal Protestantism bases religion like morality exclusively on the inner authority of conscience, reason and experience. With the coming of modern science, it rejects the supernatural in order to link religious feeling with the modern concept of a universal order." Cited in J. Garrisson, *L'homme protestant* (Paris: Editions complexe, 1986), p. 216. Garrisson goes on to observe: "What does religion itself become with such a permanent calling into question? Stripped of its mystery and its sacred character and transformed into a simple rule of behaviour, it is reduced to constraining the individual and guiding him along the proper path."

5   The radicalization of the Protestant establishment which the *progressistes* achieved through the later stages of the Algerian war was followed in November 1971 by the publication of a highly provocative, even revolutionary, tract *(Eglises et pouvoirs)* in which contemporary culture and its capitalist underpinnings were categorically condemned. This revolutionary document, so highly political, was followed by a period of spiritual disarray during which the Protestant sociologist Roger Mehl has called upon members of the Reformed community to recreate a minimal *règle de foi* to forestall an even deeper sense of moral and theological dissipation. R. Mehl, *Le protestantisme français dans la société actuelle, 1945-1980* (Geneva: Labor et Fides, 1982), p. 218.

6   The pervasive influence of Protestants in key areas of French public life led Robert Beauvais in *Nous serons tous des protestants* (Paris: Plon, 1976), to charge they were intent on establishing what amounted to cultural and moral hegemony over the nation. In *Le mal français*, also published by Plon in 1976, the Catholic Gaullist Alain Peyrefitte argued in very different vein that France had suffered enormously by its earlier persecution of the Protestant minority which had contributed so much to the development of modern culture through the propagation of the ideas of individual self-reliance, tolerance and the civic spirit.

7   For a fuller reflection on what may be seen to characterize the French Protestant
     minority, see J.-P. Richardot, *Le peuple protestant aujourd'hui* (Paris: R. Laffont, 1980),
     and Yves Bizeul, *L'identité protestante* (Paris: Meridiens Klincksieck, 1991). Richardot
     sees the French Protestants as "a people with their own history, their own collective
     unconscious, ancestral reflexes, customs and institutions and a certain method of
     educating, of affirming one's personality, of participating, working, organizing, voting,
     challenging, rejecting, hoping, fearing, closing ranks, and of opening themselves up to
     entire planet," p. 37.

Pastor Marc Boegner, president of the French Protestant Federation,
1929-1961
(Courtesy FPF, Paris)

CHAPTER ONE

ALGERIA 1830-1954: A COLONY IN ALL BUT NAME

The French expedition against Algiers in 1830 which led a generation later to the conquest of what the invaders named Algeria was motivated by a series of domestic and foreign policy problems. Jewish merchants in Algiers owed money to metropolitan French interests; and the *dey* of Algiers whose powers derived from the Ottoman Sultan in Constantinople had been provoked into striking the French consul with a fly-swatter, something the administration in Paris could not let pass. Finally, the advisers of the last Bourbon king, Charles X, calculated that a successful military expedition would shore up the radically declining popularity of the king.

French army units disembarked in Algiers on 14 June 1830. On 5 July, the *dey* surrendered the city. Over the next several decades, French army men tended to initiate, and the civil authority in Paris to follow, a policy of substantial territorial conquest as a result of which large stretches of North Africa were absorbed by France. In this effort, the invaders were challenged by the young *marabout* Abd-el-Kader. In 1834 he proclaimed a *jihad* or holy war against the conquering infidel and hoisted the green-and-white banner which 130 years later became the flag of the *Front de Libération Nationale* (FLN). In the face of this resistance, Marshal Bugeaud, commander of the invading army (as well as governor-general between 1841 and 1847) ordered his men to devastate those parts of the territory outside French control through what became known as the *razzia*.

Roughly four-fifths of the population ultimately brought under French control was Arab; some twenty percent scattered throughout the territory belonged to the original indigenous Berber culture. Whatever their ethnic background, those living in what became French Algeria adhered to the teachings of Mohammed.

French colonization in earnest began under the Third Republic when France, to compensate for her defeat in the Franco-Prussian War, pressed ahead with imperial expansion. Some 5,000 patriots, many of them Protestant, left Alsace and Lorraine when these provinces were ceded to Germany; some ended up in Algeria. Other Protestants from the *Hautes-Alpes* department were induced to relocate across the Mediterranean by the *Société Coligny*.

Many of the immigrants during the latter part of the nineteenth century came not from metropolitan France (the *métropole*) but from the Mediterranean littoral, from Corsica, Cyprus, Italy, Portugal and Spain. A law

11

passed in 1889 declared the children of these foreign-born immigrants to be "Français d'Algérie," endowing them with the rights of full citizenship. This legislation helped shape a sense of ethnic solidarity and of shared superiority to the Muslim masses at a time when racial (and racist) myths were sweeping through the European continent.

Charles-André Julien, the distinguished Protestant historian of the Maghreb (the Arabic term for extreme northwest Africa, including Morocco and Tunisia as well as Algeria) who spent much of his early life in Algeria, before World War I, offers a graphic portrait of this settler mentality:

> Reassured by a policy of repression (directed against the Muslim majority), proud of its vitality and its entrepreneurial spirit, sure of its republican and civilizing vocation, the European population felt free to impose on the territory and its indigenous masses a political, economic and social domination which nothing would be able to undo.[1]

Pierre Nora, a prominent French historian who spent two years teaching in an Algerian lycée beginning in 1958, paints a remarkably similar collective portrait: "The only common bond among French and other European immigrants was a *psychologie de déclassé* with regard to their nation of origin. In one way or another, those who came to Algeria as settlers had left a failed life behind them."[2] Nora adds that this inferiority complex brought the *colons* to make sure that the Arabs and Berbers in their midst would be humiliated as they themselves had been back in Europe. This helps explain why the European minority would feel justified in rejecting out of hand reforms being urged on them not only by the Muslim society which they had come to despise but by their metropolitan counterparts who could not share their hurt but were all too ready to condemn their retrograde mentality.

While Algeria did not become a colony in name, it was situated on the periphery of France's (and later the world's) capitalist economy, destined to export raw materials and to import manufactured goods. Early on, copper and iron were discovered by French prospectors. Towards the end, in the decade before independence, vast reserves of oil and gas were located in the Sahara.

The Europeans who settled on the land chose the fertile plains where they sowed wheat and later planted vineyards. Although the term *colons* (settlers) was often applied to the European minority in general (and will be used in this sense in what follows), in fact only a small proportion of emigrants to Algeria ended up as substantial landowners. Pierre Nora estimates that there were only 22,000 landowning *colons* compared to some 650,000 Muslim proprietors, adding that the Europeans owned perhaps as much as one-quarter of the cultivable soil. Germaine Tillion offers an even more modest figure (19,400 European landowners) and indicates that 7,432 of these possessed less than ten hectares and were in effect *petits blancs* ("poor whites"). So the *colons* in the original property-owning sense were perhaps no more than 12,000 in all of whom, according to Tillion, only 300 were rich and as few as a dozen were extremely wealthy.[3] (Charles-André Julien refers to this latter category as "settlers in yellow gloves"). At most, then, with their families, there were 45,000 *colons* or settlers in the Algerian countryside.

The overwhelming majority of the Europeans settlers lived in cities or towns close to the Mediterranean littoral. Few were proletarian although many were specialized workers. Some were solid middle-class businessmen and engineers, most had lower middle-class jobs as shopkeepers, telephone operators, taxi drivers, lower echelon civil servants, station-masters and mechanics; many were students. The vast majority of Algeria's Europeans thus belonged to social categories which would have made them the natural clientele of leftist parties in continental France. The Socialist Premier Guy Mollet on a visit to Algiers in February 1956 made this assumption and was quickly disabused.

The radical difference in socio-economic status between the large-scale landowners and the vast mass of small farmers and petty-bourgeois urban Europeans would normally have produced serious class tension and political division. The enormous pressures that this complex European society felt, however, even before the 1954 insurrection, led to a closing of ranks. Except for a tiny liberal minority, the Europeans developed a siege mentality. All became "pieds-noirs," proud of their Eurafrican roots, not altogether unlike the whites of South Africa during the same period and all tended to be denounced as wealthy and self-serving *colons* by liberal critics in continental France. By adopting an increasingly defensive attitude in the face of rising demands by the Muslim masses (who were infinitely less well off than the poorest of Algeria's poor whites) they tended to justify the negative, even caricatural, portrait of their community as privileged and well-to-do.

Religious life in French-ruled Algeria developed differently from that in most of the empire, partly because, although the population of the territory was overwhelmingly Muslim, the large influx of Christian settlers encouraged in some at least the hope of conversion in an area which had, after all, given birth to St. Augustine in the late Roman imperial era.

The evangelical dreams of some settlers were very different from the aims of the home government. It was more interested in the maintenance of social peace across the Mediterranean. Following the capture of Algiers on 4

July 1830, the newly established regime of King Louis-Philippe guaranteed Algeria's Muslims freedom of worship. Protestants who subsequently arrived in the territory were quick to demand the same assurance. Among the first arrivals were a number of Protestants from Alsace, neighbouring Swiss cantons and Germany while the French Foreign Legion, created in March 1831 had as its nucleus a predominantly Protestant Swiss battalion.

Because the conquest of Algiers coincided with the movement of religious revival within French Protestantism known as *Le Reveil*, interest in the spiritual well-being of those of the faith who had settled in the newly acquired territory was intense. This concern was apparently not unjustified. A foreign Protestant missionary visiting Algiers in the years immediately after the conquest noted the absence of appropriate arrangements for worship there, and the second pastor sent to minister to the still small parish was told by his congregants that they had come to Algeria not to win eternal salvation but to make their fortune.

In October 1839 a royal ordinance sanctioned the creation of a regular Reformed church, led by a pastor and governed by twelve elders. This church like others which followed was administered under the terms of the Organic Articles of the Year X (1802) that is, the church itself would be built with government money and the pastor paid out of state funds.

Although their numbers grew substantially through the nineteenth century, Algeria's Protestant community remained a tiny group within settler society as a whole. By the 1950s, there were twenty-one Reformed congregations with approximately 6,000 parishioners. The four parishes in Algiers and the single parish in Oran made up half the total Reformed population. The rest was dispersed all over the territory. It should be noted that during the seven and a half years of the war, roughly two percent of those soldiers despatched to Algeria (or 10,000 men) can be assumed to be Protestant in line with the proportion in France as a whole.

While there was a natural urge among Protestants to ensure the proper maintenance of their right to worship, there was also, for the zealous at least, the prospect of turning Algeria into a mission field. This fervour was fuelled in part by the creation in Paris in 1822 of the *Société des Missions évangeliques chez les peuples non-chrétiens*. Soon after the seizure of Algiers, in August 1830, the Society committed itself to sending two young Protestants into this new field preparing them in advance to have a proper understanding of Islam and a working knowledge of Arabic.

The government's coolness to this project was based in large measure on its desire not to compound the problems of administering an already rebellious population by what it saw to be a provocative campaign of conversion. That same coolness deflected the energies of the would-be emissaries of the faith elsewhere. In the end, foreigners became the chief propagators of the Protestant version of the Gospel in Algeria by default. In 1881, the Englishman George Pearse inaugurated what later became the North Africa Mission; a Methodist missionary enterprise followed in 1885, again directed by a non-French pastor. The only specifically French Protestant mission effort in Algeria, the *Mission Rolland*, was launched in 1908 by two English women at Tizi-Ouzou in the Kabylia region. It was transferred to Emile Rolland, a worker for the Renault automobile company, by French authorities worried about potential spying activities had it remained in English hands. Rolland learned and preached the Gospel in the local Berber language and built a permanent place of worship in the town.

The results of the limited involvement of French Protestants in this missionary efforts were predictably meagre. At the time of the 1954 insurrection, there were at most 800 Protestant converts from Islam. This limited harvest of souls did not discourage some. As we shall see, the Syrian-born Reformed pastor Georges Tartar pressed the cause of conversion throughout the war and beyond.

The proximity of the new territory to metropolitan France, the absence of a well-developed political or administrative structure there, and the relatively high level of European settlement made Algeria seem like the ideal testing-ground for the application of full-scale integration or even assimilation of the Muslim majority into French society. The benefits of such a policy were taken for granted: the high degree of civilization incarnated by France, including the propagation of the universalist message of the Revolution of 1789, would be brought to the Maghreb including (by implication at least) to the Muslim population.

A belief in the myth of assimilation and efforts to transform it into reality haunted French administrators until the very last days of France's presence in Algeria. Ironically, the assimilationist argument, consistently invoked by liberals and leftists in mainland France, was regularly cited by the *colons* as well. They, however, interpreted it to mean not the incorporation of Muslims into the French body politic but the legitimizing of their own privileged status in Paris as well as Algiers.

Efforts to transform the assimilationist myth into reality began following the 1848 Revolution in Paris when a coalition of liberals and leftists founded the Second Republic. On 2 March, the Provisional Government of this Republic granted the 100,000 Europeans then living in Algeria full French citizenship. Subsequently, adult males among those newly enfranchised settlers were given the right to elect three deputies to the Legislative Assembly sitting in Paris. The parts of Algeria not then under direct military control—essentially the areas along the Mediterranean coast where the European population was most concentrated—were transformed into three departments and subdivided into *arrondissements* and *communes*. Each department, like its mainland equivalent, would elect a deputy to the national parliament while *arrondissements* were given prefects and *communes* sub-prefects as in France.

This decision to assimilate Algeria politically to France gave the *colons* enormous lobbying power in Paris while the Muslim majority was excluded from any legal role in deciding the territory's future. Not surprisingly, the fully enfranchised settlers resented and resisted all subsequent efforts to modify this arrangement with a view to offering the Muslims a share of power and influence.

Although the assimilationist policy triumphed over the long term, an attempt was made in the middle decades of the nineteenth century to try a radically different approach. Napoleon III, elected president in December 1848 and made Emperor four years later, favoured a policy of close association between France and Algeria. That policy involved a clear recognition of and respect for the Muslim tradition and a serious commitment to balance the defence of the European minority with protection of the rights of the Arab and Berber majority. Some 2,000 highly skilled specialists were brought together in what became known as *Bureaux arabes*. Special army units, including a doctor and an interpreter, were despatched throughout Algeria to encourage rational farming methods, to supervise the administration of an updated version of traditional Muslim justice and to oversee an improvement in hygiene and medicine. The emperor made clear that France's first obligation in Algeria was to its 3,000,000 Arabs and Berbers. On visits to the territory, he did his best to promote racial reconciliation and an appropriate respect for the property rights of the majority which had been seriously undermined by the introduction of the individualist definition of property propagated by the Revolution and arbitrarily introduced to Algeria.

The collapse of Napoleon III's regime during the Franco-Prussian War in 1870 ended the attempt to define the relationship between France and Algeria in terms of association and ethnic balance. The *colons* who had developed a deep loathing of the "Empereur des Arabes" rejoiced at his defeat. After toying with the idea of proclaiming a "petite République française" under exclusive settler control, they ended up achieving essentially the same result without a formal rupture with the mother country. On 4 October 1870, a month after proclamation of the Third Republic, Algeria's three departments were given two seats each in the National Assembly (or Chamber of Deputies as it was then called), as well as three seats in the upper chamber or Senate. Through these six deputies, Algeria's settler minority gained effective control of the territory's political future. On 24 October, the new government in Paris designated a governor-general who was to administer Algeria's three departments under the supervision of the National Assembly to which he was responsible. At the local level, Algeria was to be governed by two types of *commune*: *communes de plein exercice* would be established in areas where settlers were sufficiently numerous to govern their own affairs, and *communes mixtes* in areas of widely dispersed or limited European settlement where their representatives (*conseillers*) would be appointees drawn from among locals *caïds* or chiefs. In the more remote parts of the Algerian interior, French military authorities served as local administrators, by and large to the advantage of the Muslim population.

Between 1871 and 1891, Paris tended to let Algeria run itself, that is, it allowed the settlers to determine policy in the three departments as they saw fit. This effective abandonment of the Muslims did not go unchallenged. The Protestant senator Jean-Jules Clamageran urged fiscal as well as political reform in Algeria to remedy a situation that was clearly not compatible with republican principles of liberty, equality and fraternity. Despite these expressions of concern for the Muslim majority, the *colons* were granted a greater degree of autonomy over Algerian affairs in 1898. The territory was awarded its own legislative assembly known as the *Délégations financières*, the members of which were to be chosen by direct election. Some 5,000 Muslims were included in the electorate.

As the tensions leading to World War I increased, France's presence in contiguous Morocco was challenged by Germany. Algeria took on new psychological as well as strategic importance. In February 1912, Muslims were made subject to recruitment by lot in the French army. At the same time the Protestant economist Charles Gide, president of the newly founded *Alliance Franco-indigène*, suggested that France's long-term presence in Algeria was not plausible unless coupled to promotion of a "mixed Franco-native Algerian nation." In February 1913, Gide launched a weekly newspaper, *La France islamique*, aimed at involving the Muslim elite in the French administration of the Maghreb. The Muslim response was essentially positive. A group calling themselves *Jeunes Algériens* proclaimed their sympathy for assimilation (or francisation) rather than for a future dominated by ideas deriving from Islam or from Arab solidarity.

The contribution of Muslim soldiers and workers to the Allied victory in the war brought Premier Georges Clemenceau and other far-sighted politicians to press the case for reform in Algeria. Legislation enacted on 4

February 1919 created a special status (semi-naturalization) for an additional 5,000 Muslims to join those already entitled to vote for the *Délégations générales*, which was divided into an assembly of two houses, or colleges, each of which represented what amounted to an ethnic bloc (European or Muslim).

The 1919 legislation was deeply resented by the *colons* and, as it turned out, only some forty naturalizations a year were sought by Muslims in the inter-war years. Reform efforts originating in Paris did not, however, cease. Maurice Viollette, an idealistic Freemason who served as Algeria's governor in the 1920s, hoped to make 1930, the centenary of the conquest, into an occasion for realizing the promise that had always been implicit in the idea of assimilation: that naturalization be extended to all those Muslims who wished and deserved it.

Although the centennial ceremonies did not bring about a new accommodation between France and Algeria, the success of the Popular Front, which came to power in 1936, offered a new chance for reform and reconciliation. Viollette was named minister of state in charge of Algerian affairs and drew up a reform proposal, endorsed by Premier Léon Blum, that would have gone far towards satisfying the Muslim elite. What became known as the Blum-Viollette reforms would have extended the franchise to the *évolués* within Algeria's Muslim community. These included army officers, holders of the *Légion d'honneur* and decorated soldiers, those holding secondary education certificates, civil servants and *caïds* or men holding elected office, and workers who had been specially recognized. Had the proposal been adopted, some 20,000 Muslims would have been enfranchised, hardly enough to threaten the power of the 202,000 *colons* then entitled to vote but certainly enough to effect a real change at the local electoral level and to offer Muslims a political training ground.

Presented to the Chamber of Deputies on 30 December 1936, the Blum-Viollette bill languished for the next eighteen months. Predictable resistance developed in Algeria's European community where the Federation of Mayors, a high-powered lobbying group, did its best to subvert any chance of reform.

The collapse of the Popular Front in 1938 and with it the shelving of the Blum-Violette proposals came on the eve of World War II which radically changed the context in which Algeria's fate was to be decided. France's military defeat in 1940, the accession to power of Marshal Pétain and the proclamation of the fascistic "National Revolution" by Vichy were greeted with a large degree of sympathy in settler circles. The victorious landing of Allied armies in Algiers in November 1942 brought with it a series of shocks.

Vicious infighting ensued between the partisans of Vichy whom the Americans for tactical reasons needed to conciliate and the Free French led by Charles de Gaulle who arrived from London to base his Provisional Government on French soil. Meanwhile, President Roosevelt made clear that Allied war aims must include the liquidation of Europe's empires.

The division and confusion within French wartime leadership and the increasing role of the United States in European affairs did not go unnoticed by Algeria's Muslim elites. In February 1943, a number of Algerian leaders, including the pharmacist Ferhat Abbas who had up to then been devoted to French culture and to the ideal of assimilation, submitted a *Manifeste du peuple algérien* to Algeria's governor, the Gaullist General Catroux. A copy was also sent to the fledgling United Nations. The Manifesto reflected a basic shift in tactics and ideology on the part of a substantial number of Algerian intellectuals. They condemned the policy of assimilation, indicated that they were proudly Muslim and wished to remain so, and insisted on Algeria's right to self-determination with its own constitution and official language (Arabic). A subsequent *Addition au Manifeste* demanded the immediate constitution of an Algerian government in which Muslims and Europeans would hold an equal number of portfolios.

General Catroux and with him Charles de Gaulle ignored the Manifesto. During a conference at Brazzaville in the French Congo in January 1944, attended by delegates from all over the French Empire, a resolution was adopted which unconditionally asserted the principle of the integrity, even the indivisibility, of the Empire: "The completion of the work accomplished by France in her colonies precludes any idea of autonomy, any possibility of their evolution outside the French imperial framework."[4] (Not surprisingly, partisans of *L'Algérie française* often cited these words when de Gaulle, as president of the Republic, was seen to be moving towards recognition of Algerian independence).

On 1 May 1945, as the war in Europe was ending, Muslim crowds demonstrated in favour of Algerian independence. On 8 May, a day on which militant nationalists had asked for a general insurrection, there was a bloody encounter in the town of Sétif, a clash which some historians see as the beginning of the war of independence. Between 8,000 and 10,000 Muslims converged on the town's war memorial, some of them brandishing the green-and-white flag inspired by the banner hoisted by Abd-el-Kader in the 1830s. When the police tried to seize the provocative flag, shots were fired and a violent clash ensued. The army brought in tanks and planes. Before the confrontation had ended, over 100 Europeans and thousands of Muslims were killed. Leading nationalist figures including Ferhat Abbas and Messali Hadj were arrested.

Political life in Algeria resumed haltingly in 1946, a year in which the French voted twice before selecting a constitution for the Fourth Republic. Ferhat Abbas founded the *Union démocratique du Manifeste algérien* (UDMA). Its platform, reflecting the aims of the moderate nationalist bourgeoisie, included a demand that Algeria become a republic with full internal autonomy in association with France. Messali Hadj, his more radical rival, helped create the *Mouvement pour le Triomphe des Libertés Démocratiques* (MTLD) which forswore any continuing link with Paris and presented a revolutionary agenda designed to appeal to the peasant masses. The UDMA ended up boycotting elections to the French National Assembly in November 1946; the MTLD whose leader was banned from running, won five seats.

This was the background for passage of the most critical legislation affecting Algeria in the postwar period, the *Statut de l'Algérie*, voted in the National Assembly on 27 September 1947 by an overwhelming majority (322 to 82, with the Communists and the Algerian deputies abstaining). Centrepiece of the law was the replacement of the *Délégations financières* of 1898 by an *Assemblée algérienne* of 120 deputies, half of whom would be chosen from a basically European electoral college (500,000 Europeans and 70,000 assimilated Muslims), the other half by a Muslim college of some 1,450,000 voters. Since the electoral suffrage was henceforth to be universal, the statute in effect decreed that, while Muslims were for the first time fully enfranchised, their overwhelmingly disproportionate demographic strength (9-to-1) would still not give them a majority voice in the territory's government. Any legislation before the Assembly could be blocked by the European college which had what amounted to a veto.

Although the statute of 1947 left the supreme legislative authority for the territory with the National Assembly in Paris, it granted the newly created Algerian body greater powers than those enjoyed by the *Délégations financières*. It could, for example, examine laws passed by the parent parliament in Paris and propose amendments; and it could vote its own budget.

In addition to creating the Algerian Assembly, the 1947 statute promised to grant citizenship to the Muslim majority, to allow the teaching of Arabic at all levels of schooling and to apply the republican principle of church-state separation, thus secularizing Algerian public life and liberating Muslim women. Finally, the *communes mixtes* were abolished so that all local government was organized as it was in France.

Unfortunately for those who saw in the 1947 statute a chance for the gradual, peaceable evolution of the territory within the French political system, both the European minority and the Muslim majority in Algeria opposed its effective implementation. In the years that followed, interference and manipulation by the colonial administration frustrated the prescribed electoral process, preventing the parliamentary dialogue which might have allowed the two communities to move towards a shared political future.

Management of the political process in Algeria by Governor-General Edouard Naegelen and his successor Roger Léonard meant that nationalists were effectively precluded from being elected. The 17 June 1951 elections to the National Assembly were so artfully manipulated that only two deputies reflecting a nationalist perspective, those running in fact under the banner of the *Parti Communiste Algérien* (PCA), succeeded in winning seats.

Feeling abandoned by the government in Paris and betrayed by the administration in Algiers, nationalists went underground or left for exile in Cairo. For a while, ideological splits and personality conflicts made it difficult for these rebellious spirits to achieve a common front, but in March 1954, a *Comité Révolutionnaire pour l'Unité et l'Action* (CRUA) was constituted in Algiers and subsequently reinforced by those nationalists who had fled to Nasser's Egypt.

The capitulation of the French army to Ho Chi Minh's forces at Dien Bien Phu on 7 May 1954, and the recognition both in Paris and elsewhere that the battle to retain France's imperial presence in Southeast Asia was lost, acted as a tonic to Algerian nationalists. With some 3,000 partisans ready to take up arms, the CRUA planned an uprising for 1 November 1954 which was to signal the beginning of the struggle for Algeria's independence. Simultaneously, from exile in Cairo, the nationalist leadership created the *Front de Libération Nationale* (FLN), which quickly became the chief political instrument of the struggle for Algerian independence.

François Mitterrand, the minister of the interior whose portfolio included Algeria, reacted by repeating the old Jacobin shibboleth that the territory was an integral part of France and by rejecting any notion of negotiating with the rebels.

Notes

1   Charles-André Julien, *Histoire de l'Algérie contemporaine. La conquête et les débuts de la colonisation, 1827-1871* (Paris: Presses Universitaires de France, 1964), p. 500.
2   Pierre Nora, *Les Français d'Algérie* (Paris: Julliard, 1961), p. 81.
3   Germaine Tillion, *L'Afrique bascule vers l'avenir. L'Algérie en 1957* (Paris: Editions de Minuit), p. 32.

4   Cited in Jacques Soustelle, *Lettre ouverte aux victimes de la décolonisation* (Paris: Albin
    Michel, 1973), p. 36.

Governor-General Jacques Soustelle
(Courtesy Mme Georgette Soustelle)

André and Magda Trocmé
(Courtesy Mme Nelly Trocmé-Hewett)

CHAPTER TWO

GOVERNOR JACQUES SOUSTELLE: THE TRIBULATIONS OF A JACOBIN PROCONSUL (1955-56)

The uprising which triggered the eight-year-long Algerian conflict began on 1 November 1954 in two key areas: the hilly Kabyle terrain to the east of Algiers and the Aurès mountain range south of Constantine. The rebels, under the overall command of an *Armée de Liberation Nationale* (ALN), were at most 3,000. The French army, which had some 50,000 men stationed in the territory, responded with a leaflet campaign dismissing the rising as inspired by agitators who were counting on foreign support. Nevertheless the army leaflets urged the population to move into designated security zones where they would be protected.

Ten days after the start of the insurrection, Pastor Maurice Voge offered a prophetic warning of what lay ahead. Voge had since 1948 been secretary-general of *Christianisme social*, the radical social action movement which stood apart both from Protestant officialdom and from all political parties. He informed readers of the organization's newspaper that, more than half a year before the outbreak of the rebellion, in May 1954, he and others had met with a group of moderate Algerian nationalists in Paris. The visiting Muslims had warned the Protestants that France faced an armed uprising if she did not deal immediately and effectively with the poverty and injustice which plagued the Algerian masses. This and other similar warnings should have alerted the administration in Paris, Voge noted. Instead, falsified election returns and the continuing refusal to apply the 1947 statute had compromised the efforts of the minority of moderate Muslims who accepted the new legislation to relay their message. For too long, Paris had been determined not to deal with such free men but with the lackeys ("Beni-oui-oui") who sat in the Algerian Assembly. Now, faced with armed rebellion, she had no choice but to effect radical change under enormous pressure or risk losing everything.[1]

Two weeks following the appearance of Voge's article, *Cité nouvelle* offered its readers a very different perspective by an eminent Protestant historian who would soon have a falling out with his colleagues over Algerian policy. Pierre Grosclaude argued that France must respond to the 1 November rising with uncompromising firmness, adding that she must prevent any foreign meddling in what remained an exclusively French problem and that she must not act in such a way as to subvert the interests of the *colons*.[2]

Voge and Grosclaude represent the diametrically opposed positions

25

which French Protestants adopted as the conflict deepened. In time, the great majority of Protestants who expressed an opinion condemned the government for pursuing the undeclared war and the army for conducting it so ruthlessly while partisans of Professor Grosclaude's position ended up as a small band of intractables with little influence.

Anxious to reflect both the essentially liberal outlook of metropolitan Protestants and the nervous preoccupations of the faithful in the settler community across the Mediterranean, the official organs of the Reformed church adopted a politically neutral attitude during the first five years of the war.

In December, the national synod of the *Eglise Réformée de France* (ERF) extended its compassionate concern to those caught up in the conflict, especially civil and military officials living in a society divided by racial and social antipathies, who might be troubled by problems of conscience. Protestants on the scene were urged "to repress all egoism, to clear up misunderstandings, and to overcome hatred."[3]

By year's end, reports of army brutality began to reach Paris. Claude Bourdet, the leftist editor of *France-Observateur*, and the liberal Catholic François Mauriac in *L'Express* condemned the army's use of torture. The Protestant lawyer Pierre Stibbe went to Algeria to see for himself and then relayed his impressions to the readers of *Cité nouvelle* and *Christianisme social*. What he witnessed was highly alarming: on 31 December he saw Muslim prisoners clearly in need of medical attention as a result of being tortured. In the lawyer's opinion, the French soldiers' methods of getting information from their captives were clearly inherited from the Gestapo. Some prisoners had been plunged naked into ice-cold water; others had received electric shocks on their genitals. And all this while Paris kept insisting that Algeria was an integral part of France. One thing was evident, even from the lawyer's brief visit: French law clearly did not obtain on the other side of the Mediterranean. Under the circumstances, Stibbe wrote, it was imperative that the authorities come down hard on those who were so grossly abusing the military code of conduct.[4]

During the first year of the undeclared war, two men of Protestant background but of very different temperament and ideological outlook, Jacques Soustelle and Pastor André Trocmé, offered radically opposing formulae for the resolution of France's last important colonial dilemma. As governor-general, Soustelle tried his best to achieve the integration of Algerians, Muslim as well as European, inside the framework of the modern French nation. Trocmé, while fully aware of the need for radical political and economic reforms in Algeria, aimed at the promotion of mass literacy and, ultimately, the propagation of the Christian gospel, among the Muslim masses. In hindsight, both efforts may be seen as at best hopelessly idealistic, at worst, imperialist. However, neither can be condemned as self-serving. Perhaps the fairest way of evaluating both enterprises is to see them as bold efforts by men of conscience to come to grips (albeit far too late in the day) with the problems created by the European colonial powers as they continued to try to impose their value system on the societies that they had only nominally absorbed into their empires.

Born in 1912 in Montpellier to Protestant parents of modest means, Soustelle was baptized in the Reformed faith. Memories of his religious upbringing, of household visits by itinerant evangelists and of stories about ancestors who had fought for freedom of conscience against Louis XIV stayed with Soustelle long after studies at the *École Normale Supérieure* in Paris had turned him into a sceptic.

Research as an ethnologist took Soustelle to Mexico in 1932. Living among descendants of the Aztecs, the young scholar developed a deep sympathy for Indian culture and a strong sense of outrage at what clerical oppression and a feudalistic landowning system had done to subvert it. At the same time, Soustelle was convinced that the integration of Aztec and European Mexicans was proceeding apace, a conviction which later influenced his policies in Algeria.

Back in Paris, Soustelle helped found the *Musée de l'homme* in 1936 while committing himself to mobilizing the Paris intelligentsia against fascism as the Popular Front took power. In 1940, already established as a scholar and political activist, Soustelle joined de Gaulle's Free French movement whose intelligence service he helped direct. After the war, the ethnologist-turned-politician remained a devout Gaullist, helping to found the *Rassemblement du Peuple Français* in 1947, then joining the leftist *Républicains Sociaux* when the RPF broke up.

Not surprisingly, given his political past, Soustelle was welcomed by champions of reform in Algeria when his appointment as governor-general was debated in the National Assembly. Just as naturally, his appointment was greeted with alarm and suspicion by supporters of the status quo.[5]

Pierre Mendès France (who had become premier in June 1954 on the understanding that he would negotiate an end to the war in Indochina) proposed Soustelle for the governorship of Algeria in the hope that forceful enactment of reform there would enable him to end the insurrection while retaining the territory for France. When Mendès fell from office, his replacement, Edgar Faure, who took office on 25 February, confirmed Soustelle in his mandate which, renewed after six months, would run for a full calendar year (26 January 1955 - 31 January 1956).

Soustelle felt eminently qualified to take on this challenging new responsibility. He was convinced that his on-the-spot familiarity with Mexico, where, he believed, the Indians had been integrated into a modern state while preserving their traditional culture, would equip him well to find a formula for integrating Algeria's Muslims into contemporary French political and cultural life while respecting their ethnic integrity.

Maurice Voge, writing in *Cité nouvelle*, hailed the appointment of Soustelle as bold and courageous. "The man has character," the left-wing Protestant noted, adding: "he has a keen intellect and he is thoroughly versed in colonial affairs. We can surely put our fullest confidence in him. Once he is on the scene, torture should cease and the big financial interests over there will be put in their place."[6]

Soustelle put together a small team of experts who might serve as interlocutors with the moderate Algerian nationalists he hoped to win over to a programme of reform and reconciliation. Foremost among these advisors was Major Vincent Monteil, a student of Muslim culture and politics who spoke Arabic and who had travelled extensively in Morocco. Shortly after arriving in Algeria, the new governor persuaded his fellow-ethnologist Germaine Tillion to give him additional counsel. Tillion had started her research career in the Aurès mountains in the late 1920s and, in the immediate aftermath of the 1954 insurrection, had witnessed the brutal methods used by the French army to repress the rebellion.

Soustelle was no political innocent but he could not have fully appreciated in advance the formidable coalition of forces in Algeria ready to oppose his kind of reform agenda. The bureaucracy in the *Gouvernement-Général*, the *Fédération des maires*, the veterans' associations, the overwhelmingly conservative European press, the student unions, were all determined to subvert what they regarded as the impending betrayal of French Algeria by the metropolitan government and its new appointee.

As for the army in Algeria, it was still reeling from the shock of Dien Bien Phu, a debacle which preceded by only a few weeks the 1 November rising. Prepared to engage in another *sale guerre* (dirty war) only if they could be convinced that the regime in Paris had the will to back their efforts to the hilt, the military was determined to take matters into its own hands if the civil authority showed signs of capitulating to the rebels.

Quite apart from its relationship to the political establishment of the Fourth Republic, the army was divided about the best means of combatting the FLN. Some, particularly veterans of Indochina, were prepared to apply a counter-insurgency strategy adapted from the Vietminh, including torture and psychological warfare. Others were intent on waging more traditional combat in the field.

The greeting accorded Soustelle on his arrival in Algiers was far from friendly. The editor-in-chief of *L'Echo d'Alger*, owned by the reactionary Alain de Sérigny, spotted the governor-general on his arrival and remarked to the newspaper photographer: "Hey there! Give me a profile shot of this faggot Ben Soussan, OK? That way people will see that he's a Jew! Even if he calls himself Soustelle!"[7]

The attempt to portray Soustelle as Jewish was clearly designed to undermine his authority by playing on the notorious antisemitism of the European minority in Algeria as well as on the widespread prejudice of the Muslim masses. The incoming governor-general was understandably bitter at the vicious effort to subvert him. He asked himself: "Was I going to be reduced to revealing my Cévenol past (a reference to a revolt by Protestant peasants against Louis XIV during the first decade of the eighteenth century) perhaps even to producing my Montpellier birth certificate?"[8]

That Soustelle had been appointed by the Jew Mendès France whose government had prepared the way for Moroccan and Tunisian independence added to the anticipatory dismay of the European community nor did his Gaullist credentials stand him in good stead in a society which had favoured Vichy during the war.

Within a week of his arrival, Soustelle set off for the Aurès region where the rebellion had been vigorously supported. His conclusions were clear and simple. The rebellion must be mastered by the army whose leadership was clearly ill-equipped to produce a decisive victory and which needed to be made subordinate to his will and policy. At the same time, the Muslim population must be won over by the forceful application of reform, even in the face of civil and military opposition. Even more challengingly, the *pieds-noirs* must be persuaded to accept basic changes in the relations between minority and majority.

Soustelle presented his reform agenda on 23 February in his first speech to the Algerian Assembly, a body dominated by *colons*. The governor-general's aim was to persuade the *petits blancs* ("poor whites") who had daily contact with Muslims to collaborate with him in helping to transform conditions throughout Algeria. Integration, which Soustelle presented as his long-term goal, required at least minimal support from this lower-middle-class constituency which made up the vast majority of Algeria's European community. If his programme were to succeed, these were the people who would have to accept the promotion of Muslims to jobs in both the private and public sectors. The governor-general indicated that he wished to see a *collège unique* replace the existing two-college system. He also promised to double the current level of Muslim school enrolments and to introduce radical agrarian reform through the creation of *Secteurs d'amélioration rurale* (SAR).

While these reforms were being put in place, Soustelle added, public order, without which no reforms were conceivable, would be guaranteed by a thoroughgoing policy of pacification, a term which soon enough became a cruel synonym for ruthless repression.

Tragically, the liberal phase of Soustelle's administration was relatively short-lived. This was in large measure because the men behind the November insurrection were determined to generate not peaceful dialogue but dialectical conflict between the administration and the Muslim majority and to liquidate (or at least neutralize) the moderate nationalists whom Monteil (and, through him, Soustelle) were trying to engage in discussion. The deliberate terrorist attacks which these radicals incited produced what their authors had hoped for: a ruthlessly repressive policy by Soustelle's subordinates which the governor-general in the end felt he had to endorse.

The strategy of the hard-line nationalists was accompanied by a concerted effort to recruit support for the Algerian cause from the increasingly aggressive bloc of Afro-Asian states whose meeting at Bandoeng (in Indonesia) in April 1955 was a key event in the campaign for postwar decolonization. Delegates from Algeria helped ensure that the final conference communiqué included a resolution to support the struggle for Algerian self-determination. Simultaneously, the nationalist leader Ben Bella and others based in Cairo were doing their best to transform the Egyptian capital into a propaganda centre for their cause.

As he met with increasing resistance from militant nationalists as well as from *pieds-noirs*, Soustelle did his best to persuade the Faure ministry to give him the funds and political will to carry out his reform agenda. At one point he even threatened to resign if Paris were not more forthcoming, a threat which his liberal supporters later criticized him for not carrying out. In order to ensure that the pacification programme could be carried out, the governor-general asked Premier Faure to authorize the declaration of a state of emergency (*état d'urgence*). This declaration, which required a favourable vote in the National Assembly was approved early in April.

Meanwhile, concerns about the government's method and policy were being expressed in metropolitan Reformed circles. On 10 February, the *commission sociale* of the *Église Réformée de France*, acting on reports from reliable eye-witnesses, expressed its concern about the use of torture by army officers in Algeria and reminded the faithful of national synod's resolution two years earlier: Christians had a civic obligation to use every lawful means available to oppose unjust practices used against those under the protection of the French flag, even when such practices were urged on them by what amounted to moral blackmail.

A clear signal of alarm about Algeria was submitted to the 24 February issue of *Cité nouvelle* by Jean Scelles, a former *conseiller* of the *Union française* and a delegate to the *Comité chrétien d'entente France-Islam*. Scelles deplored the excesses of settler reaction to the 1 November rising.[9] He reported that, in the immediate aftermath of the insurrection, Muslims suspected of being terrorists had been lynched in the town of Tizi-Renif but that no action had been taken against those responsible for this indiscriminate retaliation. The inclination of soldiers and police (most of whom spoke no Arabic) to arrest and punish without due process was simply reinforcing the ranks of the rebels.

In the 12 March issue of *Réforme*, the five-member *Comité d'Études Nord-Africaines* created in 1952 by the 16th regional synod of the *Église Réformée de France*, published an open letter ("L'Avenir de l'Algérie") which surfaced later as a "Lettre aux Métropolitains" in *L'Algérie protestante*.[10] The authors reflected an essentially reformist middle-of-the-road perspective. At one and the same time they repudiated the reactionary view that the French presence in Algeria must be preserved at any cost and the leftist argument that colonization had been responsible for all the territory's problems. If the writers expressed a moderate position, they were, however, totally opposed to outright independence for Algeria, which would at this time bring no benefits to any of the territory's communities. Here the representatives of Algerian Protestantism articulated a view close to that of the governor-general: Muslim society in Algeria was "exclusive, tribal, male-dominated, invested with supernatural (*sacral*) power and fatalistic." The poverty of the Muslim masses clearly resulted from an uncontrollable demographic explosion. The economic development needed to attenuate this poverty was problematic given the area's meagre natural resources. Under these unpromising circumstances, Algeria must remain dependent on the largesse of Paris for the foreseeable future.

The committee conceded that the European minority was not without its responsibility for this sad state of affairs. The wealthier *colons* who dominated the *Assemblée algérienne* exercised a disproportionate influence on the local administration and the media. What was required, in the view of the report, was the full implementation of the 1947 statute, together with a clearer and more coherent sense of direction for Algeria on the part of the government in Paris.

The committee members were clearly nervous about the implications of enfranchising the Muslim majority. Indigenous society, they felt, contained few genuinely creative forces; in fact, the sense of resignation which pervaded the masses and their ability to endure suffering had been a key factor in the area's centuries-old stability. Democracy, which was not an infallible method of government, might pose problems if brought suddenly to such a society but it was vital nevertheless to involve the majority in the evolution of Algerian life, something even benevolent administrators had tended to neglect. "Many things are being done *for* the Muslim population, but nothing is done *with* them or *through* them," the committee concluded, balancing caution with a prudent and imprecise expression of good intentions.

In mid-April, the Algerian question was the central theme on the agenda at the Thirtieth Congress of *Christianisme social* held at Lyon.[11] Professors Jean Bichon of the University of Algiers and Charles-André Julien of the Sorbonne opened a free-wheeling debate by presenting radically different perspectives. Bichon's views on the cultural as well as spiritual incompatibility of Christianity and Islam were already well known. He argued that Christians were impelled by conscience to agitate for reform but that any change in the existing situation must be slow and piecemeal, not radical or fundamental. Julien, whose Socialist convictions were modified by a belief that nationalism was an irresistible force in the Mahgreb, argued that, while France had clearly brought benefits to Algeria, the overall balance sheet after 125 years of domination was negative. Four out of five Muslims in the colony were illiterate. Muslims now consumed only three-fifths of what they had consumed in 1900, partly because of the mother country's failure to introduce progressive agricultural methods.

Paul Ricoeur, whose reputation as a philosopher was already established, seconded the Julien position, arguing that it was time for France to adopt a policy of "constructive decolonization," not only in North Africa but in all her overseas territories. A strong metropolitan administration sustained by a prosperous economy offered a splendid opportunity to act both firmly and generously. Two things ought to be done at once. Human dignity should be granted the colonized who still felt the sting of imperial domination and material assistance should be provided to a society suffering serious economic deprivation. Once these steps had been taken, Paris should promote the fundamental reforms needed to bring Algeria into the modern age.

At a more personal level, Ricoeur pleaded with his fellow-delegates to act as intermediaries between the Protestant communities in France and Algeria who had obvious difficulty in sharing the same perspective on events across the Mediterranean. Above all, the philosopher said in conclusion, "we must subordinate all of our judgments and consequently all the positions we end up adopting to the dictates of our conscience."

The congress, after debating these positions, passed three resolutions: (1) that Christians had an obligation to understand the Algerian dilemma before passing judgment one way or another, (2) that the solution to the existing imbroglio lay in Paris, not in Algiers, and (3) that the entire population of Algeria should elect a single electoral college which would then vote for separate Muslim and European assemblies, thus ensuring the representation of the whole community and of its two clearly different elements.

The problems of conscience raised by Ricoeur had already been addressed in very personal terms by Protestant soldiers who found themselves engaged in what they regarded as an unjust war. By the spring of 1955, some sixty conscripts had challenged the right of the state to commit them to battle. Late in May 1955, one of them, Pierre Tourne, a theology student preparing to enter the Reformed ministry, was brought before a military tribunal at Metz. When the presiding officer cited the military career of St. Paul as evidence of the Christian obligation to serve in the army, the audience, clearly sympathetic to Tourne, protested and was ordered to leave the court. The only witness for the defence, Pastor Loux, then took the stand. Noting that the accused had served as a volunteer worker in the United States and Israel, he went on to say that a recent national synod of the Reformed church had passed a resolution reproaching the government for its refusal to rule on the issue of conscientious objection.

The commissioner appointed by the government conceded that the accused was a man of high moral character and the defence attorney then argued against a judgment which would involve a violation of conscience. In the end, Pierre Tourne was condemned to a year in prison. Writing to *Réforme* following the sentence, Pastor Loux urged readers to join him in urging that France's legislation concerning conscientious objection be brought into line with the more enlightened policies in other advanced countries.[12]

Reaction to the conflict in Algeria by Protestant university students, many of whom, like Pierre Tourne, were subject to a military call-up, was expressed through the *Fédération Française des Associations Chrétiennes d'Etudiants* (popularly known as *La Fédé*) after Daniel Galland, editor of the association's bi-monthly review *Le Semeur*, brought the issue before his readers.

Galland had himself become involved early in 1955 in response to an invitation from the *Centre catholique des intellectuels français* to join in a study day on Algeria which brought together Christians and representatives of the MNA and UDMA. As a result, a group of students in the Lyon area belonging to ideologically diverse organizations (Communist and Socialist as well as Christian) formed a committee to lobby against military repression in Algeria and for democratic freedoms there.

Following his own involvement in this lobbying effort, Galland devoted an entire issue (the April-May number) of *Le Semeur* to developments in North Africa.[13] His own contribution to this special issue was a highly provocative piece ("Pour la paix en Algérie") reflecting what was at the time very much a minority viewpoint. It was clear, the student editor wrote, that France was facing, not a few scattered terrorist bands, but an army of national liberation, something which Governor Soustelle clearly understood. The options were clear: "The prior question now is to decide whether the *Algerian nation* (in italics in Galland's text) which will be brought into being one way or another, will be created through an absurd war or in friendly association with France." Soustelle talked of pacification but what was in fact happening was a pitiless police operation. The Muslim masses were in a state of generalized rebellion, provoked to desperate action by a series of broken promises. The government's proper response was to end all repression and begin serious negotiation with the nationalist leadership including those in prison, taking as a starting point a clear understanding that "Algeria is *not* France!"

Among the mostly negative responses to Galland's article was a lengthy letter from the student correspondent for *Le Semeur* in Algiers, Bernard Picinbono.[14] Picinbono was the son of a prominent *colon*; the family lived on friendly terms with their Muslim farmhands and neighbours. He began by denouncing the caricatural portrait of evil colonizers and innocent colonized which Galland, like others before him, had relayed to people living in France. Such reporting implied that the actions of wicked settlers and perverse colonial administrators fully justified armed rebellion when in fact the tough measures taken by the authorities had been provoked not by the *colons* but by cowardly bands of assassins who had (among other things) murdered European farmers.

Algeria, Picinbono went on, was not a society composed of a few wealthy *colons* and a mass of poverty-stricken Muslims. Like so many other observers from afar, Galland had ignored the thousands of *petits Français* who lived there, many of whom were descended from families which had been in the territory for generations. It might be noted, he added (prophetically, as it turned out) that these same "simple French folk" were just as capable of acts of despair as their Muslim neighbours.

Having done his best to vindicate settler society, Picinbono went on to expose what he saw to be the peculiar political problems facing Algeria which, unlike Tunisia and Morocco, had not been a formally organized state at the time of the conquest. It was hard to imagine or support the rapid introduction of democracy where a tiny minority dominated both cultural and economic life while the vast mass was both illiterate and impoverished. Such a change would necessarily mean control by the least developed element. The best solution in the current circumstances, Picinbono wrote, would be the resolute application of the 1947 statute.

As for the notion of a "Franco-Muslim community," something mainland intellectuals talked of, Picinbono dismissed the idea as sheer fantasy. Progressive-minded people ought to try instead to propagate the idea of equality in a culture which was still strictly hierarchical. They ought to insist on a shift in the Muslim attitude towards women and they should fight for the idea of *laïcité* in Algeria given that Islam, like Catholicism, was theocratic by nature. Showing some Protestant passion, Picinbono recalled for the readers of *Le Semeur* that Muslims repudiated salvation through Christ's sacrifice and hated the Jews; the campaign to liberate them was thus bound to be both long and arduous.

Galland did not publish Picinbono's letter for five months, something for which he later apologized. The apology, however, was followed by a renewal in somewhat modified form of the editor's original indictment.[15] France's Christians were not as Manichean in their view of European-Muslim relationships as Picinbono had inferred, Galland wrote. They were, however, surely justified in asking to what extent "poor whites" in the territory had in any way associated with the Muslim masses among whom they lived, especially in terms of political action. Galland suggested that Christians living in Algeria tended to see the conflict in purely spiritual terms when it seemed obvious to an outside observer that the problems as well as the solutions lay in the political sphere. Was this really a time, as Picinbono seemed to imply, to evangelize the natives when Christianity was seen as an integral part of our imperial presence? The example of Catholic worker-priests who joined assembly lines and shared the class struggle before preaching the Gospel to the proletariat was there to show where the best chance for conversion lay.

Taking up the challenge, Picinbono expressed his frustration that the gulf between the French on the two sides of the Mediterranean had become even wider since his original letter to *Le Semeur*. Christians in mainland France had a tendency to be self-righteous, he admonished, adding that "Algerian Christians have a right these days to ask for more tact and compassion from their French brethren." There were two generalizations in particular, both of them false, to which those living in France tended to subscribe: that the self-government of nations was a universal panacea and that negotiation was always the noblest, truest course of action, a belief which had led up to (and then sanctioned) the Munich conference of 1938.

The correspondence between these two idealistic young Protestants continued through the long conflict ahead. A quarter of a century later, reflecting on this exchange, Daniel Galland, who had become a Reformed pastor, remembered how Picinbono's letters had helped him to understand the deep internal conflict not only of Picinbono but of other sensitive members of the settler community such as Albert Camus and Jean Daniel, the Jewish intellectual who later went on to edit the leftist *L'Observateur*. All of these men might well be personally innocent, Galland conceded, devoid of the colonialist attitudes of the society into which they were born. The destiny of Algeria, however, was bound to be shaped without (and even against) them, as Galland had warned in the unwittingly cruel predictions he had offered in *Le Semeur* as early as 1955.[16]

While concerns about France's Algerian policy were stirring up debate within the metropolitan Protestant community, Soustelle prepared to use the special powers granted him by the *état d'urgence* which the National Assembly voted in April. To reassure the Muslim majority, Soustelle met representatives of several nationalist groups on 28 March, insisting that the emergency decree would not be used to silence political discourse. The governor repeated his commitment to basic political and economic reform and promised to work for a substantial increase in the number of deputies Algeria would send to the National Assembly. At the end of the meeting, one of his Muslim visitors described Soustelle as "a man of good faith whom one could clearly trust if only those around him would give him a free hand."

On 2 April the governor had a surreptitious meeting with Ferhat Abbas, the pharmacist-turned-revolutionary whose arrest most *colons* would have applauded. Abbas suggested that, given the obduracy of the settlers towards any change, Soustelle's only method of effecting reform would be to arrest the most reactionary elements among the *colons* and then to despatch nationalist representatives to negotiate an end to the war.[17]

Three days after this less than promising dialogue, Soustelle issued a blunt directive to all his subordinates demanding that they abandon any trace of the old colonial mindset. Words or gestures of contempt, no doubt once tolerated as expressions of rough comradeship between conquerors and conquered, were no longer admissible. Hurting the self-esteem of a proud people would leave hard to heal wounds. A policy of courtesy and respect for the Muslims was just as important as a programme of political and economic reform.

The state of emergency meanwhile allowed Soustelle to purge the schools of real and alleged communist teachers, a move which immediately clouded his relations with Monteil and Tillion and brought bitter criticism from the metropolitan leftist press. The emergency decree passed by the National Assembly also covered the governor-general's decision in the spring of 1955 to transfer suspected subversives to *camps d'hébergement*, detention centres which leftist critics in France denounced as ill-disguised concentration camps.

Without Soustelle's knowledge, right-wing army men began abusing the emergency legislation, inflicting torture on suspected terrorists and holding entire villages "collectively responsible" for FLN activity in their areas. Visiting the Aurès region in mid-May, the governor learned at first hand that this ruthless repression had not only produced great devastation but that it had engendered indiscriminately murderous retaliation by nationalist bands including the killing of a government officer, Maurice Dupuy, who had lived among the Muslims for years trying to improve their living conditions.

Maurice Voge remained highly sympathetic to Soustelle through this period of increasing violence. The radical pastor saw that the governor was caught between two fires. The wealthy settlers were angry with him on a number of grounds. He had rejected their proposal for a special citizens' militia, he had refused to arrest Ferhat Abbas, he had taken action against soldiers who pursued a policy of collective reprisals against Muslim communities, and he had liberated MTLD leaders whom the courts had judged to be innocent. These initiatives of Soustelle were without precedent, Voge noted, and they had resulted, not surprisingly, in a sustained campaign against the governor both in Algiers and in Paris where defenders of the settlers' interests were doing their best to have Soustelle recalled on the ground that he had become "the accomplice of the terrorists."

If the developments Pastor Voge was reporting on left him feeling little optimism, he was convinced that all was not yet lost because "M. Soustelle is totally committed to the achievement of peaceful coexistence in Algeria, showing the courage and character which we know he possesses. However, he has against him a situation he inherited on his arrival for which the *colons* are trying to make him responsible."[18]

Not recognizing the depth of Soustelle's rage over Dupuy's murder, Germaine Tillion urged him to contact the FLN leaders in the Aurès region where, she reported, the army's repressive measures were creating havoc. The governor-general turned a deaf ear to this suggestion and he and Tillion had no further exchange before her departure for France. Monteil meanwhile urged Soustelle to resign rather than carry out a policy with which he was surely not in agreement. In the end, on 24 June, the liberal major submitted his resignation, pointing out that there had been a fundamental change in policy with which he could not agree.

Late in May, the editor-in-chief of *Réforme* offered a critical analysis of the Algerian situation and a bold prescription for its remedy.[19] Most French citizens, Finet suggested, were unaware of the enormous wealth accruing to the nation from its imperial possessions. Faced with the insurrection of November 1954, they were in all likelihood unwilling to accept the sacrifice entailed in long-term, extensive, reform or, should reform fail, the equally costly problem posed by the evacuation and relocation of the hundreds of thousands of their fellow-citizens now living in Algeria. The nation's politicians were just as lacking in perception and vision. They intoned cryptic slogans such as "L'Algérie c'est la France!" without being willing to translate them into reality by turning the colony's three departments into fifteen with the concomitant increase in Muslim representation in the National Assembly. Nor were they ready to apply France's advanced but costly social programmes across the Mediterranean.

The most reasonable way out, Finet argued, would be to transform the existing relationship between France and Algeria into an association and the most feasible means of negotiating this arrangement would be to open a dialogue with moderate nationalists, the very people who had all too often been arrested while revolutionary terrorists took to the hills. Objective observers, Finet suggested, might well compare the Muslim rebels in the Aurès mountain range to the *maquisards* who had taken up arms against the Nazis.

Frustrated on all sides in his efforts to promote *la petite intégration* (the achievement of legal and political equality as well as economic justice for the Muslim majority in Algeria), Soustelle decided to embark on an even more grandiose project. The *grande intégration* to which the governor now committed himself involved the full administrative merger of Algeria and France. Soustelle envisioned liquidation of the Algerian Assembly and the subsequent proportionate representation of the territory's population in the National Assembly in Paris (where it would constitute a considerable bloc). He also insisted that Algerians of all backgrounds must be guaranteed the living standards and socio-economic benefits which obtained in the *métropole*. This was in effect the ultimate expression of Soustelle's Jacobin republicanism.

To help establish the conditions which would give this highly ambitious strategy some chance of success, Soustelle insisted that Muslims be brought into the Algerian administration, ultimately to constitute half of its personnel, something which would be furthered by the creation of a *Centre de formation administrative*. Efforts at literacy and higher education would be intensified so that Algerians would become truly and effectively bilingual.

The revised reform plans of the governor-general were put together in what became known as *Le Plan Soustelle*, which he submitted to Premier Faure and Interior Minister Bourgès-Maunoury on 1 June. Shortly afterwards, during an official visit to Paris, on 7 June, Soustelle declared that his ultimate aim was to transform France's three Algerian departments into "a veritable French province."

After a debate in the National Assembly, the cabinet approved the Soustelle Plan and, on 4 July, the governor's six-month mandate was extended for a further half-year.

In mid-July, following the release of the "Plan Soustelle," Paul Adeline (the nom de plume of Pierre Alexandre, a *pied-noir*, pastor, and Africanist scholar who championed the cause of emerging third world nations) in *Réforme*, published a basically sympathetic analysis of the governor-general's approach:

> Obliged to sustain a permanent and exhausting effort to break through the barrier between himself and the colony both by a part of the upper echelons of his administration and by a selfish or cynical European population, (Soustelle) cannot even turn to a large and qualified staff because the war in Indochina has decimated the ranks of officers trained in native affairs.[20]

Adeline went on to note that Soustelle's campaign to achieve simultaneous pacification and depauperization required at least 200 young and vigorous subordinates who were simply not available. Nor could the governor-general rely on native police units to maintain order in a sustained fashion. Adeline concluded that terrorists would be able to frustrate Soustelle's plan by continuing to sow panic among Europeans as well as Muslims and to create increasing division between the two communities.

The publication of the Soustelle Plan also elicited favourable responses in the pages of *Cité nouvelle*. Jean Scelles applauded the proposals as far as they went but in a show of evangelical zealotry, insisted that no real progress in Algeria was possible without a concerted attack on alcoholism and prostitution which, he insisted, the authorities tolerated. Scelles was convinced that reform from above, however well-intentioned, was insufficient. The Muslim masses needed to be engaged, something which required the intervention of those who enjoyed their confidence at the local level.[21]

Maurice Voge was pleased that Paris, by endorsing the plan, had renewed its confidence in Soustelle. This would increase his moral and political clout at a time when the governor would be called upon to impose respect for the law and the administration of social justice. By drafting his plan, Soustelle had forced the government in Paris to abandon its passivity. The governor was now pledged to pursue a policy of "moderate integration through the application of the 1947 statute, without shutting the door on a solution based on a federal association between France and Algeria," a policy bound to appeal to moderate nationalists. The governor's straightforward character and his willingness to deal with representatives of the Muslim community would be key factors in favour of success. Voge wished him well.[22]

Pierre Poujol, a third partisan of "Social Christianity," joined in backing Soustelle. The governor had avoided a serious deterioration of the situation by vetoing the creation of a settlers' militia at a time when three-quarters of the territory was still unaffected by the rebellion. As a result of this and other intelligently balanced policies, simple Muslim villagers had learned to distinguish between a European such as Soustelle and a reactionary *colon* such as Henri Borgeaud. In Poujol's opinion, the average Muslim "remains very happy that the disinterested perspective of Soustelle is being supported." It was all the more important under these circumstances, the contributor to *Cité nouvelle* added, "that skillful scheming against Soustelle not give this Muslim the opposite impression."[23]

Soustelle's liberal collaborators, one after the other, had abandoned him as a result of his shift to the right. Now the French Socialist Party (SFIO), which had condemned the 1954 insurrection and supported the maintenance of Algeria within the French Union, also began to express its critical concern about the governor-general's policies.

At the national convention of the SFIO held at Asnières, between 30 June and 3 July 1955, delegates reflected at length on the Soustelle policy of integration which in fact closely resembled the approach the party had championed since before World War II.

In the end, delegates condemned the Soustelle Plan and, influenced by the Protestant Charles-André Julien, passed a resolution urging dissolution of the existing Algerian Assembly and, in an initial phase of reform, its replacement by a body based on equal representation of Europeans and Muslims and chosen by a single electoral college. This proposal had the advantage of involving the Muslim majority in the selection of European delegates (and vice versa) and thus of reassuring the *colons* that they would not be marginalized as Algeria underwent reform.[24]

Soustelle's controversial pacification strategy faced further challenges following a series of massacres of Europeans and pro-French Muslims at

Philippeville and in other parts of the Constantine region beginning on 20 August and lasting three days.

The riposte to this calculated assault was not surprising. Some 2,000 Muslims were murdered by European vigilantes, many of them armed for the first time. This retaliation was not only predictable but a calculated part of the FLN strategy of forcing the two communities into irreversible conflict. Soustelle, who rushed to the scene of carnage, was overcome with rage and nausea.

A week after the slaughter, Pastor André Chatoney, president of the Algerian synod of the Reformed Church, addressed the European community over *Radio-Algérie*. Chatoney, one of the few pastors serving in Algeria who had been born in the territory, had been in Philippeville just before the tragedy. He offered prayers for those who had been victims of hatred and fanaticism but also for those who lived all too often in poverty in city slums or in the countryside and who, like a leaderless flock, had ended up following evil shepherds. While the settlers needed to be reassured and guaranteed security in their grief, they should, despite their distress, seek God's forgiveness for those who had left them bereaved. Christ died, Chatoney made bold to remind his listeners, for all human beings, whatever their ethnic origin.[25]

The massacre of 20 August brought a new sense of urgency and alarm to correspondents of *Cité nouvelle*. André Monnier pointed out that the victims on both sides had become the unwitting instruments of rebellion or repression. In the aftermath, the outlook was grim: "Only extraordinarily, not to say heroically, generous measures can now stop the slide into chaos," Monnier warned. He urged President Boegner of the FPF to convoke a special general assembly of the Federation including representatives from the North African churches.[26]

Writing in the same (25 August) issue, Pierre Fontanieu, who had just returned from a holiday in Algeria, reported that there was now a high level of fear throughout the territory. The Muslims had developed a new sense of unity, and Soustelle was the only person able to contain the settlers' urge towards mindless repression. Unfortunately, there was a serious lack of qualified cadres to support him in his efforts to combine control of the situation with the aggressive promotion of reform. For Maurice Voge, the 20 August slaughter put an end to Soustelle's integration policy. At best, what remained was the possibility of establishing a federal link between France and Algeria through a revised version of the French Union, something which might be thought through in a round-table discussion following a mutually acceptable truce agreement.[27]

After the 20 August slaughter, it became clear to all that the forces ranged against the French presence in Algeria were well organized, ruthless, and little attracted to compromise. As Soustelle reacted to these forces by an increasingly unconditional application of the pacification policy, the Ultras among the *colons*, including the influential newspaper owner Alain de Sérigny, shifted from opposition to support for the governor-general. Like so many of his predecessors, Jacques Soustelle was about to become the hostage of the European minority. His faith in the long-term goal of integration would remain, but his power to transform that ideal into an everyday reality would henceforth be radically reduced.

In an effort to reassure the Muslim majority that he remained committed to reform over the long haul, Soustelle presented the September session of the Algerian Assembly with a revised series of proposals. These included the implementation of the statute of 1947, the teaching of Arabic in Algeria's schools, a substantial redistribution of land to Muslim farmers, and the formal secularization of a legal system which was still governed in part by the Koranic code. However, when the president of the first, European-dominated, college countered with a more modest proposal of his own, Soustelle's effort was effectively sabotaged.

Not surprisingly, Soustelle's programme had also alienated most *colons* who now became even more determined to maintain the status quo. Sporadic terrorist attacks by the FLN through the fall of 1955 helped set the stage for creation of European counter-terrorist organizations.

The international community, meanwhile, was beginning to show an interest in the Algerian conflict. On 30 September, the General Assembly of the United Nations voted (28-to-27) to put the Algerian question on its agenda.

Early in October 1955, the council of the FPF expressed concern about "all the human and spiritual suffering being experienced" in Algeria but "did not feel itself capable at the moment of suggesting any concrete solutions."[28] At the meeting of the Assembly held at Montpellier at the end of October, delegates reiterated the council's message of compassion and deplored both terrorism and counter-terrorism but declared themselves incapable of establishing responsibility for the recent dramatic increase in violence. The text of the resolution did, however, express "humiliation for the errors and failures which are compromising the work of France."[29] No doubt the use of force might have been necessary to preserve life and civil order, but reprisals which struck at the innocent were indefensible, nor could a policy based on force without a concomitant concern for justice be supported.

Those who drew up the resolution went on to declare that Christians directly affected by events in Algeria must serve as pioneers in the search for reconciliation. The faithful in uniform were assured of sympathy at a time when many were no doubt experiencing conflict between obedience to their conscience and duty to their superior officers.

While this text was basically apolitical, it did contain an attack on French public opinion which was seen to be irresponsibly indifferent to events in Algeria. Implicitly, it also criticized the government for failing to express a clear and resolute policy concerning the nation's purpose in Algeria. Protestants everywhere were urged to prepare to make sacrifices to alleviate the social and economic misery of the North African masses whose circumstances could be improved only at considerable cost to citizens in the homeland. The text of the resolution was forwarded to President Coty and to Premier Faure.

Despite mounting criticism, the policy of integration and Soustelle's method of implementing it were defended by members of the Faure ministry in the National Assembly. Finet made his doubts about that policy known to readers of *Réforme*. Given that both Tunisia and Morocco had already been granted autonomy in close association with France, Finet argued, either the redefinition of Franco-Algerian relations on some kind of federal basis or an attempt at full assimilation of the colony into the political life of the metropolis seemed the only remaining alternatives. One had to recognize that the Algerian people had achieved a sense of collective solidarity which it would be foolish to dismiss.[30]

Of all those who wrote articles on Algeria for *Réforme* during this phase of the conflict, the distinguished theologian and social scientist Jacques Ellul proposed the most radical solution: total disengagement. Ellul began the case he put for this solution by observing that well-intentioned Protestants tended to feel a need to become committed to one or other side of any contentious moral issue. Unfortunately, he insisted, there were cases when remaining *dégagé* made much better sense, as was particularly true in the case of Algeria. Supporting radical reform in the territory, as the editors of the Catholic review *Esprit* had urged twenty years ago, had made some sense at the time. However, it was not now possible to support either side since both FLN terrorists and *colons* were using unjustifiable violence.

Ellul went on to observe that the kind of nationalism preached by the rebels and which so many French Protestants championed (while condemning its domestic expression), had always brought evil in its wake. However, the phenomenon had now become a reality in the everyday lives of North Africans, and those who wished Algeria well should try to help those living there to avoid its excesses. In fact, Ellul concluded, the wisest course of action under the circumstances would be for France to withdraw entirely from Algeria in order to let passions cool and wounds heal and then to start preparing reform in black Africa immediately before it was too late there as well.[31]

Ellul's intellectual disenchantment with the conflict was matched by a growing reluctance to serve in Algeria on the part of young men called up to join the increasingly large contingent battling the FLN. There had been a serious incident at the Gare de Lyon early in October. The police had been brought in to make arrests after 600 protesters blocked a troop-train to demonstrate their opposition to an old-style colonial war. The socially radical Pierre Poujol disapproved of this act of disobedience, arguing that citizens must either oppose war in general or serve the nation when called upon. He hoped, however, that those heading for Algeria would resist any order involving them in an atrocity.[32]

At the end of November, Soustelle called the Algerian Assembly into extraordinary session in a further effort to gain consent for the reform agenda which he had earlier set aside. To his great distress, the same group of Muslim deputies repeated their opposition both to his specific reform proposals and to the integrationist philosophy which lay behind them.

On 2 December, Edgar Faure dissolved the National Assembly and its counterpart in Algiers, thus removing any opportunity for either body to explore more fully (not to say endorse) Soustelle's reform plans.   The dissolution of parliament also automatically carried with it the end of the emergency decree which had permitted the governor-general to detain suspected terrorists.   After summoning Algeria's prefects and gaining their support, Soustelle decided to defy Paris and maintain the state of emergency.

What hurt Soustelle most as his administration intensified its parallel pursuit of repression and integration was an outburst of substantial criticism from the French intellectual community.   At the end of the year, Francis and Colette Jeanson, whose opposition to the handling of the Algerian issue later brought them to engage in illegal support for the FLN, published *L'Algérie hors-la-loi*, a forthright indictment of Soustelle's administration.[33]   At about the same time, a manifesto was published by the *Comité d'action des intellectuels contre la poursuite de la guerre* which had been founded in the fall of 1955 with a double aim: to condemn the government's Algerian policy and to influence voters in the forthcoming election.

Soustelle's response to this indictment, published in the 3-4 December issue of *Combat*, was as incisive as it was swift.[34]   The veteran ethnologist began by establishing his own substantial intellectual credentials. "Even when fully committed in action, I remain an academic, a teacher and writer. I believe in the intrinsic worth of thought, of research and of reflection." His critics were wrong on all counts of the indictment they had brought against him. They referred to the "war" in Algeria when no such state of affairs existed: they had made no analysis of the origins of the rebellion which they mistakenly assumed was inspired by the same principles which had guided the French masses in 1789. In fact, Soustelle pursued, adopting an argument which would be taken up (albeit from a different perspective) by defenders of French Algeria, the aim of the rebels was "the creation of a theocratic and racist state." Even more outrageously, those who attacked him had slandered their countrymen in uniform by calling them "killers." They spoke a great deal about honour, something he reminded them it was possible to defend in other ways than by penning slanderous manifestos.

The governor-general ended his response with a vigorous resumé of his own consistent opposition to tyranny, whether during the Popular Front experience, the Resistance, or during the current battle against reactionary terrorism. "*I* have not changed," Soustelle proclaimed to his adversaries. "If now, in the name of medieval totalitarianism, France is asked to renounce not only Algeria but in effect herself as well, I will not be a party to such a betrayal."

While Soustelle felt increasingly under attack by the French intellectual community, he was able as governor-general to count on Paul Adeline, whose sympathy and support surfaced again in a lengthy review of the Algerian situation published in *Réforme* at the beginning of October.[35] Ever since issuing the statute of 1947, the pastor reminded his readers, France had vacillated between the traditional Jacobin policy of centralization and an effort to accord Algeria a measure of autonomy. And since the 1954 insurrection, the administration in Paris had been even more irresponsible, simply letting the governor-general puzzle out policy on his own, without giving him the appropriate means to implement what he chose to do. The Soustelle Plan, inspired by a genuine search for justice, had been subverted by insufficient funding and delays in execution. The result was an increasingly costly mix of repression and reconstruction.

If Adeline concluded that a way out of the political dilemma in Algeria was hard to find, he was equally pessimistic about the military situation in the fall of 1955. Conscripts called up for duty had little faith in the cause they were asked to serve. Most had equal disdain for "dirty Arabs" (*sales bicots*) and self-interested *colons*. Non-commissioned officers had a tendency to engage in indiscriminate methods of fighting while their superiors were nervous about the way French public opinion would react if they risked soldiers' lives. The rebels meanwhile had established control over a large part of Algeria and were intimidating the population in many other areas. Any long-term solution would clearly depend on the Muslim majority. Winning their confidence was essential if the course of the conflict were to be reversed and such a change was in turn dependent on generous sacrifice from the French population at large.

Late in October, Adeline returned to the defence of Soustelle, the only person to have evolved a comprehensive plan to solve the Algerian dilemma.[36] If given strong support, the governor-general had perhaps six months in which to achieve his aim; he was fully aware that there were *colons* ready to hold on to their privileges by any means, including the importing of 1,000,000 new Italian immigrants. Adeline agreed with Soustelle that, whatever solution might issue from any elections following the pacification the governor-general was striving for, the double college in the Algerian Assembly ought for the moment to be retained, since most Muslims were insufficiently assimilated and tended to be reactionary in outlook.

At the beginning of December, Jean Czarnecki, regular contributor to *Cité nouvelle* until the end of the conflict, brought a radically new perspective to bear on events. Czarnecki had been a professor of philosophy in Algeria for sixteen years and was an active member of the Reformed church. He made two key points in this first article. To begin with, he argued that the governor had lost all credibility:

> All Algerians are disappointed in Soustelle. On the one hand, there are those for whom *ratissages* ("the combing out of terrorist nests"), concentration camps and collective reprisals are inadequate methods by which to contain the situation and who want him to commit himself unconditionally to the use of force. On the other hand, there are those who reject him because he is promoting a programme of reform and integration which are no longer seen as sufficient.

Czarnecki went on to describe more fully what he summed up as the overall disappointment of the liberal community in Algeria at Soustelle's capitulation to the forces of reaction:

> People are clearly surprised that a man who is obviously as honest as he is intelligent should show himself to be so blind to reality and to let himself be stopped in his tracks by the least admirable private interests. All those who once placed their hopes in him have now abandoned him.[37]

Some liberals in the European community, Czarnecki added, were turning for leadership to the progressive mayor of Algiers, Jacques Chevallier; others had given up and were ready to leave but could not sell their property. For Czarnecki, the lesson of all this was clear. Paris must recognize the FLN and begin negotiating while there was still time.

At the very end of his mandate, Soustelle faced a special moral and political challenge from one of France's most prestigious writers, the Algerian-born Albert Camus who, abandoning a resolutely neutral stand, published a series of articles in *L'Express* (September 1955 - February 1956). Friends of the existentialist writer, Muslim as well as European, supported the case he made in these articles for a truce in the conflict, followed by reconciliation and the working out of a new federal relationship between France and Algeria.

Camus visited Algiers briefly during the last weeks of Soustelle's administration. The novelist was convinced that a show of support for a "civil truce" on the part of his friends in both the Muslim and European camps might prepare the way for the spiritual and political reconciliation he wanted so much to sponsor.

A remarkably ecumenical group came together to arrange a mass rally in favour of the truce: the abbé Tossot, a close advisor to Cardinal Duval of Algiers, the Reformed pastor Henri Capieu, and a number of Muslim intellectuals. The rally itself, on 18 January, was attended by between 1500 and 2000 persons from all sectors of Algerian society (including Ferhat Abbas, who arrived late). Outside the hall, a crowd of European Ultras called down curses on Camus (and Mendès) and threatened to disrupt the meeting. In the end, those attending the rally dispersed to avoid what might have been a bloody racial encounter.

The Algerian question preoccupied politicians and voters on both sides of the Mediterranean as elections to the National Assembly scheduled for January 1956 got under way. On 8 December, the Socialist Guy Mollet joined Pierre Mendès France, François Mitterrand and the Gaullist Jacques Chaban-Delmas in a coalition known as the *Front républicain* whose platform included calls for peace and by implication the recall of the army in Algeria. One of the winners' vote-catching slogans was: "Let's put an end to the war in Algeria!," a phrase which implied to many a negotiated solution to the conflict and thus gave considerable encouragement to those trying to subvert Soustelle's reform efforts. The governor-general, who had run successfully under the Gaullist banner in 1951, returned twice to Lyon to campaign for his own re-election.

On 20 December, to forestall the uncontrollable turbulence of an electoral campaign in Algeria, Soustelle ruled that elections to the territory's seats in the National Assembly be postponed. This meant that, until the collapse of the Fourth Republic in May 1958 and subsequent fall elections, parliamentary deliberations over the territory's future were held in the absence of any direct representation from those most obviously affected, Muslims as well as Europeans.

The French parliament which emerged from the 2 January 1956 vote (during which Soustelle triumphed in his own Gaullist bastion in Lyon) was deeply fragmented. Pending efforts by the Socialist Guy Mollet to form a new government, Soustelle sent a memorandum to outgoing Premier Faure which was somehow leaked to the press.

In this memo, Soustelle revealed in full and explicit terms his integrationist formula for Algeria which the public could see meant the effective assimilation of the territory into France within six years. Implementation of this plan was, to say the least, radical. Among other things, it amounted to the application of French law and the equalization of living standards on both sides of the Mediterranean through the guarantee of equal salaries and social security provisions for Muslims. At the political level, the plan included the disappearance of the office of governor-general, the suppression of the Algerian Assembly, and the election of one hundred deputies from Algeria's departments to the National Assembly in Paris, based on a single electoral college. Not surprisingly, when details of Soustelle's grand design were leaked to the press, they caused the outgoing governor considerable embarrassment.

Revelations of Soustelle's grand design for Algeria caused serious disquiet in the settler community, Czarnecki observed, adding that Muslims seemed equally unwilling to endorse it. The correspondent for *Cité nouvelle* concluded that Soustelle had drawn up the plan to force his successor to face his responsibilities to all Algerians. The problem was that the departing governor had put forward an utterly unrealistic scheme. Speaking for himself, Czarnecki perceived the real options facing the administration in Paris and Algiers as increasingly clear but limited. One could try to defend the status quo which would bring an inevitable intensification of the conflict or one could negotiate a form of autonomy for Algeria in federation with France. This latter was something which the former governor had seen as nothing more than a prelude to full-blown independence (but which Czarnecki favoured as a status that might be achieved through secret negotiations).[38]

Soustelle's report to the government at the end of his second six-month mandate was given a generally favourable reception by Paul Adeline who noted that its tone "reflects fairly clearly the pseudo-Cartesian philosophy of assimilation which dominates public opinion."[39] Seen in abstract terms, Adeline remarked, Soustelle's plan was inspired by "an unambiguous generosity, recalling certain aspects of the conquering yet liberating

Jacobinism of the Year II." Had it been implemented in the aftermath of World War II when France was triumphant and Islam divided, it would have had a much clearer chance of success.

On 19 January, after learning that his successor was to be the Socialist Robert Lacoste (who would be named resident minister rather than governor-general), Soustelle submitted what he thought of as his Algerian testament to Mollet. He urged the new prime minister to do two things: to extend the mandate of the deputies who had represented Algeria in the National Assembly since 1951 until June 1956 and to promulgate a *loi-cadre* in which the government's policy concerning Algeria would be clearly set forth and then to mandate the appropriate authorities to implement it. Such a policy, Soustelle recommended, should clearly recognize the peculiar cultural personality of Algeria, and it should guarantee equal rights to all Algerians as individuals.

Two weeks after the electoral triumph of the Republican Front, the SFIO held a special national convention in the course of which party divisions, buried during the campaign, resurfaced. André Philip urged his colleagues in the new government to seek a political solution to the conflict across the Mediterranean by fashioning a new federal relationship between France and Algeria. In the immediate term, there was an urgent need to implement reforms in a territory where, the Protestant deputy insisted rather dramatically, some 8,000,000 men and women were on the verge of starvation.[40]

By contrast with the hostility which had greeted his arrival, Soustelle's departure from Algiers was accompanied by mass demonstrations. Crowds singing the Marseillaise and crying: "Ne partez pas! Ne partez pas!" blocked the route taking him to the ship waiting at anchor in the harbour. The *colons* who had greeted his arrival with such open hostility a year earlier and who had done their best to subvert his efforts at reform, now hailed him as their champion. The governor-general, no doubt giving way to the kind of political intoxication to which he was so susceptible throughout his career, convinced himself that he was in the presence of "an elemental and ardent collective will.... The entire multitude blended into one immense being whose heart spoke directly to my own."[41]

Soustelle's tenure as Algeria's governor-general may be seen as the last effort to impart to France's overseas empire the great Jacobin vision of 1793. Soustelle regularly referred to de Gaulle's Brazzaville declaration as testimony to the promise made by republican France that her relations to the once-colonized would be transformed by principles derived from the Revolution, thrown aside by Vichy and then resuscitated by Free France. A little more than two years after his return to power in 1958, De Gaulle would renounce this pledge, thereby definitely breaking with one of his most ardent but at times most restive supporters.

Jean Czarnecki offered the readers of *Cité nouvelle* a mixed review of the governor's administration.[42] Soustelle was admittedly a man of good intentions but he had not displayed the will needed to effect basic change. When the government in Paris refused to back him unconditionally, he had offered his resignation but had then withdrawn the offer a few hours later. Had he possessed a proper sense of his own dignity, Soustelle would have stood by his original decision and given up his post. Instead, by staying on, he had made himself responsible for all the faults of official policy throughout his time in office.

During the early spring of 1955 at a time when Governor-General Soustelle's policy of pacification had begun to excite protests in the French intellectual community, the territory had been witness to an extraordinary pilgrimage by a Protestant of a very different type.[43] Pastor André Trocmé, on six-weeks leave from the Geneva-based *Mouvement international de Réconciliation*, left Marseille at the end of April on what he admitted to himself might well be a rather quixotic enterprise. His aim was to apply the Laibach method, a technique by which adults who had received little formal education could learn a new language phonetically, and then transmit this knowledge to others. Trocmé was distressed that the education of Muslim boys ended automatically as soon as they reached military age and that girls were even less likely to be properly schooled. This resulted all too often in laziness among adult males and prostitution among females. So, the pastor told himself, "my arrival answers a real need!" Beyond this initial resolve lay the even more ambitious dream of winning devotees of Islam to the Christian faith.

On board ship crossing the Mediterranean, Trocmé got a precocious view of the Algerian drama: the Muslim passengers were all in fourth-class cabins, out of reach, while officers and men of the dreaded *Compagnie Républicaine de Securité* (CRS or riot police) strutted about on deck.

In Algiers, when the pastor met his first Muslim interlocutor, an equally ardent partisan of the Laibach method, they chatted in French (Trocmé's first lesson in Arabic would be on the following day) about the local situation. The Muslim described the young generation of Algerian Muslims as disoriented, adrift, susceptible to the propaganda they heard on the radio. Algerians were no longer confident in France's will or in her capacity to protect them. The pastor's contact remarked that there was even a sense, based on reading the French press, of a kind of "capitulation in advance" which encouraged young people to turn to pan-Arabism or to the United States or even to communism as a source of guidance and inspiration.

Within a few days of his arrival, after listening to panicky *colons* as well as Muslims, Trocmé was already coming to the conclusion that France and Algeria must ultimately go their separate ways. The Algerian majority, he sensed, was looking for a radical new form of leadership,

> a popularly based dictatorship, drawing its strength from the latent energy of the masses, stimulated by rudimentary slogans; a system which will force everyone to become literate and to work (even if this has to take the form of forced labour) and to profess the same faith. Democracy will have little to do with this inevitable development except perhaps to sow confusion between individual and collective liberty. Proud to be "freed", North Africans will forget to insist on personal liberation.

A week after his arrival, as his contacts with the Muslim population widened, Trocmé asked himself first of all whether it was not too late for "westernization" to take hold across the Mediterranean and secondly whether such a development would in the end be advantageous. The answer to the second question, which the pastor committed to his diary, was a qualified affirmative:

> Yes, in order that Islam, a rational religion which nothing in theory separates from the modern world, might become, like post-Reformation Christianity, a real seed-bed of sincere believers and cease trying to regulate and thereby to paralyse the social system of which it is a part.

Trocmé added, with a peculiar mixture of logic and naïveté: "Yes too, if one hopes some day to evangelize Algeria" something which he felt could not be undertaken as long as the Christian faith was seen to be synonymous with colonization.

Trocmé's politics were clearly liberal. He was a partisan of Pierre Mendès France and a regular reader of *L'Express*, the ex-premier's vehicle of expression following his resignation from office. He believed that France should give its support to Algeria's *nationalistes raisonnables*. At the level of communal life, Trocmé envisioned (again rather naively) that he and other Protestants should come together socially with Muslims on a one-to-one basis. On reflection, he had to admit that pairing Europeans and Muslims in this fashion was rather like trying to match peasants from the very Catholic Vendée with students from the *Collège cévenol* (a school founded by radical Protestants at Chambon-sur-Lignon in 1938). In practice, Trocmé discovered that the average *colon* and his usually illiterate Muslim neighbours neither came together socially nor understood each other when they did. The result was clearly tragic. "So the gunsmoke speaks out instead, as does senseless brutality, gratuitous crime and monstrous torture.... Everything, language, skin texture, general demeanour, clothing, status, religion, conspires to make contact and comprehension impossible."

Most *colons*, Trocmé began to feel, had become convinced that the Muslim majority, if allowed to prevail and assert their own authority, would throw all Europeans into the sea. As a result, they supported the most vigorous possible application of French military power. Even the liberal minority among the Europeans had a depressing message. One progressive-minded acquaintance told Trocmé that the policy of assimilation set forth in the Blum-Viollette formula might once have worked but it was far too late to attempt such a strategy now.

The failure to effect what had seemed like promising political linkages had obviously helped motivate many young Muslims to join guerrilla bands under the aegis of the FLN which in turn brought the army to intensify its pacification efforts. The powerful landowners ("féodaux") in the European community continued to clamour for the indiscriminate bombardment of villages where the rebellion was gaining momentum, Trocmé noted, adding that Governor-General Soustelle was so far resisting this demand.

In the face of the extremely discouraging evidence about Christian-Muslim and Franco-Arabic relations, Trocmé somehow managed to pursue his efforts at reconciliation. In the end, however, he was forced to agree that "Algeria is not assimilable to France." For the Europeans he came to know and befriend, this meant that Algeria must be returned to dependency under a strong paternalistic authority; for a majority of the "emancipated" (*évolués*) Muslims he encountered, this just as obviously implied the need for independence.

Trocmé's conclusions reflected at one and the same time Christian compassion and political realism. Most of the Europeans he had talked to, unlike the "féodaux," were objects of sympathy rather than anger: they were not privileged, nor were they living in luxury. In the main, they were "very humble folk indeed, nervous about their future, concerned about their pensions."

As for France's administrators in Algeria, whom Trocmé had assumed on arrival to be brutal and domineering, they were in fact well-meaning enough but hopelessly paternalistic when such an attitude had long since ceased to be effective. The real tragedy was than an impasse had been reached out of which no clear issue seemed possible, especially given the lack of any clear policy emanating from Paris. Trocmé might have added that the campaign for Muslim-Christian dialogue based on mutual respect and comprehension and, beyond it, the dream of Muslim conversions to Christianity which had taken him to Algeria in the first place, were illusory in the extreme.

The effort to promote language learning had not, however, been abandoned. A year after Trocmé's visit to Algiers, the *Association nord-africaine pour la lutte contre l'Analphabétisme* was still functioning with the aid of learning materials sent from Switzerland.

André Trocmé's brief visit to Algiers had no doubt been a rather quixotic enterprise from the beginning, at least from the evangelical point of view. Pastors who came to the territory to serve settler congregations brought a different perspective and faced a quite different set of challenges. The experience of Max-Alain Chevallier who arrived in Algeria in September 1955 illustrates the peculiar tension which liberal pastors faced as they did their best to understand the mindset of the European minority and tried to change it.[44]

Chevallier administered the parish of Hussein-Bey, an eastern suburb of Algiers, between the fall of 1955 and the summer of 1961 when he was named president of the Algerian synod. His wife Marjolaine, born in Tunisia, was the granddaughter of an ophthalmologist who moved to North Africa in 1897. When, presuming the new pastor and his wife to be French-born, parishioners commented with surprise at their openness towards Muslims and suggested that this positive approach would soon change, Mme Chevallier responded that, as a *pied-noir*, she was quite familiar with Muslim ways and not at all disconcerted by them.

The favourable disposition towards Muslim society and culture which the Chevalliers brought with them was reinforced by their contact with sisters of the Protestant community known as Deaconesses of Reuilly. They comprised an ecumenically minded group of women who lived in the poorest quarters of Algiers, the shanty-towns and outer suburbs where they would be able to witness police brutality and military repression used against Muslims in the years ahead.

Dealing with a congregation made up for the most part of hard-line settlers was taxing in the extreme for the pastor and his wife. As Mme Chevallier explains it:

> My husband and I often found ourselves at sixes and sevens with
> parishioners, feeling utterly helpless, trying our best to listen to

multiple points of view and quite capable of understanding them all, but unable to persuade the faithful in our own parish (and certainly not the greater number of them) to modify their position.

Like others in the tiny group of European liberals in Algeria, the Chevalliers were at first encouraged by the arrival of Governor-General Soustelle and then deeply disappointed when he shifted towards support of partisans of French Algeria.

Notes

1   CN, 11 November 1954.

2   CN, 25 November 1954.

3   A. Lazerus, "Natures et formes des interventions politiques des Eglises protestantes de France, 1945-1975." Typewritten M. A. thesis. Protestant Faculty of Theology, Strasbourg, 1975, p. 16.

4   CN, 27 January 1955. RCS, January-February 1955.

5   JOC, 2 February 1955.

6   CN, 10 February 1955.

7   Yves Courrière, *La guerre d'Algérie*, 2 vols. (Paris: Laffont, 1990).

8   Jacques Soustelle, *Aimée et souffrante Algérie* (Paris: Plon, 1956), p. 9.

9   CN, 24 February 1955.

10 REF, 12 March 1955.

11 RCS, May-June 1955.

12 REF, 11 June 1955.

13 SEM, April/May 1955.

14 SEM, Summer/Fall 1955.

15 Ibid.

16 Daniel Galland, *L'espérance maintenue. Chronique d'un homme du commun* (Paris: Le Centurion, 1979), p. 91.

17 Ferhat Abbas, *Autopsie d'une guerre* (Paris: Garnier frères, 1980), p. 75.

18 CN, 26 May 1955.

19 REF, 28 May 1955.

20 REF, 16 July 1955.

21 CN, 23 June 1955.

22 Ibid.

23 CN, 9 June 1955.

24 SFIO, *Bulletin intérieur* #81 (July 1955), pp. 12-13.

25 LAP, October 1955.

26 CN, 24 August 1955.

27 CN, 6 October 1955.

28 Arch. FPF., "Conseil de la FPF. Afrique du Nord. 4 octobre 1955."

29 Ibid., "Assemblée générale du Protestantisme. Montpellier octobre 1955."

30 REF, 15 October 1955.

31 REF, 22 October 1955.

32 CN, 6 October 1955.

33 Colette et Francis Jeanson, *L'Algérie hors-la-loi* (Paris: Seuil, 1956).

34 Combat, 3/4 December 1955.

35 REF, 1 October 1955.

36 REF, 22 October 1955.

37 CN, 1 December 1955.

38 CN, 2 February 1956.

39 REF, 21 January 1956.

40 OURS, "48eme congrès national de la SFIO, 14-15 janvier, 1956."

41 Soustelle, *Aimée et souffrante Algérie*, pp. 256-257.

42 CN, 2 February 1956.

43 CPED, André Trocmé, "Viens et vois," typed letters from Pastor Trocmé, 26 April-26 May 1955, recording impressions of trip to Algeria.

44 The information which follows derives from a letter to the author from Mme Marjolaine Chevallier, 1 September 1994.

André Philip
(Courtesy of Monsieur Loïc Philip)

CHAPTER THREE

1956—MOBILIZING AGAINST MOLLET:
THE RESTIVENESS OF THE PROTESTANT LEFT

Early in January 1956, following elections to the National Assembly, the Faure government gave way to a coalition known as the National Front, led by a new prime minister, the Socialist Guy Mollet. A month into his mandate, on 6 February, a date full of ominous resonance for French leftists (because of the failed fascist putsch against the Third Republic on 6 February 1934), Mollet visited Algiers. There he was treated to a humiliating verbal as well as physical assault by a crowd of 50,000 angry *colons*, many of them belonging, ironically, to the same lower middle-class constituency which regularly supported the SFIO in France. This rage had a variety of sources: the recent success of the FLN in seizing part of the port city of Oran, the appointment by Mollet of the liberal General Georges Catroux to succeed Soustelle, and the premier's suggestion that new elections for a single college be held in Algeria and that "la personnalité algérienne" be recognized.

The creation of a *Comité de défense de l'Algérie française* by Soustelle after his term as governor-general and the rallying to this organization of a number of distinguished intellectuals should have forewarned Mollet of deepening divisions inside France, even within normally solid republican lines, over the government's Algerian policy. However, it was his reception at Algiers which forced the premier to decide whether to pursue or abandon the Soustelle line of conduct. Mollet opted for the first course, dismissing Catroux, but had great difficulty finding a replacement. The new appointment went in the end to the Socialist Robert Lacoste who was named *résident général* rather than governor-general. In announcing his choice Mollet declared that the government's aim was to create a "Franco-Moslem community" but, as it turned out, the prime minister ended up supporting whatever measures Lacoste adopted. The newly appointed resident minister, for his part, travelled to Algiers determined to be the "Clemenceau" of the Algerian war, the resolute civilian who would bring the enemy to his knees while keeping the army under control.

Having named a tough-minded new administrator, Premier Mollet at the same time tried to keep open the possibility of a peaceful resolution of the Algerian conflict. On 28 February, the premier proposed a cease-fire, to be followed within three weeks by free elections to a body which would negotiate Algeria's constitutional future. Although the FLN balked at this formula, insisting on France's recognition of Algerian independence before any agreed upon cessation of hostilities, there were informal contacts between representatives of the premier and the FLN late in July in Belgrade and early in September in Rome. Unfortunately, these led nowhere.

Another series of confidential contacts with the FLN which began at this time, and which were sanctioned by Mollet, involved Jean Carbonare, a Protestant engineer, and Ferhat Abbas.[1] Carbonare was a graduate of one of France's most prestigious engineering schools whose political education as well as spiritual vocation had begun in 1943 as a sixteen-year-old in Besançon. During a visit to the city's Hôpital Saint-Jacques in 1943, he ran across some 300 Senegalese infantrymen who had been wounded fighting for France, then crowded together in the hospital's death-ward (*mouroir*), in effect an antechamber to the morgue. It was clear to the young Protestant that these African *tirailleurs* had been left to die by a country which was showing them neither gratitude nor compassion. Scandalized, Carbonare stood up at the end of the next Sunday service in his church asking for 300 volunteers, "godmothers" (*marraines*), to tend to the needs of the stricken Senegalese.

The spiritual shock which he had experienced during that hospital visit helped transform the young Carbonare into a radical pacifist. After a brief detention in a German prison camp for illicit border-crossing, he returned to France in 1945 where he again ran into large numbers of Senegalese soldiers. This time they had been demobilized, given ribbons for service rendered and then told to fend for themselves (*"Débrouillez-vous!"* their officers had instructed them, peremptorily, as they were discharged). To help remedy this situation, Carbonare founded an *Association d'accueil aux travailleurs immigrés*, the first of its kind in France. It was through this Association that the Protestant activist encountered Algerians from the Constantine area who were working in the Peugeot automobile plant near Besançon. When the Algerian insurrection began on All Saints' Day 1954, Carbonare felt immediately implicated. From the beginning of the conflict, he sensed that the only way to peace would be through granting political self-determination to the Algerian people.

When the Mollet government was formed in February 1956, Carbonare was reassured by the mayor of Besançon that the incoming prime minister was going to Algeria and would soon bring the conflict to an end. Following his public humiliation at Algiers on 6 February, the premier indicated through his colleague from Besançon that he would like Carbonare (who had established a reputation for friendliness towards Muslim Algerians and their cause) to go on a confidential mission to the Aurès region. He was to make contact with the FLN cadres there with a view to sounding out their demands.

Carbonare took on his secret mission without hesitation. He spent two weeks in the Aurès talking with the FLN leaders who relayed to him their three-stage formula for ending the conflict. This involved a clear recognition of *le fait national algérien* by the French parliament, the proclamation of a cease-fire, and subsequent discussions leading to a pacific resolution of Franco-Algerian relations. These conditions were of course unacceptable to the Mollet government which, instead of opening negotiations, mobilized more troops to put down the insurrection.

Despite what he felt had been a missed opportunity, Carbonare pursued his informal efforts at mediation between Paris and the FLN until he and Lacoste had a violent exchange. When Lacoste accused him of soft-heartedness, Carbonare replied: "But I live according to my sentiments!" and broke off all relations with the Socialist government which he felt had betrayed its mandate to end the conflict.

Carbonare was not alone in feeling sceptical about Mollet's Algerian policy. Recalling how Soustelle had arrived in Algeria with the best intentions which were soon frustrated, Paul Adeline worried that Mollet, too, would back way from supporting reform as a result of this first grim encounter.[2]

In the aftermath of Mollet's visit, Marcel Niedergang, a well-known student of Third World politics, offered the readers of *Réforme* a deeply pessimistic prognosis about the territory. Four out of five *colons*, he reported, repudiated in advance any political initiative emanating from Paris while a great many Muslims, convinced that force was their only hope of a better life, were already armed. Some of those who had given Mollet such a grim reception had indeed planned to kill Catroux and to proclaim their own de facto government. They were now persuaded that they had won a decisive victory and that the new prime minister had lost his nerve. As a result, Niedergang concluded, "the Algerian war has begun in earnest and it will be pitiless." The initiative in what the journalist described as "a proletarian revolt" lay with the rebels; the hope for pacification followed by the implementation of basic reform had become a pipe-dream.[3]

Niedergang's pessimism was echoed in the comments of regular contributors to *Réforme*. Paul Adeline noted that *colons* had proven themselves incapable of rising above parochial concerns. Soldiers in Algeria had little heart for the type of combat in which they were engaged. Domestic policy disputes, including reactivation of the old quarrel within Republican ranks over public support for the mostly Catholic *écoles libres*, prevented the government from making bold decisions about Algeria's future. Finally, French workers and intellectuals had too manichean a view of the world to see any justice in the position of Algeria's European minority. At a recent Paris rally of students, representatives of the FLN had been hailed as heroes at a time when the press was reporting new massacres of *colons* near Algiers.[4]

René Courtin (a Protestant law professor and regular contributor to *Réforme*) offered a truly apocalyptic vision of what lay ahead if France did not take steps to hold on to Algeria at whatever cost. Pan-arabism would triumph over European interests all around the Mediterranean. A holy war against the West was probable and black Africa would follow the Mahgreb in severing its links to France. Finally, a flood of refugees would pour into France, full of xenophobic sentiments, forming the basis of a fascist movement which might in turn engender a new Popular Front. Courtin clearly saw the latter as the most devastating consequence of French abandonment in Algeria.[5]

Jean Czarnecki, who had begun his regular column for *Cité nouvelle* with an indictment of Soustelle, denounced both "the astonishing ineptitude" which Premier Mollet had shown during his visit and the "emotional versatility" which the *colons* had displayed towards Soustelle. They had moved from an irrational antipathy at the beginning of Soustelle's mandate to an equally irrational endorsement at the end. Given the turbulent situation which the premier's visit had exposed, Czarnecki pleaded with the liberal minority of settlers to speak out in favour of peace and reconciliation and to commit themselves to staying in Algeria over the long haul.[6]

In the month following Mollet's ill-fated visit, Czarnecki openly urged negotiation with the FLN. His colleague among contributors to *Cité nouvelle*, Pierre Grosclaude, took the opposite tack, deploring the tendency of so many of his compatriots to engage in indictments of the government's policy concerning the territory. The loss of Algeria, Grosclaude argued, would not only be a catastrophe in itself; it would be highly damaging to the nation's economy, especially in the Marseilles area. Worse still, it would inevitably lead within a couple of years to the emergence of a fascist regime in France. The Protestant scholar repeated the conventional argument that Algeria, by contrast with Tunisia and Morocco, had had no independent political existence prior to the French conquest and was thus entirely a "French creation." Invoking the rationale that inspired government policy throughout much of the conflict, Grosclaude insisted that France was doing battle against "a barbarous insurrection supported from abroad."[7]

Czarnecki's appeal meanwhile did help bestir the progressive minority in the settler community. The *Fédération des libéraux d'Alger* was founded in March and deputed a group of its members to meet Lacoste on the 28th of the month. On 10 April, the Federation published a bulletin in which it repudiated racism in all its forms, proclaimed its faith in the possibility of peaceful coexistence among all of Algeria's ethnic groups, and asked for a dialogue with the rebels, followed by a cease-fire and discussions designed to redefine Algeria's place in a *Union Française* reconstituted along federal lines.[8]

During his tenure as resident minister, Lacoste persuaded the Mollet government to obtain special powers from the National Assembly so that he could police the situation while delivering reform by fiat in the face of Ultra and FLN opposition. As a result, on 17 March a decree was issued limiting freedom of the press and of movement in Algeria as well as sanctioning arbitrary house arrest and the collective punishment of whole communities where FLN terrorists had been active. Administrative reform followed these tough measures. Algeria's three departments were divided into twelve and at the local level, Muslims were brought into municipal politics. In order to promote economic change, some large European-owned estates were nationalized with a view to their transfer to Muslim proprietors.

Lacoste's efforts to promote reform from above did little to create the "Third Force" which, like Soustelle, he hoped would emerge once his good intentions became clear. Instead, terrorist acts continued. To those the resident minister responded with punishment by death, refusing appeals for clemency from Catholic and Protestant clergy. This resolute repression did nothing, however, to arrest the insurgency which gathered momentum and broadened its social base during Lacoste's mandate.

The personal humiliation experienced by Guy Mollet at the hands of Algeria's *petits blancs* had brought into sharp focus a developing crisis within Socialist ranks. Differences within the party over France's Algerian policy were only one aspect of an overall malaise. There was general restiveness about the tendency of the party executive to increase its control over local organizations during the Mollet years. There was concern about the drift to the right in French politics since the early 1950s which the SFIO had been unable to arrest. There were divisions about the advisability of joining the movement towards European unity and there was debate about the tactical advantages that might come from an alliance with the left-leaning Radicals grouped around Pierre Mendès France.

During this four-year crisis within the SFIO, Protestants played a leading role in defining and debating the options available to the party, including those affecting Algeria's future. Despite his personal dislike of Mollet, Gaston Defferre remained within the party mainstream and fashioned a *loi-cadre* which provided for the liberal restructuring of the *Union française*. Francis Leenhardt, like Defferre a veteran of the wartime Resistance, also supported an essentially reformist position within the Party. By contrast Robert Verdier, who had been editor of the Socialist newspaper *Le Populaire* until 1954 when he became a deputy and then president of the SFIO group in the National Assembly, together with André Philip and Charles-André Julien, argued for a radical reorientation of the party's colonial policy. Among other things they sought a clear recognition of the need to come to terms with what they perceived to be the irresistible (and essentially just) force of Algerian nationalism.

The government's Algerian policy was subjected to a particularly critical analysis by Julien, the leftist Protestant who had grown up in the territory and who, from adolescence through his career as an historian, condemned France's imperial presence there. Julien had been dismayed at the ruthless repression of Algerian rioters in 1945, correctly perceiving that it had only served to intensify the nascent nationalism of the Muslim masses. That same year, his fellow-Socialist Edouard Depreux had recommended that Julien be made under-secretary of state in charge of Algerian affairs in the Bidault government but the MRP prime minister had rejected him as too foolhardy for the post. Then, almost two years before the insurrection of November 1954, Julien had participated in a colloquium devoted to the nascent crisis in the Maghreb sponsored by the *Centre des intellectuels catholiques*. In an open letter to *Le Monde* following the conference, Julien noted that he had participated as a "non-believing Protestant" in a show of solidarity with other Christians whose consciences were troubled by France's policies in North Africa.

Early in 1956, as the Mollet government turned its attention to the North African situation, Julien resumed his public reflections about developments in Algeria, the hardest of the three parts of the Maghreb for France to deal with. In the professor's view, the problems with Algeria were multiple. It was very hard to find "valid interlocutors" in a part of the world where France had succumbed to her own myth, taking for granted that Algeria's three departments were an integral part of the motherland. French opinion refused to acknowledge that the Muslim majority was not represented proportionately as were citizens in France itself. Neither was it recognized that Muslims had radically different views concerning church-state relations and that they were undergoing a demographic explosion and increasing pauperization. In the immediate circumstances, he wrote, the use of military force against the insurgency was totally unproductive. The obvious solution, Julien concluded, was to follow the course already adopted in Morocco and Tunisia where the leadership of the rebellion had been recognized and bargained with.[9]

On his return from Algiers in February, Mollet had sought the advice of Julien, then teaching colonial history in Paris. When the premier expressed his determination to carry out a policy of unremitting firmness and revealed that he intended to name Robert Lacoste to implement this policy, Julien strongly advised against the appointment. Mollet never again sought the professor's advice.

In a letter to *Le Monde* at the beginning of May, Julien made a blunt public attack on the *colons* and by implication on the Mollet government. The European minority, the professor wrote, was consistently reactionary in outlook, easily given to racism as had been apparent in the antisemitic outpourings which occurred on D-Day and in the repeated opposition to the granting of any rights to the indigenous majority. Under these circumstances, reform was out of the question. Citing his hero Léon Blum, Julien went on to say that "colonizers do not have rights but rather duties, the first of which is to prepare the native population for self-government." In any event, the expert on the Maghreb added, it was foolhardy to deny the existence of *le fait national algérien*. Trying to arrest this reality by force of arms (especially when this force was being used at the discretion of a Lacoste) was fruitless. "Perhaps the Sultan of Morocco and Bourguiba (President of Tunisia) could be asked to act as intermediaries in ending the conflict. Subsequent free elections in Algeria followed by negotiations with the winners, is the best solution."[10]

While older left-wing Protestants were making known their dissent from the government's Algeria policy, Protestant youth on both sides of the Mediterranean continued to express the divergence of views which had already been revealed in the 1955 correspondence between Daniel Galland and Bernard Picinbono.

Le Semeur, the organ of the national Protestant student organization ("la Fédé"), kept its readers abreast of efforts made by the Federation in collaboration with its Catholic counterpart the *Jeunesse étudiante chrétienne* (JEC) to maintain a dialogue with the *Union générale des Etudiants musulmans* (UGEMA). A meeting held at the national level on 25 April at Montpellier had been encouraging, the national Protestant leaders believed.

The Algiers branch of the *Fédé*, meeting on 16 June, made clear that they thought otherwise. Analyzing the responses given the two Christian student groups by UGEMA, the Algiers executive concluded that the Muslims' responses to questions posed by their Christian colleagues proved there could be no meeting of minds. The Muslim students had revealed themselves to be intolerant and undemocratic; they always ended up identifying French colonial policy as the scapegoat for all the problems facing contemporary Algeria, thus making further exchanges of view pointless.

The bitterness which the Algiers group relayed to the editors of *Le*

Semeur when referring to UGEMA was replaced with a quite plaintive tone at the end of their comment. They declared that, while they deplored the excessive nationalism of such late nineteenth-century thinkers as Paul Déroulède, they felt as intensely French as they did Algerian. Finally, they declared themselves to be under enormous psychological pressure and urged their mainland comrades to pray for them.[11]

On 25 April, in an effort to heal the growing rift within SFIO ranks, Lacoste met a group of Socialist deputies including members of the party's executive committee. One of these was André Philip, who had voted for the granting of special powers to deal with the Algerian crisis on the ground that they would be useful not only in bringing the FLN to the negotiating table but that they might also help contain the Ultra element in the European minority. He questioned the resident minister at great length while making clear his own increasing doubts about the wisdom of the party's hard-line attitude.

The conversion of André Philip from support of the party (and government) position on Algeria to outright opposition prefigured the major crisis which would shake the SFIO to its foundations. This reorientation occurred in slow and subtle stages during the spring of 1956. Having earlier defended the award of special powers, Philip concluded in mid-April that the *petits blancs* were making the process of de-colonizing "explosive." Since these "poor whites" were unalterably opposed to the emancipation of the Muslim masses, leftists, he wrote in the weekly *Demain*, should recognize this. They should abandon the Marxist-inspired notion that the solution to the Algerian dilemma lay in a common front against the big interests based on class rather than ethnic lines.[12]

Bit by bit, Philip came to concede that there were "two nations living on the same soil" in Algeria, "two national consciences." Under these circumstances, the maintenance of French troops in the territory could be defended only if it were understood that they would be fighting on two fronts, against both FLN and the Ultras. They would be doing so, he urged, in order to act as arbiters between Algeria's European and Muslim communities. By the end of May, Philip had rejected the Mollet formula for ending the war in favour of direct talks with the nationalists.

For Philip, Guy Mollet's decision to reverse course following his ugly encounter with the crowd in Algiers was not only a betrayal of Socialist principles, it put the republican regime itself in peril. The Protestant deputy from Lyon was quite categorical. "The first gesture of the incoming *président du conseil* was to consecrate the collapse of the republican state by yielding unconditionally under the pressure of a fascist-style riot."[13]

Addressing the forty-eighth annual convention of the SFIO at the end of June, Philip combined a masterful analysis of the Algerian situation with a passionate exhortation to his comrades to change course. Algeria had always been poorly endowed, Philip began. What fertile soil there had been had been seized and developed by European landowners large and small while the native population was pushed back into mountainous areas or stretches of desert. The result was that, while the *colons* had by and large prospered, Algeria's overall agricultural production had in fact declined over the last one hundred years and erosion threatened what small tracts of cultivable land remained. The idea of remedying this grim situation through intensive industrialization was theoretically attractive but a lack of energy resources, together with the problem created by the vast distances between areas of potential development, made this option illusory. In any event, such a shift in strategy would bring no benefit to France and, as it was, the trade between metropolis and colony was less than that between France and the Saar.

In part as a result of circumstances, Philip went on to argue, the *fellagha* of Algeria, unlike their counterparts in Morocco and Tunisia, could never hope to achieve real independence. Here lay the nub of the dilemma: the nationalists were unable to attain their central aim while France was in no position to hold on to the territory indefinitely, something which would require sacrifices her citizens were clearly unwilling to make. The longer Paris waged war against the rebels, the more other nations, especially the United States and the Soviet Union, were bound to establish an economic as well as strategic presence there. Philip dismissed as unrealistic the government formula (cease-fire, free elections, negotiations) for ending the conflict. For one thing, in those areas supporting the FLN, its partisans would dominate the vote, if only through intimidation, and negotiations made little sense given that Algerian nationalists were insisting on prior recognition of the territory's independence. What the administration needed to do was to put forward a concrete offer such as the creation of an Algerian federation along Swiss lines with a series of cantons having either Muslim or European majorities, perhaps following a period of population transfers.

Philip went on to say that, while a long-term solution to the Algerian problem was being worked out, France should accelerate the reform efforts begun by Lacoste. These would include the redistribution of land owned by Europeans who should be compensated and the replacement of Algeria's current judges, civil servants and police officers most of whom came from the *métropole* and tended to end up representing the interests of the *colons*. In the present circumstances, the dispatch of more troops to Algeria would be counter-productive. Philip estimated that, for every 10,000 new soldiers sent across the Mediterranean, ten times that many Muslims transferred their loyalty to the FLN. As for the notion that, by remaining in the territory, France was serving the interests of modern-day capitalism, it would be more accurate to describe such a course as calculated to sustain a feudal and racist minority.

Philip insisted that Paris must act firmly and swiftly to shore up those liberal elements among the *colons* which the resident minister seemed intent on silencing and which would prove indispensable if some accommodation with the majority were to be hoped for. As it stood, the administration's support for right-wing, even fascist, elements in Algeria constituted a serious deviation from Socialist principles, all the more tragic because it was being offered at a time when the party's focus ought to be on improving the condition of the working class on both sides of the Mediterranean. Meanwhile, France's youth were becoming more and more disenchanted with politics in general. This was not surprising, Philip argued, since:

> our current Algeria policy is leading bit by bit to an abandonment of the very notion of a Socialist ethic.... We are abandoning the moral scruples which are at the very heart of socialism and we have put in their place respect for brute force and petty-bourgeois realism which cannot excite enthusiasm, not to speak of active support, in the nation.[14]

Other Protestant voices expressing opposition to the government's Algeria policy on both moral and political grounds joined Philip at this stage. In the 3 May issue of *Cité nouvelle*, the editors reprinted an open letter to Prime Minister Mollet from ten pastors from the Gard department. The appeal began with a dramatic expression of contrition in which the pastors confessed to feeling "a deep sense of shame at having hidden the great suffering of the Algerian people through their complicitous silence." The authors of the text urged the prime minister not to send any more troops across the Mediterranean and pleaded with him instead to consider the FLN as among the interlocutors with whom to discuss a cease-fire.[15]

Two weeks later Czarnecki declared that the army, which had pursued a policy of collective repression against the rebels until 20 August 1955, was now waging all-out war, applying the tactics of *razzia* (pillaging) which had been used during the conquest. To make matters worse, Ferhat Abbas, who might have become "the Algerian Bourguiba," had now joined the FLN. In Czarnecki's view, this grim intensification of the conflict left Paris no choice but to negotiate.

In the same issue, reflecting the degree to which even radical Protestants were divided on the Algerian question, André Monnier insisted that Algeria's Muslims were not yet ready for self-government. Pending their political education (which France should do everything to promote), the best solution, in Monnier's view was a form of protectorate for the territory.[16] Writing a month later, Czarnecki advocated a variant on this proposal, urging that something like the dominion status accorded members of the British Commonwealth might be a more appropriate solution.[17]

Pastor André Trocmé, who had visited Algeria in the summer of 1955 to propagate the Laibach method of second language learning, submitted three letters to *Cité nouvelle* a year later describing a seriously worsening situation. What had begun as a revolt, Trocmé observed, was now a full-blown revolution which no armed force could arrest. If this revolution succeeded, Algeria would throw off not only the evils of French imperial domination but also the benefits which included the transmission of the Christian Gospel, French mediation of universal cultural values, and technical as well as administrative competence. The Algerian intelligentsia had itself become infected by the hatred and fanaticism which welled up from the Muslim masses, men and women who still lived in conditions of deplorable poverty which it had taken the French people centuries to overcome.

The psychological transformation which the increasingly bitter conflict had produced was appalling, in Trocmé's view. French soldiers who had been conditioned by Christian teachings to show restraint in combat had seen their comrades butchered and were subsequently themselves brutalized, capable of hatred and of mass slaughter. Meanwhile, the typical francicized Muslim of 1954 who eagerly sought assimilation and was without any particular religious commitment had lost faith in France, joined the FLN and started turning up at the mosque for worship. Tragically, what had occurred during the height of the French Revolution, was repeating itself in the Algeria of the 1950s: "the exalted national hero subtly changes into the sadistic brute."

Taking the long view of developments not only in Algeria but elsewhere in the world, Trocmé was traumatized by what he saw as a grim paradox for the Christian West, at one and the same time overwhelmingly powerful in Africa and Asia yet doomed in both continents as far as spiritual impact was concerned. What wounded the pastor grievously was that the Christian message brought to these continents by their European conquerors had been from the beginning "a Gospel tinged with our baseness, our authoritarianism, our money and our violence." Yet, true to his faith, Trocmé found at least some grounds for hope. If Christians would only abandon their domineering ways and adopt the style of the Catholic Charles de Foucauld and the ecumenical Brotherhood of Taizé, approaching people of other cultures with humility and addressing themselves to the poor and downtrodden, they might yet reverse what seemed like a spiritually catastrophic exit from the Third World.[18]

Trocmé's views were echoed elsewhere in the radical Protestant press. In their lead editorial of 7 June and again in July in collaboration with the editors of *Christianisme social*, the staff of *Cité nouvelle* urged readers to abandon the superiority complex which jeopardized relations with Muslims and to join in urging UN intervention in the conflict so that free elections in Algeria could be impartially organized. The two editorial boards described the Algerian insurrection as an integral part of the irresistible impulse towards decolonization which had swept through the world since 1945, adding that the rise of pan-arabism had given the rebellion an added impetus.[19]

As reports of renewed violence and counter-violence reached Paris, Pastor Henri Roser condemned the "inadmissible acts" being committed by France's men in uniform. This criticism was given special validity by a letter from a conscript written from the field of battle. He suggested that at most 5 percent of those serving with him had paused to reflect on the cause they were defending, making his own view perfectly clear: "even when he becomes a soldier, a man remains a man and as such should reflect and make conscious decisions."[20]

Even Finet, the middle-of-the-road editor of *Réforme*, tended to share this pessimistic reading. Underlying the military conflict between the French army and the FLN he argued, was a fundamental incompatibility of mentalities. Modern France took for granted the universal validity of her pluralistic culture which Islam was simply unable to understand. If given their independence, Algeria's Muslims, while borrowing the technology of the former mother country, would eliminate all traces of French culture and sooner or later would expel Christian missions. Thus the battle should be seen as a war to defend western civilizational values against an Islamic threat to establish a regressive intellectual hegemony over all of Africa.[21]

True to its self-appointed role as a journal of broad-based Protestant opinion and defender of the *juste milieu*, *Réforme* published letters from moderate and liberal as well as conservative subscribers. A conscript called up to serve dismissed the *colons'* view that the Algerian problem was a treatable infection; it was a deadly cancer eating away at the health of France. His conscience told him to oppose the war which could not be won, given the attitude shown by French troops in the field.[22]

The most radical as well as idealistic letter came from "R.P." who urged his fellow-citizens to apply Christian ethics to the Algerian problem, to show love to those wrongly characterized as enemies, something he had done personally with great success. Unfortunately, most *colons* kept their distance from their Muslim neighbours. In fact, visitors from France seemed better able to make contact with members of the dominant culture.[23]

The national synod of the Reformed Church, meeting at Royan in 1956, noted that, while force might unfortunately be necessary to prevent a repetition of the recent massacres, a durable peace could not be achieved except on a foundation of justice, mutual respect and love. The delegates made a point of observing that those who dwelt in Algeria, whether they came originally from Arabia or from Europe, had the right to coexist with native Berbers; only together could the three ethnic groups make the land fruitful. The synod passed a resolution urging the government to put an end to the tragic conflict by making public a series of concrete proposals which would demonstrate to the Muslim masses as well as to world opinion France's determination to promote a just and peaceful co-existence among its Algerian citizens.

During this same synod, the delegates urged that prayers be offered during Sunday services for soldiers stationed in Algeria as well as for all those, friend and foe alike, who were suffering as a result of the conflict. Finally, in cities with a large North African immigrant population living in socially degrading circumstances, members of *Conseils presbytériaux* were exhorted to assist these Muslims in a variety of ways—through *Comités de secours*, job offers, and evening classes, as well as through help in mobilizing protests against arbitrary dismissals, police brutality and the exclusion of Muslims from student organizations.[24]

Soustelle was meanwhile keeping a watching brief on the Mollet government's handling of Algeria. Early in June, following a declaration by Premier Mollet that the territory would in the future be "neither a Muslim state nor an Arab state nor a French province," the ex-governor expressed his concern about the government's sense of direction. The lack of an explicit policy was particularly worrisome given the defeatist propaganda inside France. What Soustelle found especially troubling were protests against the despatch of conscripts to Algeria, leftist flirtations with Egyptian "neo-fascism," and references to *le peuple algérien* by politicians such as the leftist Radical Pierre Cot which implicitly excluded the European minority from membership in the Algerian community. In these circumstances, it was important for the government to confirm Algeria's status as an integral part of the French state by using the National Assembly as the key instrument of policy-making for the territory.[25]

In the fall of 1956, Soustelle published *Aimée et souffrante Algérie*, an apologia of his role as Algeria's governor-general and a vigorous defence of France's right to maintain her sovereignty there. In this powerfully argued tract, the ex-governor repeated the central theses which had inspired his policies during his year-long administration. The concept of an Algerian nation was a fiction; most of the population in the territory was passive rather than anti-French, waiting to see whether the government or the FLN would gain the upper hand. Integration (which should not be equated with assimilation since it included recognition of the peculiar ethnic complexity of Algeria's population) was the best moral as well as political solution for the Muslim majority and European minority alike, he argued. The federal formula advanced by some of his critics was wrong-headed because it was simply a stepping-stone on the way to independence. The rebels, who knew that they could not win on the field of battle, were now counting on a treasonous campaign against the government by the French intellectual community and on intervention by the United Nations. France's abandonment of Algeria and withdrawal to the continental hexagon, he continued, would signal the renunciation of her role as a great power. Finally, the Algerian insurrection depended on Cairo for its sustenance. With regard to this latter argument, Soustelle summarized the plot thesis which gave London and Paris a pretext to launch the Suez expedition in November: "The truth is, we are faced with an armed insurrection of a totalitarian type, inspired, paid for and sustained by Nasser's Egypt, a rising whose organizers reject a priori any solution except one based on force."[26]

Because the Mollet government assumed (wrongly as it turned out) that Cairo (where Ben Bella and others had established an FLN contact point) was the nerve centre of the Algerian revolution, President Nasser's 26 July announcement of the impending nationalization of the Suez Canal brought a furious reaction from the defenders of France's Mediterranean interests. This angry response reached a new intensity on 16 October when the Egyptian yacht *Athos* was intercepted off Oran carrying a cargo of arms for the Algerian rebels together with evidence of Nasser's support for the FLN.

On 22 October, just six days after the *Athos* incident, a Moroccan airplane carrying a number of key FLN leaders (Ben Bella, Mohamed Khider, Ahmed Aït, Mohamed Boudiaf and Lacheraf) to Tunis was apprehended flying over Algeria. This action was taken on the orders of local French military commanders without the approval of their civilian superiors. The five nationalist leaders were arrested. This act of insubordination was the first in a series of provocations by army men culminating in the 13 May insurrection which effectively destroyed the Fourth Republic. It also effectively frustrated for the next four years any meaningful contact between the French government and the FLN.

In November, the Protestant study group noted a sharp increase in terrorist activity coinciding with a school boycott decreed by the FLN at the beginning of October. The capture of Ben Bella and four of his colleagues and the tough policy adopted towards Cairo by Paris, had brought a probable slowdown in external support for the insurrection. The Soustelle/Lacoste policy of endorsing the *collège unique* had been swallowed by many members of the European minority but in the view of the signatories of the report, it was what lay beyond this concession that troubled the *colons*: "the Europeans are going along (without enthusiasm) with the idea of genuine equality with the Muslims but they are experiencing a nightmare at the thought of finding themselves living under an Arab government."[27]

Meanwhile prolonged secret negotiations between the British prime minister, Anthony Eden, Israel's Ben Gurion and France's Guy Mollet culminated in a decision to move collectively against the Egyptian government. From the official French point of view, the overthrow of Nasser would bring down an antisemitic and dictatorial leader before he became a new Hitler. It would erase the shame of Munich, when France had furthered the policy of pre-war appeasement and, in the more immediate sense, the headquarters of the FLN in Cairo would be destroyed, thus severely undermining if not liquidating the presumed headquarters of the Algerian insurrection.

The military operation which emerged from this diplomatic conspiracy began brilliantly when French and British troops seized Port Said and Port Fuad at the beginning of November. After two days, however, the attack was stalled in its tracks as a result of warnings that the Soviets might intervene militarily and signals from President Eisenhower that American oil supplies might be cut off from the Allies and that there might be a Washington-inspired run on sterling.

Although Paris and London yielded to Big Power pressure and withdrew from Suez, the National Assembly renewed its confidence in the Mollet ministry on 20 December. A majority of the deputies were, it appears, convinced that the Suez gambit had seriously weakened the FLN and that it had rescued Israel from an impending pan-Arab assault.

The nationalization of the Suez Canal in which so many French citizens held shares, brought the focus of Protestant editorial opinion to shift temporarily from Algeria to Egypt, which was already seen by many French commentators as the nerve centre of FLN activity. Jacques Ellul, always ready to see nationalism as a major scourge, took the opportunity to indict at one and the same French Socialists for attacking nationalization abroad while favouring it at home and Egyptian nationalists for implementing a policy which would bring little or no benefit to the peasant masses in whose name it was allegedly intended. Nothing was worse, Ellul observed bitterly, than the coming together of nationalist and socialist ideologies: "When socialism goes nationalist, it is nothing more nor less than national-socialism."[28]

At the beginning of December, Paul Adeline was still hopeful that the Suez crisis had not precluded negotiations in Algeria. Editorially, he urged Lacoste to take advantage of the abduction of the five key Algerian nationalist leaders by opening negotiations in which Tunisia and Morocco might serve as mediators. Meanwhile, France's European partners should be invited to join in exploitation of newly discovered oil wealth below the Sahara.[29]

The Council of the French Protestant Federation (FPF), meeting in extraordinary session on 6 November, deplored Egypt's violation of the UN Charter before going on to condemn the unilateral intervention of Britain and France as "extremely regrettable, even deplorable." The highest body in French Protestant officialdom expressed the hope that the crisis might force the United Nations to remedy those weaknesses and ambiguities which had so far paralysed its capacity for decisive action.[30]

André Philip, writing in *Réforme*, produced what was perhaps the most categorical indictment of the Suez expedition by a French Protestant. The attack on Egypt, he warned, had roused the underdeveloped nations, in fact the whole world, against France. Of even more critical importance, it had alienated the United States while enhancing the prestige of Nasser and opening the path to Soviet influence in the eastern Mediterranean. It had also brought into sharp relief a fundamental principle of contemporary politics, namely that "any purely national action is both ineffective and absurd."[31]

Jacques Maury, general secretary of the "Fédé," published a letter in *Réforme* damning the hypocrisy of "a military expedition whose avowed aim was the separation of Israeli and Egyptian forces. Behind the complex tragedy was the raging fury called nationalism which afflicted him personally as a Christian."[32]

In mid-December, as the focus of French opinion shifted back from Egypt to Algeria, Jacques Soustelle urged the government to reject a proposed reorganization of the Sahara region on the ground that it undermined the perception of the area as an integral part of Algeria. The statute of 1947 had, after all, included a recommendation that the Sahara be divided into departments so that it might be represented in the National Assembly. But, beyond that, ever since the pacification of the area in the nineteenth century, France had taken on the responsibility of guaranteeing the rights of the ethnically diverse populations living there (as an expert in the field, Soustelle cited precise tribal groupings). Even since 1954 these populations had manifested their loyalty to the mother country. French missionaries, civil servants, army officers and (more recently) prospectors, had done much to transform Saharan life. Schooling had been radically expanded since 1945, hospitals had been built and training centres established to form local cadres. The response to Soustelle's plea was sarcastic: the Sahara was "no Eldorado, no second Canada" replied one critic.[33] Meanwhile, the grim conflict in Algeria continued. On 28 December, the FLN ordered the assassination of one of the most notorious representatives of the European Ultras, Mayor Amédée Froger of Boufarik. On the following day, to avenge Froger, mobs of European vigilantes went on the rampage, indiscriminately slaughtering Muslims in the area. At the same time, right-wing elements conspired in a plot to isolate Lacoste, arrest his associates and transmit power to two generals, Raoul Salan and the air force commander, General Frandon. The conspiracy failed, but its near-success brought Lacoste to surrender all police power in Algeria to the army.

Among other developments, the last months of 1956 brought the first formal involvement in the Algerian conflict of the *Comité Inter-Mouvements auprès des Évacués* (CIMADE), one of the most original and creative instruments of Protestant social action in modern France. CIMADE, which was to play a significant role in attenuating suffering and attempting reconciliation during the Algerian conflict, began functioning in 1939 as an ad hoc organization created to help the thousands of Alsatian civilians evacuated from their homes behind the Maginot Line at the start of World War II.[34]

The signing of the armistice with Nazi Germany and the establishment of the Vichy regime made the situation in the camps where these refugees had been housed increasingly dramatic. Madeleine Barot, an archivist and historian who had helped cope with the refugee crisis of 1940, together with other Protestant volunteers, did what they could to improve the lot of these hapless prisoners throughout the occupation, often providing false identification papers or smuggling men and women across the borders to safety in Switzerland or Spain.

At the war's end, CIMADE teams turned up not only in bomb-wrecked French towns and among returning prisoners of war and forced labourers but also in devastated German villages in what was no doubt the first gesture of postwar Franco-German reconciliation. In the generation that followed, the Committee offered aid to East European refugees, helped generate support for the movement towards Christian ecumenism and endorsed the process of decolonization. The presence of CIMADE in Algeria was thus a logical prolongation of its earlier commitment to be present in situations requiring compassionate Christian activism.

Although CIMADE became totally committed to attenuating the

multiple crisis engendered by the conflict, the initiative in drawing the attention of the French Protestant community to this crisis lay with an outsider. Late in 1954, soon after the beginning of the insurrection, Willem A. Visser't Hooft, the distinguished Dutch theologian and leading figure in the ecumenical movement, expressed his concern about the apparent indifference to the crisis on the part of Protestants in France and Algeria to Madeleine Barot, secretary-general of CIMADE. Mlle Barot having agreed that something ought to be done, Visser't Hooft sent a Genevan from the World Council of Churches, André-Dominique Micheli, to conduct an on-the-spot inquiry. The Swiss visitor was appalled at the indifference of the Protestant community in Algeria regarding the condition of the surrounding Muslim population and the de facto colonial context in which they were still living.

After reading Micheli's report, Visser't Hooft urged Pastor Boegner to assemble the council of the French Reformed Church to consider developments in Algeria. When the council demurred, Visser't Hooft, Madeleine Barot and Marc Boegner agreed that under the circumstances CIMADE would be the most appropriate instrument through which the French Protestant community might express its commitment to those on both sides of the Mediterranean who were suffering as a result of the Algerian conflict.

To direct CIMADE in this challenging new assignment, a new secretary-general, Jacques Beaumont, was chosen. In retrospect, he was the ideal person. Born in Alsace, Beaumont had followed an intellectual itinerary that prepared him well for his role as the guiding intelligence behind CIMADE between 1956 and 1968. As secretary-general of the Protestant University Students' Association (the *Fédé*), and vice-president of the Protestant Political Science Students' Union (when Michel Rocard was its president), he had helped develop the Grenoble Charter of student rights, a landmark document which added substantial coverage to undergraduate insurance coverage, among other things.[35]

In the letter of acceptance addressed to the president of CIMADE, Pastor Marc Boegner, in April 1956, Beaumont made clear that he preferred to consider his responsibilities in an ecumenical context. In fact, he soon succeeded in adding the phrase *"Service ecuménique d'entraide"* to the organization's logo. He expressed the hope, based on his experience in the United States, that this interdenominational perspective would be adopted by his colleagues through collaborative social action at the parish level.

Beaumont confided to Boegner that he thought one of the key priorities of CIMADE in 1956 must be to respond as best it could to the crisis in Algeria and the parallel but clearly linked problems facing North African workers in France itself. The new secretary-general went on to argue that how the organization coped with these related crises might well shape its future.

As president of the CIMADE and at the same time president of the FPF, Boegner proved to be an invaluable ally, providing Beaumont with an effective cover when the secretary-general engaged in activities which were bound to antagonize either the *pied-noir* community or Protestant officialdom in Paris. Boegner, who had learned the art of subtle diplomacy while negotiating with Vichy during the war, was ready when necessary to separate his role as president of CIMADE from that of his function as chief executive of the FPF, sometimes informing the latter only after the fact when Beaumont had committed CIMADE to a particularly bold course of action. He advised the secretary-general to combine vigour with discretion: *"Il y a des choses qu'il faut savoir ne pas dire,"* he suggested early on in Beaumont's mandate. Pastor Boegner's deep commitment to what Beaumont proceeded to do in Algeria was confirmed by visits to the centres which CIMADE established across the Mediterranean as the war intensified.

As important to Jacques Beaumont in the successful implementation of his Algerian mission was the role played by Madeleine Barot; she spent her weekdays in Geneva in regular contact with the World Council of Churches and her weekends in Paris where she could meet with Boegner as well as the executive committee of CIMADE. As Beaumont puts it, whenever he tended to go beyond his mandate in ways which might even embarrass the well-intentioned Boegner, Mlle Barot was ready to soften the shock or deflate potentially critical reactions.

As master strategist of CIMADE operations in Algeria, Beaumont was bound to deal with political and military forces in the field. Often operating in areas where the French army and the ALN were in combat, the Protestant relief organization needed a protective cover, something frequently provided by sympathetic local prefects such as the Protestant Robert Poujol who facilitated contact with the military. Proximity to Liberation Army units posed an equally serious problem. For Beaumont and some of his chief collaborators who came to feel the inevitability (and even the desirability) of Algerian independence, direct contact with FLN leaders in Tunis or Geneva seemed eminently sensible. Cécile Lacheret, who served as Beaumont's stenographer and secretary from 1959 until the end of the war, became a member of *Solidarité*, an underground organization which promoted Algerian independence in the hope that the new state would be genuinely pluralistic, open to Jews and Christians as well as Muslims. Towards the end of the war, Beaumont himself joined the executive committee of *Solidarité* in order better to safeguard himself and his co-workers against violence from extremist elements in the European minority.

During the period of the conflict and, to a degree, beyond 1962, Jacques Beaumont divided his time between France and Algeria. He met regularly in Paris with an executive committee which, apart from Pastor Boegner, included three Protestants—Madeleine Barot, Suzanne de Dietrich and François de Seynes-Larlenque (from a prominent banking family whose interest focused elsewhere soon after Beaumont's arrival)—and one Orthodox Christian, Paul Evdokimov. The impecunious situation of the CIMADE when Beaumont took it over was changed substantially when he persuaded Rémy Schlumberger, scion of a prominent Protestant banking family, to purchase a property on the rue de Grenelle to give the organization appropriate headquarters.

Jacques Beaumont assumed effective direction of CIMADE in October 1956. Almost immediately, he and his colleagues found themselves dealing with the refugee flow which followed the abortive Hungarian Revolution. The commitment to attend to the problems raised by the Algerian conflict did not, however, go unattended. Concerned about the serious difficulties being faced by Algerian workers in France's major cities, Beaumont decided to commit his organization's limited resources to Marseilles where some 70,000 of these workers were living, the great bulk of them in sub-human conditions.

Before choosing a site for their first hostel (*foyer*), the secretary-general and his colleagues contacted other religious and charitable organizations already working with North Africans including the ecumenically structured *Frères de Taizé* and Catholic groups such as the *Petites Soeurs de Jésus*. The deacons' office of the city's Protestant churches, which normally assumed responsibility for the poor within its own constituency, did not feel ready to commit itself to helping North Africans; but Beaumont got a sympathetic response from a local left-wing colleague, Pastor Démeret. The prefecture was helpful as was the dominant figure in postwar Marseilles political life, the Protestant and Socialist Gaston Defferre (who had married into wealth and could thus afford personal benevolence).

Two study days were held at the end of October to which all interested groups were invited, including the president of the city's Reformed churches. A decision was made to open a hostel, in the heart of what had become the North African part of Marseilles. Thanks to help from foreign churches as well as gifts from friends of CIMADE, an abandoned building at 43, rue d'Aix was acquired and a nearby apartment rented for the organization's team-workers.

Two tasks were taken on by those running the hostel. Literacy lessons for adult males were placed in the hands of a Kabyle Christian, Hassen Kébaïli, who had worked for years with the Methodist church in Algeria.

Children's activities were taken over by two women, Marie-Hélène Délye, a nurse of European Algerian background who spoke Arabic, and Valentine de Saint-Blanquart who had worked with CIMADE in Paris and Berlin.

Many of those whom Kébaïli invited to the hostel had been in Marseilles for years; others were adolescents without resources or employment; those from his native Kabylia tended to be more enterprising; some of them had opened cafes or small shops. What distressed Beaumont and his colleagues was the degree to which so many of these North Africans had drifted into alcoholism, drug abuse, petty theft or pimping. For those whom Kébaïli was able to contact, the hostel became a social club. Some thirty were soon taking literacy lessons or accepting jobs as dock-workers, bakery assistants and the like which CIMADE was able to arrange. Meanwhile, about eighty children turned up every evening for an hour of singing, story-telling and lessons in manual skill.

The popularity of this first experiment led to the creation of a second hostel, this time in an area known as the Grand Arénas where some 180 North African families lived in squalor. Adopting a technique first used by the abbé Pierre, the well-known champion of the homeless in postwar France, CIMADE workers transformed an old cattle-car into a second hostel where literacy lessons and paramedical services were offered and a kindergarten opened for Muslim children.

A third centre followed, in the rue des Dames. It was run by Evelyne Ries, a Protestant, in collaboration with Bernard Dauphinet, an ex-Dominican, thus realizing in the most concrete possible way Beaumont's dream that CIMADE function as an ecumenical enterprise at the base level.

As CIMADE proved its worth, it developed a routine strategy: normally, teams of two people would move into place to open each new centre of operation. French cities with large numbers of North African workers such as Lyon, Strasbourg and Paris were soon provided with CIMADE teams and bases. And, no doubt inevitably, the process was replicated across the Mediterranean, beginning at Diar-es-Sems, a suburb of Algiers where between 10,000 and 15,000 dispossessed Muslims were offered the same basic forms of social relief and educational opportunity.

The concern of Jacques Beaumont and his colleagues for Muslims inside France was not limited to the hundreds of thousands who lived in squalor in or around France's major industrial cities. The secretary-general and some of his closest associates were determined to investigate at close hand the circumstances in which members of the FLN or those suspected of nationalist sympathies were being held inside French prisons. Since, as a pastor, Beaumont would normally have been expected to do chaplaincy work, it was easy for him to secure a card authorizing him to visit French prisons (from Marc Boegner) which allowed him to contact all those inside, including political prisoners and to chat with them alone. Befriending them through the loan of books or, on occasion, even smuggling out correspondence, provided an invaluable means of getting to know their political perspective. Following the arrest (in 1957) of five key FLN leaders, Beaumont was able to visit three of them and to establish a close bond with Ahmed Taleb, a future foreign minister of Algeria.

Beaumont's work in this ultra-sensitive area of human contact with leading Algerian nationalists was complemented by the prison visits of Étienne Keller, a pastor's son and CIMADE *équipier*, who would in this way meet and befriend several key personalities in the FLN, including Ben Bella. Two remarkable women participated in these prison visits: Tania Metzel, one of France's first female pastors, and Jacqueline Peyron, daughter of the founder of the French branch of the Salvation Army. Both women were commissioned to this service by the chaplaincy committee of the FPF.

The year that ended with the fiasco of Suez saw a renewed focus on armed conflict in Algeria. It also witnessed the arrival of CIMADE team-workers among Algerians on both sides of the Mediterranean conveying a very different Christian message to the Muslim world.

Notes

1 What follows is based on a conversation with Jean Carbonare in New York on 2 October 1994.
2 REF, 11 February 1956.
3 REF, 18 February 1956.
4 REF, 3 March 1956.
5 REF, 17 March 1956.
6 CN, 1 March 1956.
7 CN, 16 February 1956.
8 CN, 17 May 1956.
9 Charles-André Julien, "L'Algérie n'est pas la France," *Demain*, 4 January 1956.
10 *Le Monde*, 2 May 1956.
11 SEM, April/May 1956; Summer 1956.
12 André Philip, *Demain*, 12-18 April 1956.
13 Philip, *Le socialisme trahi* (Paris: Plon, 1957), p. 173.
14 OURS, "48eme congrès national SFIO, 29 juin 1956."
15 CN, 3 May 1956.
16 Ibid., 17 May 1956.
17 CN, 7 June 1956.
18 CN, 18 May; 21 June 1956.

19 RCS, July 1956.
20 REF, 28 April 1956.
21 REF, 19 May 1956.
22 Ibid., 14 April 1956.
23 Ibid.
24 REF, "Synode national. Royan 1956. Décisions XXV et XXVI concernant l'Algérie."
25 JOC, 5 June 1956.
26 Soustelle, *Aimée et souffrante Algérie* (Paris: Plon, 1956), p. 221.
27 CPED, "Comité protestant d'études nord-africaines. Groupe d'Alger. Chronique du mois de novembre 1956."
28 REF, 25 August 1956.
29 REF, 1 December 1956.
30 FPF "Suez 6 novembre 1956. Procès-verbal de la séance extraordinaire du Conseil de la Fédération Protestante de France."
31 REF, 17 November 1956.
32 REF, 24 November 1956.
33 JOC, 13 December 1956.
34 A brief history of CIMADE is offered in Arlette Domon et Alain Guillemoles, *Aux origines de la CIMADE*, published as a special edition of *CIMADE-Information* (Paris: Cimade, juillet-août-septembre 1990).
35 What follows is to a large extent based on taped conversations with Pastor Beaumont in New York on 15-16 October 1994.

Jacques Beaumont and Jean Carbonare
(Photo by author)

CHAPTER FOUR

1957—FULLY ENGAGED: PROTESTANTS TAKE
SIDES IN THE BATTLE OF ALGIERS

At the beginning of 1957, the Protestant commentator Paul Adeline scolded Premier Mollet for a series of blunders which had made the search for peace harder to undertake: the premier had capitulated to the mob on 6 February 1956; he had thrown away a chance to accept Moroccan and Tunisian mediation in the conflict and a third opportunity to begin negotiations had been lost following the arrest and abduction of the five FLN leaders. What was needed now was a courageous effort to rise above the immediate political crisis and reach for the kind of sublime understanding that had occurred between Christians and Muslims during the reign of Saladin at the time of the crusades or, more recently, the proconsular career of Marshal Louis Hubert Lyautey in Morocco early in the twentieth century.

The Ultra threat, meanwhile, had in Adeline's view been greatly exaggerated. There were perhaps 200, at most 300, right-wing extremists involved, most of whom were wretched souls, too ignorant to be feared or respected. Mollet could deal with this riff-raff by sending them off to some remote part of the Algerian countryside and then begin serious negotiations with the various groups of nationalists who would thereby be forced to clarify their long-term aims.[1]

André Philip relayed his deep concern about the direction the SFIO was taking over Algeria in a passionate declaration before the party's *Comité directeur* in January 1957. Motions coming up from the base through regular conventions and transmitted to Socialist administrators such as Lacoste had been regularly disavowed or subverted, the ex-deputy charged. The party had thereby not only betrayed its own teachings; it was in the process of undermining republican institutions and alienating public opinion. In a series of devastating phrases, the Protestant Socialist summed up his indictment:

> Right-wing policy made by men who say they are on the Left will lead to the disappearance of any effective public opinion throughout the country. The Right is currently silent because its ideas inspire those in power; while the Left has no comment precisely because its leaders are in charge.

To the suggestion made by some comrades that he was simply undergoing a personal crisis of conscience, Philip replied that he had joined the SFIO thirty-five years earlier because of the ideals to which he remained faithful. In the present circumstances, his Protestant heritage left him no choice but to join the minority in denouncing the party's policy in Algeria: "More than 300 years ago, my Cévenol ancestors, in spite of the king's dragoons, defended the principle of free criticism against all forms of clericalism and cesaropapism. You will forgive me if, today, I remain faithful to their memory."[2]

Philip's salvo against Mollet and the party leadership during and after the January meeting of the *Comité directeur* of the SFIO was matched by the creation of a *Comité Socialiste d'Étude et d'Action pour la Paix en Algérie* (CSEAPA) that same month. Among the militants who brought their energy and intellect to the first general rally called by this fledgling organization on 29 January were the young Protestant Michel Rocard and the veteran leftist C.-A. Julien. The aims of the CSEAPA were those which Philip had already made his own in the inner councils of the SFIO: to work for a peaceful resolution of the Algerian crisis which would satisfy the aspirations of the Muslim masses while guaranteeing the basic rights of the European minority and to rehabilitate the party.

While Adeline urged a shift in government policy and a determined minority of Socialists was fighting both inside and outside the party for a change of course, the Socialist resident minister Robert Lacoste was moving in the opposite direction. Confronted by a shift in FLN tactics from rural to urban warfare, including a determined effort to shut down Muslim schools through a boycott, Lacoste committed the defense of Algiers to the parachute general Jacques Massu, whose reputation had been enhanced during the aborted Suez expedition. What followed was the "Battle of Algiers" which began early in 1954 and which by October had effectively restored French military control in the territory's capital.

To help achieve the effective restoration of French civil as well as military control in Algiers, Massu made the liberal Catholic Paul Teitgen his deputy for police matters. As the city was purged of FLN supporters, it was divided up into small sectors whose surveillance was put in the hands of veterans' organizations. In the short term, this method was effective enough. In the long term, it made relations between Muslims and Europeans untenable.

To counter the military operation launched by Massu and to draw the attention of the international community to their cause on the eve of a United Nations debate on Algeria scheduled for 29 January, the FLN called for a week-long general strike by its supporters. French soldiers broke the strike ruthlessly before it had a chance to gain momentum.

On the eve of the UN debate, a group of prominent Christian intellectuals including André Philip, Paul Ricoeur and Pastors Henri Roser and Maurice Voge and a number of leading Catholic personalities (J.-M. Domenach, Henri Marrou, André Mandouze, Louis Massignon and François Mauriac) gathered for a demonstration in front of the Invalides. Having met the press, they issued an appeal to the premier, Guy Mollet, to abandon the politics of brute force and to acknowledge Algeria's right to self-determination. Since media access had effectively been denied them, the protesters took this occasion to declare publicly: "We will oppose by our silence a policy which we repudiate, a tragedy which must be brought to an end."[3]

In the end, thanks in large part to Jacques Soustelle, whom Premier Mollet chose to put France's case, the General Assembly rejected resolutions which would have recognized Algeria's right to self-determination and urged Paris to begin negotiations with the FLN to achieve Algerian independence. Instead, the delegates adopted a motion urging peaceful cooperation between the parties in conflict, thus offering Paris a period of grace during which she might resolve the conflict on her own terms.

News of the ruthless methods being employed by Massu and his men trickled into France throughout the year. Albert Finet, writing in *Réforme* in mid-March, expressed grave concern about the behaviour of French army units. In his view they had begun acting like the instruments of the most chauvinistic element among the *colons*, resorting to summary executions, conducting arbitrary searches and creating what amounted to concentration camps. "Pacification" was clearly not leading to peace. A week later, Finet wrote that the testimony about the cruelty of the methods being used by police and military, which had been brought before the public by Jean-Jacques Servan-Schreiber and the Catholic intellectual Pierre-Henri Simon, could no longer be ignored.

On 20 March, a deputation representing 357 signatories (including 90 professors, 65 priests and 19 pastors) forwarded an open letter to President Coty. Among the well-known Protestants who affixed their names to this appeal were Roger Mehl, Paulette Meunier, Gustave Monod, André Philip, Paul Ricoeur and André Trocmé. Those who signed the letter then formed a *Comité de Résistance spirituelle* to continue expressing their grave concern about the psychological impact on the nation's youth of a war during which so many of them were being ordered to commit atrocities.

Declaring that it was the responsibility of an older generation which had known genocidal conflict at first hand to testify against the army's role in Algeria, the Committee produced a *Dossier Jean Muller*. Named after a

Catholic scout leader killed in Algeria, the dossier contained evidence of atrocities committed by French forces. In April, two parallel groups of intellectuals came together to form ad hoc committees (the *Comité de vigilance universitaire pour la défense des libertés* and the *Comité universitaire pour la paix en Algérie*) to sustain the campaign against the increasing brutalization of the conflict.

Writing in *Foi et Vie* in March, Gustave Monod noted that, while it had been possible up to that point to ignore what was going on across the Mediterranean, the cumulative evidence about the nature of the war there had become overwhelming. "We have been drawn into an adventure in which repression and reprisals far outweigh any effort at real pacification" he declared. What was particularly tragic for members of the older generation like himself, he said, was the apparent abandonment of traditional republican values.

The all too evident deterioration had begun, Monod suggested, with the nation's paratroops who were at the centre of the current military operation in Algeria. Learning how to become hard and brutal towards themselves, some of them had applied the same brutality to others. Their consciences, invaded by fear or vengeance, had often ceased to provide a brake on their wills; many would return to France having lost their humanity, affecting to despise others but in fact really holding themselves in contempt.

Monod clearly felt that the situation of the nation at large, not just the youth, was grave, even catastrophic. In his view there was only one way out of the moral crisis: France must put an end to the war, no doubt by recognizing the existence of an Algerian national entity, an acceptable solution so long as clear guarantees were offered the European minority.[4]

The mobilization of public opinion against the war and the means by which it was being waged intensified through the early spring of 1957. An ad hoc committee based on key members of *Christianisme social* and the Parisian committee of the *Fédé* wrote to the nation's pastors, urging them to inform their congregations about the true nature of the war, asking them to alert public opinion and to lobby their local deputies with a view to encouraging moves towards negotiations with the FLN. The best solution to the ongoing crisis, the members of the committee suggested, would be to work towards the creation of a North African Federation linked to France.

On 25 March, the executive of the *Fédé* joined representatives of the Radical Party's student organization (the *Fédération Nationale des Étudiants Radicaux*) and the *Union des Étudiants Juifs de France* in addressing an open letter to Prime Minister Mollet following the suicide of a prominent Muslim lawyer, Maître Boumenjel, and the resignation from his teaching post of the eminent jurist (and Gaullist) René Capitant on the ground that he could no longer try to impart principles of justice in Paris when they were being so grossly violated in Algeria. The student petitioners urged the premier to shed light on the behaviour of French forces in Algeria and to mete out appropriate punishment to those who had clearly violated the fundamental tenets of the nation's law code.[5]

While Protestant students in France were increasingly active in the campaign to end the conflict, the same was far from true of their European counterparts in Algeria. Jean Czarnecki, who knew the university scene at first hand, reported to readers of *Cité nouvelle* that a small minority (800 out of some 8,000 he surmised) of fanatics had effectively seized control of the student movement in the University of Algiers. Unless the government moved in fast to arbitrate between the *colons* and the Muslim majority, Czarnecki predicted (accurately as it turned out), this mobilization of student energy, combined with a coming together of other subversive elements in the European community, risked permitting a fascist coup in Algiers.[6]

Jacques Ellul, joining in what had become a national debate on the use of torture during the conflict, noted that, ever since Thomas Aquinas, Christian thinkers had tried to humanize war, hypocritically disguising or even rationalizing its underlying brutality. No doubt brutal conflict was a fact of life; the Resistance (which Ellul had supported) was evidence enough for modern France. But the church had no obligation to develop a rationale for war which, for Christians, must remain an abomination.[7]

These attacks on the army's methods did not go unanswered by readers of *Réforme*. One correspondent deplored the lack of clear directives given France's men in uniform (in Algeria as in Indochina) while pointing to the grim losses suffered by the officer class on behalf of the nation since 1945 and damning the mainland press for undermining army morale while regularly rejoicing in enemy victories. The army, this correspondent wrote, was still dedicated "to the kind of clear and pure Republic which was proposed to us on the morrow of the Liberation."[8]

The Algerian Protestant study group had produced one of its intermittent reports at the end of February in which developments of the previous three months were reviewed. The European minority had been badly shaken by a number of events, the authors reported: the atmosphere between the failed Suez expedition and the conclusion of the UN debate on Algeria had been one of rising tension. A bazooka attack on General Salan in January had been deeply upsetting especially since the authors of the attack were unknown. Settlers were upset by the decrees of 5 and 13 December abolishing the Algerian Assembly and the implication, despite Premier Mollet's pronouncement about "the French character of Algeria," that the proposed new single-college Algerian assembly and its executive complement would be dominated by Muslims.

On the other hand, the study group noted, there were some grounds for optimism in the European community: the reputation of former governor-general Soustelle had been greatly enhanced, partly as a result of his performance on their behalf at the UN; General Massu was acting with determination and energy in the battle for Algiers. Finally, the discovery of oil in the Sahara raised hope over the long term.[9]

Some *colons* who stayed in Algeria would pay a heavy penalty. During the intensive army assault against the FLN early in 1957, settlers known to be on friendly terms with their Muslim employees or neighbours became a target. Thus the substantial farm property of the Picinbono family in the Mitidja region was torched on the ground that the high regard in which they were held by their Muslim farmhands identified them in and by itself as sympathetic to the nationalist cause.

The impact of this savagery on Bernard Picinbono, who had urged a sympathetic understanding of the settlers' situation on Daniel Galland, president of the *Fédé* early on in the conflict, was devastating. His last illusions about government policy and the methods used by the army in the field dissolved away. He made his changed feelings known in a letter to Galland, his regular correspondent since 1955, who had since become a pastor. "Did sending in the army, even if it was to defend a not altogether unworthy cause, have to lead fatally to the use of inadmissible methods, methods which rendered this just cause indefensible?" Picinbono added with what was a clear sense of impending tragedy: "I remain convinced that pacification, which does not in itself imply repression, was justifiable provided that one did not practise the obverse policy, that is, a policy which was bound to transform a heretofore calm region into a hotbed of *fellagha*."[10]

The battle to control the administrative capital of Algeria involved a block-by-block sweep aimed at purging the city of FLN elements and their sympathizers, including the tiny group of Europeans who had developed a close relationship with Muslim nationalists. One of these rare but resolute *sympathisants* was Maurice Causse, a professor at the Franco-Muslim Lycée and a *conseiller presbytéral* of the Reformed church in Algiers.[11] Causse was the son as well as grandson of Reformed pastors and in his youth had considered a career as a missionary, studying theology as well as what turned out to be his chosen field, science. During the Second World War, he served in the Resistance, then with the French army in the Vosges campaign as the war ended.

Causse's first contact with Algeria came in 1945 while he was completing his tour of duty as a soldier at the military school at Cherchell. The Muslim manifestation at Sétif in May took place while he was still in the territory. Causse felt instant scepticism about the officially low estimate of Muslim casualties suffered during the repression which followed.

Following his demobilization, Causse spent some time teaching in Madagascar where he ran afoul of the school authorities by expressing sympathy for the demands of *Malgache* leaders that they be granted more political as well as linguistic autonomy. In October 1953, he returned to Algeria where, since the territory was an integral part of France, he had the job security granted state employees.

In Algiers, Causse developed a close friendship with another member of the Reformed communion, François Hauchecorne, a graduate of the prestigious École des Chartes who had been named chief librarian of the *Bibliothèque Nationale d'Algérie*. Hauchecorne had a keen interest in Islam and in Christian-Muslim relations over the long term, an interest he not only maintained but expressed in writing as the conflict in Algeria intensified. Causse came to share this interest as well as the librarian's conviction that the best, in fact the only, method of surmounting the divisions between Christian and Muslim culture was not through an attempt at theological dialogue based on differences of dogma but through direct personal contact founded on the assumption by each that the faith of the other was based on spiritual integrity.

In his own reflection on Islamic culture, particularly in its relations with the Christian West, Causse came to believe that the prevailing anti-Muslim prejudice among Europeans was totally ill-founded. The science professor was well-equipped to take such an approach. He was (and remains) the quintessential Protestant. He holds no particular brief for John Calvin. He feels in fact a decided affinity for one of Calvin's most serious challengers, Michael Servetus who (among other qualities) read the Koran and learned from it but who for this insolence (as well as for his openly professed anti-trinitarianism) was burned at the stake.

Reviewing the long history of tension and conflict between the Muslim East and the Christian West, Causse found ample evidence to counter negative myths concerning Islam and excessive celebrations of Christianity's role in the relationship. The Huguenot in Causse could not resist pointing to the compassion shown by Muslim fellow-prisoners to Protestant galley-slaves who had been condemned to a life in chains on the ships of the Catholic Louis XIV for daring to profess their faith openly after the Revocation of the Edict of Nantes.

Reflecting years afterwards on the Battle of Algiers, Causse notes bitterly that it was a Socialist government (which included Protestant ministers, he might have added) that sanctioned the ruthless methods used by Massu in 1957. One of these methods was to carry those arrested in airplanes high above the Mediterranean, then drop them to their death at sea, following which they were simply listed as *disparus*.

Causse's own encounter with Massu's men came in March 1957 as French paratroops raided homes of Europeans known to be sympathetic to Muslim Nationalists. At the professor's house, they found and tortured Chafika Meslem, a young woman who had sought refuge there after distributing FLN leaflets. The professor was arrested as well and taken off to the Villa Susini, a notorious internment camp. Thirty-four others were apprehended in this military operation, twelve of whom were Europeans, including a doctor, a priest and some social workers, men and women who, unlike the overwhelming bulk of the settler population, had been in regular contact with the surrounding Muslim society.

After subjection to the *baignoire* treatment (her head being immersed in a full bathtub for prolonged periods in order to induce a full confession) Chafika Meslem was ultimately released, following which she fled to Switzerland to establish contact with the FLN network there.

Maurice Causse, while awaiting trial, was transferred from the Villa Susini to a holding camp (*camp de triage*) where prisoners of various types were kept pending a decision about the nature of their offense. While detained, he was able to give evidence of the tortures he witnessed during a visit to the camp by Paul Teitgen, Massu's civil deputy.

The trial of Maurice Causse and his thirty-four fellow defendants took place four months later in July. Bertrand Poirot-Delpech, sent to provide readers of *Le Monde* with a full account, reported that the formal charge against the accused was that they had "engaged in an effort to undermine French territorial integrity by printing and distributing separatist tracts and by giving aid to militant nationalists being sought by the police."

As Poirot-Delpech reported it, the indictment against the small band of "progressive Christians" proceeded with relative serenity (the case against the Muslims was another story). The defense argued that "friendship born in the course of social action in the Muslim shanty-towns (*bidonvilles*) is the only link between the nationalists and most of the accused." The lawyer for the defendants conceded that his clients had committed "imprudent acts" but argued that these had been motivated by fidelity or charity.[12]

Like most of the Europeans in the court, Maurice Causse was freed at the end of the trial. His fellow-parishioners appear to have passed over his act of complicity with a young nationalist woman as evidence of naïveté. The cadres of the FLN, on the other hand, correctly saw Causse's act as a gesture of genuine support if not of open commitment to their cause. In the months ahead as independence approached, they regularly appealed to him to serve on committees being formed to provide guidelines for the new Algerian state. It is worth noting that, during the final phase of the war, the brother of Maurice Causse, a magistrate known for his fair-minded treatment of Muslim defendants, was assassinated by members of the OAS.

Like his friend Maurice Causse, François Hauchecorne, custodian of the *Bibliothèque Nationale* in Algiers, established a number of close friendships with Muslims while at the same time examining in a scholarly fashion the long-term relationship between Christianity and Islam. As the librarian saw it, the essential compatibility between the faiths which had arisen, parallel-fashion, from the teachings of Christ and Mohamed had been lost to view over the years. Tragically, present-day adherents of both religions, mostly through ignorance, had subscribed to caricatural views of the other.

Hauchecorne found fascinating historic linkages between Christian heresy and Muslim faith. He suggested that fifth-century Arianism with its denial of Christ's divinity may well have prepared the way for the Berber conversion to Islam two centuries later. In fact, he went on to speculate, had it not been for the conquest of the Maghreb, the Berbers might well have gravitated in time towards Christianity.

This brief but provocative study of Christian-Muslim relations over the centuries was published as a series of articles in *L'Algérie protestante* in the early 1960s and then as a book. In its final chapter Hauchecorne issued a plea for a genuine encounter between proponents of the two faiths with a view to dispelling prejudice and hatred, stressing the advantage of personal friendship over theological debate. In Hauchecorne's view, the Reformed were particularly well suited for such contacts because they were unconstrained by hierarchical authority and because, like Muslims, they founded their convictions on the word of their founder rather than on tradition. The ecumenically minded scholar even made bold to suggest that, to further the kind of dialogue he was proposing, Christians might consider recognizing Mohamed as a prophet, a quality which, after all, Muslims had always seen in Jesus.[13]

Hauchecorne did not limit his intellectual engagement to the consideration of the relationship between Christians and Muslims over the centuries. His personal friendship with Muslims and his revulsion at the methods being used by Massu's men in their effort to crush the FLN together with the information he garnered from his friend Maurice Causse, led him to conduct a personal inquiry into the French army's strategy in the Algerian conflict.

As chief librarian of the *Bibliothèque Nationale* of Algeria, Hauchecorne was well-placed to review the extensive literature on the techniques of psychological warfare which the military had learned at such cost in Indochina and which it was adapting for use in Algeria against those fighting for Algerian independence. The documentation consulted by Hauchecorne revealed a combined political and military strategy which sought to apply the revolutionary principles of Mao and Ho Chi Minh in counter-revolutionary fashion. During the first phase of this strategy, implemented throughout 1956, the army proclaimed the will of France to stay in Algeria indefinitely while doing its best to detach the population at large from the *fellagha*. In some instances, Hauchecorne discovered, the army had effectively used brainwashing techniques with those it apprehended, turning erstwhile rebels into seemingly docile villagers.[14]

In a separate unpublished essay dealing with the origins of the 1954 insurrection, Hauchecorne rejected the official contention that the FLN was motivated either by the Muslim notion of a *jihad* or by the pan-arabist movement based in Cairo. "The Algerian revolt," he wrote, "would quite clearly appear not to be a holy war but a nationalist-style insurrection along the lines of those which took place during an earlier phase of European history and which Asia and Africa are now experiencing."[15] In any event, the contention that the insurrection had found its source in pan-arab sentiment or in calls for a *jihad* was not only misleading, it was highly dangerous. It deflected the government's attention from the deeply felt grievances of the Muslim population which were at the heart of the uprising and away from the need to deal with these grievances through a programme of basic reform.

Early on in the battle of Algiers, before Maurice Causse was arrested but when he and his friend Hauchecorne had already become incensed at the army's methods in dealing with their Muslim friends, they and their families welcomed into their midst Pastor Tania Metzel, who had come to Algeria on a special mission to visit prisoners in the many camps which the military had set up in the Algiers region.[16]

Born in Berlin in 1923 to Russian emigré parents, Tania Metzel moved with them to Paris while still an infant. During the 1930s, she was active in the equivalent of the Girl Guides (the *Éclaireuses unionistes*), then in the Protestant student movement. During the Occupation, she worked as a parish helper, then joined the Resistance along with Pastor Georges Casalis. At the war's end, Mlle Metzel became a team worker with CIMADE, helping inhabitants of towns devastated by the war. In 1947, still with the Protestant volunteer organization, she served as a social worker at Hangenau in Alsace where France's long-term female convicts were housed. Between 1948 and 1952, Tania Metzel studied for a licentiate in theology in Switzerland following which she was appointed titular chaplain to two large prisons including the women's division of the notorious jail at Fresnes, a suburb of Paris.

Her ministry inside the French prison system provided Tania Metzel with the experience needed for the three missions she was to undertake in Algeria—in 1957, 1958 and 1962. The first of these visits began in February 1957 in response to an appeal by the *Conseil presbytéral* of the Algerian synod. In the Maison Carrée prison near Algiers, Muslim detainees had not only begun to attend Protestant services of worship, but were even partaking of communion in the Reformed rite. The *Conseil* was sufficiently troubled by this clear evidence of a spiritual hunger among Muslim prisoners which they felt unable to satisfy that they appealed to the French Protestant Federation to allow Mlle Metzel to come to Algeria and see what she could do to remedy the situation.

Although familiar enough with conditions in French prisons, Mlle Metzel knew nothing of conditions in Algeria or of the larger context of European-Muslim relations there. Her education in the larger social context of Algerian life and in an understanding of Muslim-Christian relations came following meetings with Maurice Causse and François Hauchecorne whose views on the inevitability of the territory's independence she soon came to share.

Mlle Metzel discovered that to visit detention centres in what had now become a war zone around Algiers she needed a special permit from the director of the territory's prison network who directed her in turn towards Paul Teitgen. Teitgen, who had been a prisoner of war in the 1940s, was immediately sympathetic. Metzel presumed, perhaps naively, that, as a victim of arbitrary imprisonment herself, the director would see her experience as a spiritual counsellor to those in jail a valuable asset in her current mission.

Tania Metzel's first camp tour, in the company of Pastor Chatoney of Algiers, produced mixed reactions. Some Muslim prisoners explained to her, very gently, that they had never spoken to a foreign woman and that, even in their grim circumstances, they felt unable to overcome this taboo. Others crowded around her to tell her that they were denied visitors and that they had been robbed of everything they had brought with them into the camp. On a few occasions, Tania Metzel was joined in her camp visits by Professor Jean Bichon. While she quickly identified him as a man of right-wing opinions, he spoke fluent Arabic and could thus serve as translator when she wanted to communicate directly with prisoners.

The Battle of Algiers did more than provoke acts of defiance by Maurice Causse, a critical analysis of French army methods by François Hauchecorne, and an anguished visit to detention camps by Tania Metzel; it forced the highest-ranking Protestant army chaplain to publicize his concern about the impact of the Algerian war on young recruits. While the battle for Algiers was raging, Pastor Albert Nicolas shared his concern about the psychological and moral trauma brought on by the war in the pages of the Protestant bi-monthly *Foi et Vie*. The chaplain was clearly anxious to reassure relatives of soldiers at the front; he was also eager to anticipate and if possible deflect some of the criticism about the army's use of torture which was bound to surface during a forthcoming meeting of the General Assembly of the World Council of Churches.

Part of the moral dilemma for Nicolas and his fellow-chaplains was that France had never officially declared war against the FLN, insisting instead that the operation in Algeria was aimed at repressing a domestic rebellion. Nicolas noted that the Protestant churches had as a result been at a loss to define their position; synods had condemned gratuitous violence on both sides, but had not taken a position on the conflict itself.

There were of course secular protocols to which one might refer, beginning with the creation of the Red Cross and continuing through the Geneva conventions of 1949 which dealt among other things with the treatment of war victims, including prisoners taken in combat. Precedents had been set since World War II for charging individuals with responsibility for crimes committed by organizations of which they were a part. All this was very fine but all a bit hypocritical at a time when mass means of destruction were not only tolerated by openly manufactured and sold on the international market.

Above all, the chaplain reminded his readers, it must be stressed that military operations of any type were inconceivable unless absolute obedience were imposed throughout the chain of command. "It would be unthinkable, even criminal," he wrote, developing this conventional argument, "to place soldiers in the position of permanent or potential conscientious objectors by leaving them to assume on their own the risk of interpreting any orders or written commands or to take the consequences which might result from their adopting a peculiarly personal position."

Given the ambiguity in the public mind about the nature of the war, the church had a special obligation to make its own position clear. In any event, Nicolas wrote, showing evident irritation, "Let her not remain in this attitude of latent conscientious objection (*objection de conscience larvée*) which is placing Christians in uniform in an impossible situation." What the church should do at the very least was to remind the secular power of the solemn declarations regarding the laws of war which France had signed.

In an effort to reassure the readers of *Foi et Vie*, Nicolas pointed out that Protestant military chaplains had published a *Guide du chrétien aux armées*. Among other injunctions, the guide urged soldiers:

> To avoid any useless violence, any kind of pillaging which would make of you not a soldier but a brigand. Thus, although a soldier's duty to obey may be absolute, no one has the right to order you to take action against civilians, especially against women and children or against wounded soldiers who are no longer able to fight. Whoever commands such actions would put himself outside God's law as well as the true law of the army.[17]

While the Protestants on both sides of the Mediterranean were wrestling with the moral problems caused by the paratroop assault on Algiers, CIMADE resolved to establish a base for its operations in the city. In June, Isabelle Peloux, who would become one of the organization's key volunteers, travelled to Algiers to canvass possible sites for a CIMADE hostel. CIMADE, Mlle Peloux concluded, had a clear opportunity to work among the city's women and children, especially in those parts of Algiers where Muslims and Europeans lived in close proximity; the Casbah, she noted, was quite another matter. The best arrangement, she wrote in a letter of 24 June to Madeleine Barot, would be for CIMADE to establish a hostel staffed by three or four women to deal with such matters as household management and social services as well as to continue the work begun by Tania Metzel, going back and forth between Muslim prisoners and their families.[18]

The small band of potential supporters encountered by Isabelle Peloux in Algiers formed the nucleus of what would in time become a substantial CIMADE operation in Algeria. Jacques Beaumont, during his many visits to the territory, would come to rely on this original nucleus together with a few other men and women ready to engage in active cooperation with the Muslim majority. Pastor André Chatoney was, in the secretary-general's mind, a well-disposed pastor whose liberal views were not always fully thought through. Robert Poujol, who served in a variety of prefectures during the war, could always be counted on to provide political cover. Professor Jean Bichon was an Arabist whose ability to communicate directly with the population CIMADE aimed to help was invaluable. Louis Mermier was a wealthy settler of progressive mind who was always willing to lend a hand.[19]

As CIMADE prepared to commit itself to the relief of a population terrorized by French paratroopers, Marjolaine Chevallier saw clear evidence of a radical shift in mentality on the part of her husband's parishioners in the eastern suburbs of Algiers. Members of the congregation were increasingly influenced by the popular, right-wing press.

During these troubled months, Pastor Chevallier and his wife had regular conversations with Pastor Capieu, one of the few *pieds-noirs* in Algeria to have joined the Reformed ministry. Because of his origins, Mme Chevallier had hoped to find in her husband's colleague a fellow-spirit, someone ready to accommodate to the shifting realities of Algerian society. In her view, the pastor was not dogmatic by nature, but when she suggested to him one day that the arrest of a committed FLN member must create the same reaction among Muslims that members of the French underground felt in the 1940s when one of their comrades was apprehended, he bridled. For Capieu, as for most other members of the Protestant community, "Members of the FLN were, after all, terrorists and assassins. And the French army was not for sure the Gestapo!"[20]

On 5 April, at the instigation of Gaston Defferre, the Mollet government created a *Commission de Sauvegarde* to look into the methods being used to deal with alleged Muslim subversives, many of whom had been mistreated even though they were clearly men of moderate views. Members of this commission scheduled a visit to Algiers but cancelled it when Ultra elements there manifested their opposition. A month later, on 10 May, Premier Mollet appointed a number of distinguished personalities, including the lawyer Maurice Garçon and the North African expert Robert Delavignette to a *commission d'enquête* to take a look at what was transpiring in Algiers. Two delegates from this commission, Professor Richet and General Zeller, visited the city between 23 May and 20 June but found no clear evidence of activities which would lead them to challenge official policy.

Ironically, Richet and Zeller were on the scene at a time when scandalous examples of arbitrary action by the military were taking place. On 11 June, a twenty-five year old assistant professor in the Science Faculty at the University of Algiers, Maurice Audin, was abducted from his home on the ground that he belonged to the outlawed Algerian Communist Party and that he had engaged in bombing activity in collaboration with the FLN. Four days after his disappearance, the rector of the university demanded to know his whereabouts. A week later, Paul Teitgen reported that Audin had died of strangulation on 21 July while being interrogated by soldiers. Apparently he had been mistaken for for Henri Alleg, director of the leftist newspaper *Alger* *républicain.*[*]

Audin's murder became something of a cause célèbre in Parisian academic circles; a *Comité Audin* was organized in posthumous defense of his intellectual integrity and in outraged opposition to the methods of psychological warfare which were being used against opponents of official French policy in Algeria.

L'Affaire Audin, for some at least, took on the proportions of a second Dreyfus Affair. Two years after the murder, Professor Paul Ricoeur of the Sorbonne addressed a general meeting in the *Salle de la Mutualité*, denouncing not only the murder of Audin but the torturing of students during the repression in Algeria. An end must be put to the atrocities which the government's abdication to the military has produced, Ricoeur insisted. Even more important, negotiations must be started which would permit the Algerian people to obtain their independence. In the changed circumstances which this was bound to produce, the European minority should be encouraged to stay in Algeria but with a new outlook based on a thoroughgoing examination of conscience as well as a radical change of status: "Stay on! You have a reasonable future with the Algerians in Algeria. Having been masters, you must now become equal partners, even servants, all of which of course requires a fundamental shift in attitude."[21]

Throughout the year, religious leaders as well as liberal intellectuals were increasingly troubled by reports of police and military brutality in Algeria. At the December meeting of the council of the French Protestant Federation, President Marc Boegner reported on a recent meeting with President René Coty during which he had expressed the council's distress at the failure of the government to publish the report of the *Commission de la sauvegarde des dignités humaines.*[22]

While French intellectual and spiritual leaders had become increasingly concerned about the basic freedoms of their Algerian compatriots throughout 1957, the regime in Paris had become more vulnerable as the Battle of Algiers moved into high gear.

On 21 May, the Mollet government fell, partly due to financial strains placed on the economy by the Algerian conflict. The defeat of a government dominated by the SFIO was accompanied by increasing restiveness in the ranks of the Socialist minority. At the *Conseil national* of the party held in

---

[*]Those guilty of his murder will in all likelihood never be identified because of an amnesty issued later which forbade any official inquiry into this and other similar outrages committed by the army during the Algerian conflict.

May, Charles-André Julien, one of the key speakers articulating the minority point of view, urged his colleagues to abandon the traditional prejudice against nationalist movements in the Third World which was blinding them to the realities of the Algerian situation.[23]

Maurice Bourgès-Maunoury, who succeeded Mollet as premier on 12 June, was a strong supporter of Lacoste, as was the Socialist Max Lejeune, given the new portfolio of Minister of the Sahara region. Encouraged by the new prime minister, Lacoste drew up the text of a proposed *loi-cadre* for Algeria which would have divided the territory into a number of autonomous regions governed by assemblies chosen by single electoral colleges while a *"parlement fédératif"* chosen either by direct vote or by members of the regional assemblies would in turn choose an executive council. Finally, the proposal would have left Paris in charge of the army, diplomacy, finance, justice, and education. While the tiny minority of European liberals in Algeria endorsed Lacoste's ideas, the vast majority rejected them outright as did the FLN. The notion of the *collège unique* remained a red flag to the Ultras who called for a general strike in protest against it on 18 September.

In June 1957, on the eve of the annual SFIO convention at Toulouse, André Philip published *Le socialisme trahi*. It was a devastating indictment both of the leadership of the SFIO and of the policies it was pursuing, with special attention to the Algerian case. Early in his essay, recalling his personal commitment to the Popular Front and to the Resistance, Philip defines a socialist as one who always seeks to make "a political choice ... in the name of an ideal universal ethic which one must look for elsewhere than in a simple analysis of social realities ... in reacting to any problem, one identifies with the social group that is suffering the most injustice."[24]

Like many others, Philip wrote, he had been convinced that peace in Algeria was at hand when the Socialists took power at the beginning of 1956. These hopes had been dashed as a result of a series of moral as well as political blunders. The attack on Egypt, inspired by "an anti-Munich complex which had no connection to reality" (Nasser was no Hitler) had been in fact in clear violation of France's international commitments. The results of the Suez expedition were equally deplorable: the army's *complexe d'humiliation*, already intense following Dien Bien Phu, had been deepened; France's investments in Egypt had been liquidated and her reputation in the Third World seriously diminished; Nasser had become a hero in the Arab world, and Soviet influence had been dangerously augmented.

In a lengthy chapter entitled "Un crime: La 'pacification' en Algérie," Philip returned to the argument he had made at the Lille congress of the SFIO a year earlier. The Muslim masses of Algeria, emerging from the feudal era, were experiencing "their 1789 revolution" which brought with it the development of an Algerian national conscience. The situation differed from that elsewhere in colonial Africa, however, because the substantial minority whom Philip described as *Eurafricains* also possessed "an Algerian national conscience of their own." Any realistic assessment of the Algerian situation would bring one to conclude that the area was evolving towards semi-sovereignty, if not full scale independence.

In the short term, Philip insisted, France must be seen as acting the part of honest broker between the Algerian majority and the Eurafrican minority, pursuing reform while restraining the hotheads in both Muslim and European communities. Herein lay the moral lapse as well as the political miscalculation of Guy Mollet following the 6 February incident in Algiers.

Philip went on to say that France's functionaries in Algeria had done their best to subvert any hope of reform. Those in charge of the *Caisse d'accession à la propriété* had been stalled in their efforts to speed up land redistribution. Only minimal changes had been made in the predominantly reactionary staff of the *Gouvernement général* and the right-wing press was still tolerated, even when it encouraged conspiratorial action while liberal Eurafricans were regularly persecuted, as was their newspaper, *L'Espoir*.

Philip expressed concern about the ruthless prolongation of Soustelle's pacification policy, but he was equally distressed at the impact the conflict was having on young conscripts. They were being called upon to act against their conscience and against the best traditions of their nation. "We risk in this way corrupting a whole generation by making our youth abandon the historic sense of values which constitutes the very essence of France.... We are presently creating for ourselves the instruments of a future fascist adventure."[25]

In these worsening circumstances and given the forthcoming meeting of the UN General Assembly, it was necessary to take action on the Algerian issue. France might help her own cause and the cause of peace by publicly recognizing the "national vocation of Algeria" and the logical inevitability of its realizing this vocation. In the short term, the Eurafrican and Muslim communities in Algeria might be granted a common nationality which would allow both over time to evolve a shared sense of belonging to a single fatherland.

In the final chapter of *Le socialisme trahi*, Philip repeated his attack on the flag-waving nationalism, the petit-bourgeois conservatism, the bureaucratization and the intellectual impoverishment of the SFIO. The Protestant Socialist ended his text with a solemn warning which (as it turned out) came just one year before the 13 May 1958 insurrection in Algiers. A fascist attempt on their nation's democratic institutions was increasingly likely he pointed out, adding: "The sad thing is that the unprincipled and unscrupulous minority which is quite capable of carrying out such a threat is coming together as of now in Algeria."[26]

Not surprisingly, Philip's fulminations against the Socialist Party establishment brought retaliation; in March 1957, the veteran of many left-wing battles was excluded from the *Comité directeur* of the SFIO; then, a year after the publication of *Le socialisme trahi*, he was banished from the party itself.

While André Philip had been condemning Guy Mollet over the government's Algeria policy, an equally powerful indictment of the prime minister had been drawn up by Michel Rocard. A member of the SFIO since 1949 and linked through marriage to Pierre Poujol, a strong champion of *Christianisme social*, Rocard later became the leading Protestant Socialist of the younger generation.[27] Because he was at the time studying at the prestigious *Ecole Nationale d'Administration* for a career in the public service, Rocard was not in a position to advertise his political views openly. Instead, borrowing (with consent) the name of a close friend, Henri Frenay, who was also a member of the Sixth Paris Section of the SFIO, Rocard drafted a forty-page assessment of the government's Algeria policy, including a series of resolutions designed to transform it. His hope was that the text would be adopted at the section level and that it might ultimately provide the basis for a series of motions at the party convention late in June. As Rocard readily admits, his would-be policy paper had little impact. Although it had been preceded by the substantial criticism of veteran Socialists such as Julien and Philip, it still stands apart as the most thorough and most damning assessment of the party's position on Algeria produced at this stage of the conflict.

Rocard began by pointing out that, because Algeria remained juridically part of France, public opinion had refused to see developments there as part of the nationalist explosion which had occurred throughout the Third World since 1945. Algerian nationalism had been rendered all the more difficult to deal with because France had for over a century proclaimed a policy of assimilation while in fact practising what amounted to racial segregation, denying all but a handful of Muslims any sense of responsibility in their own land. Although it had been possible to apply an assimilationist strategy for Corsicans and Bretons with whom the dominant majority in France shared an underlying sense of community, such was not possible in North Africa: "Because, although between Islam and the world shaped by Christianity and humanism, there can and should be a good relationship there can be no assimilation or its corollary, integration, except in the dreams of jurists." In any event, Rocard remarked, assimilation was never desirable since it threatens the very soul of a people and the individuals of which it is a part; it forces a renunciation of traditions and values without replacing them with new ones. Politically, the young Socialist added, assimilation, if implemented, would give majority rule in the National Assembly to overseas deputies, clearly something which partisans of this policy never intended and would never permit.

Developments in Algeria were grim enough in themselves, but, as Rocard pointed out, they were also jeopardizing France's relations with Tunisia and Morocco (where the increasing ferocity of the war across the border had resulted in the accelerated exodus of French settlers and capital, vital to these newly independent states).

As crucial as any other element in Rocard's indictment was his analysis of the war's impact on public morality. The war, he insisted, was being conducted with little regard for republican morality or, for that matter, legality. The parliamentary commission which had reported on the interrogation methods used by the army in Oran had effectively rationalized these methods; and one of the signatories was treasurer of the SFIO.

In Rocard's view, the failure of Socialists to act in the current crisis and their paralysis in the face of a government of their own stripe carrying out a reactionary policy meant that an opportunity to take advantage of the existing crisis in communist ranks following the Hungarian Revolution was being thrown away. As a result, the SFIO was likely to suffer the same loss of prestige and faith which had struck the Catholic MRP over its prosecution of the war in Indochina. In fact, wrote Rocard in obvious anguish, "The protest which the Left is honour-bound to express is instead being taken up by Radicals and Catholics, replacing by default the party of Jaurès."

Rocard ended his analysis with a series of proposals for a peaceful solution to the Algerian problem. They included: the recognition of an independent Algerian republic; the negotiation of a federal relationship between France and this new entity; the preservation of French nationality for the European minority in the new Algeria; the creation of a mutually recognized federal court to adjudicate questions of human rights brought before it by citizens of the new state; and the free movement of citizens from one state to the other.

The forty-ninth congress of the SFIO which both Philip and Rocard hoped to influence was held at the end of June 1957. Three separate motions concerning the Algerian situation were submitted, two of them by prominent Protestant members of the party.[28] In separate resolutions, Robert Verdier and Gaston Defferre both urged a modification of the hardline policy which the party had earlier defended and which Christian Pineau in the end persuaded the delegates to reendorse. The minority text presented by Verdier openly proposed recognition of the "national vocation of Algeria." Defferre suggested that the government should take the initiative and propose that the territory be given substantial autonomy, including its own parliament and government. Having listened to Verdier and Defferre as well as Christian Pineau who put the case for leaving party policy on Algeria unchanged, the delegates voted massively for the Pineau position (2547 votes versus 779 for Defferre and 498 for Verdier).

While French politicians engaged in a lively debate about their future, the Protestant study group produced its seasonal report on Algeria on 1 July. The news it conveyed on the military front was upbeat. Massu's men were not only winning in the field, they were escorting Muslim children to school and thereby breaking the school boycott launched in the fall of 1956. The result was that more young Muslims than ever were getting a basic education; only at the level of secondary schools was there a continuing commitment to the strike.

There were some problems with Massu's operation, the writers of the report conceded: paratroopers were often gratuitously rough and there had been a particularly nasty outbreak of violence following the killing of one of their comrades when European youths had gone on the rampage. Despite these unfortunate developments, day-to-day relations between Europeans and Muslims had not been adversely affected.

On 17 July, two weeks after the annual Socialist convention and a month into the new ministry formed by Bourgès-Maunoury on 12 June, the National Assembly debated the wisdom of renewing the emergency powers concerning Algeria granted to the Mollet government on 16 March 1956. Jacques Soustelle supported the request for an extension on the ground that France was now facing terrorist attacks at home as well as in Algeria, including murder and extortion being visited upon recalcitrant Muslim workers by agents of the FLN. The ex-governor made a point of stressing that, whatever their ethnic origin, these victims should be thought of and treated as French and protected as such. As Soustelle put it: "the murder of a Muslim Frenchman is not a mere settlement of accounts or a simple news item. It is the assassination of a Frenchman, a Frenchman who just happens to be Muslim."[29]

Soustelle urged his fellow deputies to act swiftly on Algeria, to pass legislation clearly defining the territory as an integral part of France in anticipation of increasing pressures to internationalize the issue coming especially from Senator John Kennedy, who had condemned French military conduct in Algeria in a July speech, and from the American labour movement.

Tough speeches on Algeria's future made by Soustelle's successor Lacoste and President Coty in July did not impress Albert Finet. No doubt the "virile language" the two men had used had impressed their audiences (veterans' associations and *colons*); but the evident disdain they had shown towards the FLN was not helpful in the long run. It was absolutely vital for those representing France to do everything in their power to win over the Muslim elite if the reform measures France was proposing (the promotion of birth control, monogamy and agricultural improvement) were to be implemented.[30]

On 26 September, four days before the fall of the Bourgès-Maunoury ministry, Soustelle made another passionate speech in the National Assembly in defense of French Algeria. Some defeatists in parliament he noted, were already proposing compensation for Europeans who might choose to leave the beleaguered territory. Such a policy amounted to

> a kind of Revocation of the Edict of Nantes, to the detriment of the non-Muslim community of Algeria. The Republic would be branded with an ineradicable stigma if it abandoned more than 1,000,000 Christians and 140,000 Jews to the discretion of a fanatical tyranny.[31]

Citizens of France should stop letting themselves feel guilty about Algeria, Soustelle argued. After all, as Charles-André Julien had noted, there had been a slave market in Algiers when French troops first arrived whereas now all children in the territory, whatever their background, were being educated in French schools. Soustelle reminded his fellow deputies that his party had always supported the passage of a new *loi-cadre* for Algeria. Nothing, however, should be done to set in place the institutions of a potentially independent state.

Four days after making these comments, following the passage of the government's bill (one of the last acts of the Bourgès-Maunoury ministry), Soustelle issued a solemn warning to his compatriots: "There are moments in the life of individuals as in that of nations when one's conscience must be fully alert to decisions being taken."[32] The party to which he belonged, Soustelle added, out of a concern to help reach a national consensus on the Algerian issue, had swallowed the government text despite the fact that it contained the elements of separate state institutions, that it would excite new demands from the nationalists, and that it sanctioned the creation of a *collège unique* in which it was not yet clear that minority rights would be fully guaranteed.

On 30 September, largely as a result of the parliamentary crisis provoked by Soustelle's persistent attacks on Lacoste's proposed *loi-cadre*, the Bourgès-Maunoury cabinet fell. After a long hiatus, Felix Gaillard became premier on 5 November, following which Lacoste and his advisors were mandated to prepare a revised version of their earlier proposal. This new text called for the creation of territorial councils on which the European minority would have de facto veto powers but, since the hated single electoral college was retained, the Ultras again balked, this time aided by *Lycéens* and university students who turned the annual 11 November ceremonies in Algiers into a demonstration against the revised text and its author.

Despite this opposition on both sides of the Mediterranean, the *loi-cadre* was adopted in the National Assembly by a 269-200 vote. In line with the new legislation, elections were to be held in Algeria within three months after the restoration of peace and order. Two years after that, the act provided for setting in place a federative organization.

In theory at least, the passage of this bill gave Lacoste a period of grace. When neither Europeans nor Muslims gave it their support, the resident minister turned to the army as the last available instrument of reform and thus of retaining Algeria in the French orbit.

By the fall of 1957 there were some 500,000 French soldiers in Algeria. General Salan's pacification strategy involved the creation of forbidden zones in the countryside inside which army units would use intensive bombardment to extirpate the FLN while thousands of Muslim peasants were herded into concentrated areas supervised by a specially developed *Service d'action psychologique*. In many instances, the young officers in charge of these areas brought basic literacy, medical services, public works projects as well as a restoration of faith in France's good intentions. Unfortunately, in other cases, what developed were concentration camps.

News of conditions in the worst of these camps prompted members of the *Commission de sauvegarde* to make a series of on-the-spot investigations. Robert Delavignette drew up an indictment of abuses he had witnessed at first hand and of the abdication of civilian authority in the face of arbitrary military management of these camps. When the government paid it no heed, Delavignette resigned on 30 September, the day the Bourgès-Maunoury government fell.

Abuses by the military continued, and in some ways worsened, following Delavignette's resignation. Late in November, Maurice Voge brought the arrest and subsequent torture of the twenty-year-old Muslim woman Djamila Bouchired to the attention of the readers of *Cité nouvelle*. Djamila had been apprehended for distributing FLN tracts. She had a gifted defense attorney, Jacques Vergès, who appealed to President Coty on her behalf. What was needed was full disclosure by the *Commission de la sauvegarde* of this and other abuses of police power in Algeria so that public opinion could be made fully aware of the methods being used to maintain French control of Algeria.[32]

In late November, as the National Assembly debated institutional changes affecting Algeria, Soustelle urged the passage of legislation which would clearly establish the sovereignty of the French parliament there. As it stood, the government's proposal included the establishment of a council of communities and a single assembly with equal representation of Europeans and Muslims, something which he and his parliamentary group had earlier recommended. However, there was still no legislation guaranteeing minority representation and no reference to the unitary French Republic as the continuing sovereign power. Nor was a second obvious means of binding Algeria to France (namely, the direct election of Algerians to the French National Assembly) provided for. Above all, Soustelle complained, the concept of integration which seemed again to be making progress among the Muslims and to which the European minority was now converted, must not be eliminated from consideration, as the proposal seemed to imply.[33]

Following lengthy debate, the text of a new *loi-cadre* affecting Algeria was voted but not before Soustelle had repeated his party's condition for supporting the bill—that no election be held in Algeria so long as armed bands of the FLN were still roaming the countryside.

On 12 November, while the National Assembly was debating Algeria's future, the Algerian Protestant study group published a peculiarly optimistic report on the rapidly changing situation. Terrorism had all but disappeared from Algeria, the authors noted; at the same time, relations between Europeans and Muslims had improved considerably. On the economic front, the prospects of profitable gas and oil exploitation in the Sahara were encouraging and agricultural production for the market was progressing apace. The most serious problem was the rise in unemployment which an increased emphasis on industrialization would no doubt alleviate. The administration was clearly doing its part to cope with the demographic crisis: the production of new housing units had quadrupled during the last four years.

On the political front, the authors of the report had less positive news to relay. Algeria's Europeans were nervous and uncertain about the impact of the *loi-cadre*. They were convinced that control of local government was about to slip out of their hands and that further loss of power was bound to follow. "In any event," those who signed the report concluded, "the Europeans will cease to be and to feel fully 'in France' and they find it particularly bitter that for three years they have accepted so much sacrifice and suffering for this result."[34]

At the beginning of December, Albert Finet, having been invited to visit Algeria by the governor-general, relayed his observations to readers of *Réforme*. There were some positive developments to report, Finet wrote. Massu had clearly won the Battle of Algiers; many of the SAS officers were doing a good job in local communities, and basic education was being expanded. However, there was disturbing evidence of FLN control of much of the countryside. More alarmingly, a civil servant had confided to him that "everything is happening as though the people who pull the strings here—not the government or the army but those who own the popular press—were trying to eliminate the entire Algerian elite so that we would be faced by only a disorganized proletariat."[35]

Meanwhile, the battle over the soul of the SFIO reached a new level of intensity following a meeting of the National Council on 14-15 December. Two decisions were made during this meeting which helped turn what had been an internal party debate into open schism. On 27 December, the *Comité Socialiste d'Étude et d'Action pour la Paix en Algérie* (CSEAPA) was dissolved and on 23 January 1958 André Philip was excluded from the SFIO for systematically violating party discipline and for this wholesale denunciation of the party's leadership in the pages of *Le socialisme trahi*. Philip responded to his removal from the party by demanding his reintegration in a letter to the National Council and by resuming his polemical assault on the SFIO establishment in the pages of *La Tribune du socialisme*.

At the year's end, Pastor Georges Casalis, one of French Protestantism's most radical personalities, a champion of an "inductive theology" which sought to combine Marxist analysis with the teachings of the Christian Gospel, arrived in Algiers for a few weeks to take charge of the congregation of Pastor Capieu while the latter was on leave in France.

One day the visitor found himself at Ouchaia, a remote village where masses of Muslim men, women and children were living in sub-human conditions. All of a sudden, while distributing flour to the destitute, the pastor, (whose political education had begun in 1933 in reaction to the triumph of Hitler when: "I understood that I was joining the resistance and that my whole life would be one of struggle for humankind"), was overwhelmed at the sight of those who were lining up before him to receive this minimal daily sustenance.

Casalis tells us that he felt at that moment an irresistible wave of class hatred well up inside him. The poverty and misery he saw all around him in Algeria was after all, he told himself, the direct result of France's conquest and occupation. The radical pastor experienced not just guilt at being an accomplice and beneficiary of his nation's colonialism but also a kind of self-hatred which might drive him to commit a "terrorist act in support of those to whom he was at that moment ministering."[36]

Notes

1   REF, 9 February 1957.

2   André Philip, "Déclaration devant le comité directeur de janvier 1957," in Philip, *Le socialisme trahi* (Paris: Plon, 1957), *Annexes*, p. 219; p. 225; p. 227.

3   CN, 7 February 1957.

4   *Foi et Vie*, March 1957.

5   SEM, 1956-1957 issue.

6   CN, 23 May 1957.

7   REF, 4 May 1957.

8   REF, 3 April 1957.

9   CPED, "Comité protestant d'Études nord-africaines. Groupe d'Alger. Chronique de l'hiver (3 novembre 1956-20 février 1957)."

10 Daniel Galland, *L'espérance maintenue. Chronique d'un homme du commun* (Paris: Le Centurion, 1979, p. 91.

11 This account of his experiences in Algeria is based on a taped conversation with Maurice Causse on Orleans on 9 September 1994 as well as on a subsequent extensive correspondence.

12 *Le Monde*, 23/24 July 1957.

13 François Hauchecorne, *Chrétiens et musulmans au Maghreb. De l'Église d'Afrique à la présence chrétienne* (Paris: Les Bergers et les Mages, 1963), pp. 92-99.

14 Bernard Vollet (pseud. F. Hauchecorne), "Guerre psychologique en Algérie," REF, 26 July 1958.

15 Personal archives Fr. Hauchecorne, "Algérie. Guerre sainte et panarabisme," n.d.

16 The account which follows is based on a taped interview with Pastor Metzel in Paris on 29 October 1994.

17 Albert Nicolas, "Quelques réflexions sur l'emploi de la force en Algérie," *Foi et Vie*, March-April 1957, pp. 137-146.

18 ACIM, Isabelle Peloux to Madeleine Barot, 24 June 1957.

19 What follows is based on a taped conversation with Pastor Beaumont in New York on 16 October 1994.

20 This information was relayed to the writer by Mme Chevallier in a letter of 1 September 1994.

21 CPED. Paul Ricoeur, "Aux enseignants. Texte de l'allocution de M. Paul Ricoeur, professeur à la Sorbonne, prononcée au meeting à la Mutualité," in *Textes et Documents*, August/September 1959, pp. 15-16.

22 FPF. Rapport du President Boegner au Conseil national 10 December 1957.

23 Cited in G. Morin, "De l'opposition Socialiste à la guerre d'Algérie," p. 305.

24 Philip, *Le socialisme trahi*, p. 43.

25 Ibid., p. 187.

26 Ibid., p. 208.

27 Michel Rocard, "Le drame algérien. Rapport présenté par Henri Frenay (pseud.) au nom de la VIe Section de la Fédération de la Seine (SFIO)," s.d., unpublished typescript.

28   OURS, "49eme Congrés national, 27-30 juin, 1957."

29   JOC, 17 July 1957.

30   REF, 13 July 1957.

31   JOC, 26 September 1957.

32   JOC, 30 September 1957.

33   JOC, 26 November 1957.

34   CPED, "Comité protestant d'études," November 1957.

35   REF, 7 December 1957.

36   Georges Casalis, *Les idées justes ne tombent pas du ciel* (Paris: Cerf, 1977), p. 9.

Etienne Mathiot
(Courtesy Mouvement International de Réconciliation, Paris)

Tania Metzel
(Courtesy Mme Janine Philibert)

CHAPTER FIVE

1958: PROTESTANT REACTIONS TO
THE *13 MAI* AND THE COMING OF DE GAULLE

On 11 January 1958, the internationalization of the Algerian conflict came a step closer when a French army patrol was attacked near the Tunisian border. Fourteen French soldiers were killed and five more taken prisoner. Paris charged Tunis with complicity in the attack and demanded the immediate return of the captives. President Bourguiba not only rejected this demand but refused even to receive the emissary sent by France to negotiate their release.

French commanders in the field were determined to retaliate for what they were convinced was official Tunisian collusion with the FLN. On 8 February, responding to anti-aircraft fire which had been coming from inside Tunisia just across the Algerian border for many days, French planes bombarded the Tunisian town of Sakiet-Sidi-Youssef at market time, killing sixty-nine civilians and wounding 130 others, including some Algerian refugees who were being looked after by the International Red Cross. The officers who directed the attack had not bothered to get prior authorization from their civilian superiors, most notably Resident-General Lacoste, who was understandably outraged when the news reached him.

Writing in *Cité nouvelle*, Jan Czarnecki speculated that, apart from seeking military retaliation, the perpetrators of the assault were anxious to put an end to what had appeared to be a rather promising opportunity for detente between Paris and Tunis. The left-wing journalist expressed the hope (in vain as it turned out) that the bombardment would be followed by mass protests throughout France.[1]

The Sakiet incident was a significant moment in the evolution of the Algerian conflict for three reasons: it exposed the impotence of French civil authority in dealing with the military who were determined to wage war on their own terms after what they saw to be a political sell-out following Dien Bien Phu; as a corollary, it undermined the legitimacy and credibility of the Fourth Republic (Yves Courrière notes: "It was at Sakiet-Sidi-Youssef on 8 February 1958 that the death-knell of the Fourth Republic first sounded");[2] and, because of the clear violation of the air space of newly independent Tunisia, it forced the issue of France's continuing presence in Algeria onto the United Nations' agenda.

Tunisia's President Bourguiba, whose hold on power was less than absolute, took his grievance about the attack to the Security Council of the

United Nations where, given the American desire to outdo the Soviet Union in championing the cause of decolonization, Washington would be under pressure not to offer Paris unconditional support. Enormous strains were thus imposed on the Atlantic Alliance and, to avoid its rupture, the United States, supported by Great Britain, offered its "good offices" to resolve the tension between Tunis and Paris. The subsequent presence of the veteran American diplomat Robert Murphy outraged the European minority which saw this as just another signal of their forthcoming abandonment by the home country in the face of American and third-world manipulation.

The Sakiet incident and its aftermath evoked considerable comment in the pages of *Réforme*. Paul Adeline remarked that the crisis had once again made clear that France was unable to deal with the Algerian problem by herself. Her diplomatic isolation during the crisis and the feeble state of her economy made it necessary to review the situation which could best be resolved through a comprehensive North African arrangement involving Morocco and Tunisia.[3] The managing editor of *Réforme*, Pierre Bungener, agreed with this view, suggesting the creation of a Franco-African federation, an "occidental Mediterranean community" which could, among other things, undertake a common exploitation of Saharan oil resources.[4]

Albert Finet wondered why a night raid by commandos had not been used in response to the FLN assault at Sakiet; the air raid against innocent civilians which had been launched instead reminded the editor of *Réforme* of the indiscriminate kind of aerial bombardment used by Americans in the 1940s. Finet concluded that the whole unhappy episode had resulted from the visceral reaction of a middle-level civil or military officer who had not thought through the consequences. Some expression of regret by Paris together with an offer to compensate the victims would no doubt have limited the subsequent damage in France and her interests.[5]

In the 6 March issue of *France-Observateur*, André Philip offered a devastating indictment of the government's Algerian policy. Under the title "Le suicide de la France," Philip argued that Sakiet, like Dien Bien Phu, would prove to be the turning-point in this latest colonial conflict. A few months earlier, France might have negotiated with the FLN from a position of strength; now, alas, the most intractable elements on both sides had dug themselves in. The FLN had limitless possibilities of recruitment among Muslim youths; arms were more and more available from the Eastern bloc; and the Americans, seconded by the British, were being drawn despite themselves to intervene in the conflict; in fact, Philip concluded gloomily, "Following the bombardment of Sakiet, we have the whole world against us."

Although the situation was very depressing, it was not altogether hopeless, Philip continued. There was still a chance for the government to effect a volte-face. The good offices of Tunisia's Bourguiba and the King of Morocco might be appealed to, in an effort to influence the political leadership of the FLN which tended to be more open to reason than its military arm. A second option would be to turn to the European allies of France for mediation. Otherwise, the Algerian issue would inevitably be internationalized; and, if this should happen and Paris were to reject the views of the UN Security Council, the Soviet Union was clearly all too ready to intervene. The ultimate result of this latter development, Philip asserted, would be the total removal of French influence in Algeria, paralleling what had happened to the Dutch in Indonesia.

André Philip was equally concerned about the domestic implications of the Sakiet incident. By encouraging a flag-waving national sentiment, the government risked stirring up a violent reaction in the army; and if, in what might well become a worsening situation across the Mediterranean, the United States were to impose French capitulation to the FLN, there was a real danger of an internal fascist rising.[6]

Philip's comments had been motivated in part by the appearance of Henri Alleg's *La Question*, a graphic account by the left-wing Algerian journalist of his arrest and torture by the French military. Alleg's tract also inspired an anguished commentary from Pastor Henri Roser who compared the revelation in Alleg's work to the disclosure by the leftist reporter Andrée Viollis of ruthless French colonial practices during the 1930s; worse still, Roser suggested, Alleg's revelations conjured up memories of the dehumanizing methods of the Nazis. By what unconscionable complicity have we come to this, Roser wrote; how have we been so negligent that we have not seen that our soldiers are being turned into sadists as a result of indoctrination by experts in brainwashing and in psychological warfare?

Readers of *La Question*, Roser continued, were bound both to share the writer's agony and to join vicariously in his resistance to torture through which all humanity was ennobled. Henri Alleg was Jewish, or so it was said, but so had Jesus been! Roser hints here in his own comment at the antisemitism which may well have made Alleg a special target of the military. Christians, as Roser pointed out, had much to do penance for in their historic treatment of Jews; he went on to say that they should in the present circumstances also seek pardon from Muslims "by opposing humility to violence" and by vanquishing "the ultra-nationalism by which France is in her turn today being infected."

After asking rhetorically whether the logical consequence of the shifts in French mentality would culminate in a recognition of Algerian independence, Roser replied: "If we had the requisite vision for this, we would soon discover that France would thereby gain in good will all that she is currently losing by her stridently warlike posturing."[7]

The graphic revelations about the use of torture by the French military in Algeria which Henri Alleg had brought to the public intensified the debate on the subject in Paris. Albert Finet was moved by the detached, clinical style of Alleg's essay but worried about the motives which drove the French Left to focus on the negative side of the military operation across the Mediterranean without ever querying the methods of the FLN.[8]

Meanwhile, the grave embarrassment caused by the Sakiet incident, especially the American meddling in what the French Right considered to be an area of exclusively national interest, was a key factor in the fall of the Gaillard ministry. In the weeks preceding this development, Soustelle had given a series of speeches on behalf of the *Union pour le salut et le renouveau de l'Algérie française*, the organization he had founded following his return to Paris early in 1956. Moved in large measure by Soustelle, who condemned Washington's mediating efforts (after Sakiet) as biased against France, the National Assembly denied Premier Gaillard a vote of confidence on 15 April.[9]

While Jacques Soustelle was leading the assault on the Gaillard government following the incident at Sakiet, liberal and leftist elements in the French Protestant community had become deeply involved in the arrest and trial of a Lutheran peace activist, Pastor Etienne Mathiot of Belfort. Mathiot had developed a reputation with the authorities as a result of harbouring local derelicts as well as refugees from the Hungarian Revolution of 1956 and Algerian workers from the local Alsthom plant. He was apprehended by the gendarmerie on 12 December 1957 on the charge that he had given shelter to Si Ali, a prominent FLN leader sought by the police. A young Catholic militant, Françoise Rapiné, was arrested shortly afterwards on the same charge.

Although the full story behind this arrest was not revealed until after the pastor's death in 1983, in fact Etienne Mathiot was not responsible for the offence for which he was charged and later tried. Two days before the gendarmes showed up at the door of his presbytery, he had sent Si Ali to see his brother-in-law, Pastor Jacques Lochard whose parish lay close to the Swiss border, phoning ahead to make sure that his colleague would welcome the Algerian nationalist. Lochard had in turn spoken with a member of his congregation who had some experience in guiding people across the border into Switzerland without benefit of passport. As a result, Si Ali had already slipped across the frontier on foot at the time when Mathiot was being interrogated at his front door.

Concerned not to implicate his brother-in-law in the escape, Mathiot had blurted out a confession of his own guilt as soon as the gendarmes appeared on his doorstep.   He noted that his action did not signify philosophical support for the FLN, that he was in fact against all forms of violence and that he had acted as he did in order to spare Si Ali the physical abuse he presumed such prisoners were bound to suffer at the hands of the authorities. Finally, he said, he would not have intervened had he believed his visitor to be capable of murder.[10]

Once Mathiot's arrest became known, the Protestant community began to mobilize. Pastor Boegner, president of the French Protestant Federation, went to see the minister of justice, Robert Lecourt, to denounce his colleague's arrest and plead for government intervention.

Pastor Henri Roser paid tribute to his colleague Mathiot in the pages of *Cité nouvelle*: "It is immediately evident to us that (Mathiot) acted simply in accord with the dictates of his conscience and in order to remain faithful to the love of the Lord whom he serves and to whom he belongs." Mathiot had given asylum when it was asked for; he was in any event justified in not surrendering his guest to the torture which might well have awaited him if apprehended. As a pastor and as a human being, Etienne Mathiot could not have acted differently, Roser wrote, adding rather grandiloquently: "The issue is clear. Either they restore Etienne to his ministry or they lay charges against Jesus Christ and banish Him from our midst.[11]

On 26 January, the Algerian study group, meeting to discuss reports of continuing abuses by the French military across the Mediterranean, concluded that Pastor Mathiot's action should be seen in this context. Not surprisingly, the Belfort pastor had been deeply troubled by the atmosphere of heightened violence on both sides of the Mediterranean. As the members of the study group wrote: "This climate of anguish and moral disarray has been brought to our attention by the gesture of Etienne Mathiot, whatever judgment one might make about that gesture in and by itself."[12]

From his prison cell in Besançon, Mathiot wrote exultantly about the new constructive relationship between settlers and Muslims which was sure to develop through the love and shared suffering he and others like him were experiencing.[13] Meanwhile, concerned about the pastor's welfare, Henri Roser gathered a group of close friends and associates at Protestant headquarters on the rue de Clichy in Paris to discuss the forthcoming trial of Mathiot and the ways his pastoral colleagues might rally support.

Among those present at this meeting was Tania Metzel who set off at once for Besançon.   After staying overnight at the pastor's house, she borrowed bread and wine from Mathiot's wife before travelling to the prison so that she might offer her friend and colleague communion. Etienne Mathiot was understandably delighted by the surprise visit but when Metzel proposed that they share communion, he hesitated, asking whether his visitor was able to pardon him for the action which had led to his arrest. When Metzel reassured him by telling him: "I'm here, Etienne, isn't that assurance enough!," the two partook of communion together in the prison's barber-shop which the jail authorities set aside for them.

The March 1958 trial of Mathiot and his co-defendant Françoise Rapiné attracted a good deal of press attention, no doubt in part because a number of key Protestant personalities turned up as witnesses for the defense. These included Professor Paul Ricoeur, Pastors Georges Casalis and Charles Westphal of the *Fédération Protestante de France*, and André Philip.

Mathiot's defense was in the hands of a prominent Protestant lawyer, Jean-Jacques de Félice, who later became vice-president of France's leading civil rights organization (*La Ligue des Droits de l'Homme*), founded during the Dreyfus Affair, as well as a member of the board of CIMADE. Mathiot, speaking in defense of his action in providing shelter for Si Ali, declared: "I tried to convert an enemy into an open-minded human being because I know that, by contrast with acts of violence, any gesture of love brings with it the potential for change."[14]

Ricoeur recorded his impressions of the trial for the readers of *Cité nouvelle*, beginning with a description of the dramatic court appearance of Mathiot and the Algerian Si Ali, symbolically shackled together. The distinguished Protestant philosopher saw Mathiot and Rapiné as "guilty yet pure, actors in a drama which has arrested our attention as vividly as burning brands tossed into icy water." Mathiot and Rapiné had been pushed to their extreme action by government policy and the perverse use of the law. They deserved indulgence, if not acquittal "in the name of the purity of their intention which has been lost to view because of the ineptitude of their action."[15]

Protestant conservatives were as outraged by Mathiot as leftists had been moved. "S.D." rejected what it saw to be pure casuistry in Philip's argument. "There *is* an enemy;" the journalist insisted, "There *is* treason here. And there *is* justice to be done!" The writer went on to argue, as though out of respect to Philip, that there were clearly guiltier parties than Mathiot and Rapiné in the case, including members of a government which was prepared to send young French soldiers to die in Algeria while permitting members of the intellectual elite to sap their morale, becoming accomplices of the enemy with absolutely no risk to themselves. Mathiot's courage, the journalist pursued, was not in question; after all, he was currently serving out his sentence. But an argument cited in the pastor's defense that one must love one's enemies could never be made to mean that one becomes a willing partner of those who are killing one's brethren![16]

Mathiot's action in rescuing Si Ali was greeted with equal indignation by the *Conseil presbytéral* of Boufarik in Algeria, whose presiding officer, Pastor Georges Tartar, condemned "certain pastors and representatives of the church who mix politics with their spiritual mission." In a series of messages to his co-religionists inspired by *L'Affaire Mathiot*, Tartar indicted the "so-called progressivist tendency which pretends to speak in the name of Algerian Protestantism" and made clear that the congregations he spoke for wanted politics to be left to politicians and military operations to army men. In any event, France was not persecuting Algerians in any way; if people such as Si Ali were being arrested, it was because they were clearly identified as belonging to terrorist cells; they were criminals and murderers whose prosecution Christ himself would sanction. Thanks to the army, Tartar concluded, the work of reconciliation and reconstruction was going ahead apace.[17]

When, inspired by Tartar, the conservative synod of Boufarik rejected any effort to engender collective support for Mathiot, and decried the "martyr's status" which some Protestants were assigning him, Henri Roser challenged readers of *Cité nouvelle* to ask themselves if Jesus himself had been a model of prudent behaviour vis-a-vis the authorities of His day.[18] In the end following a guilty verdict handed down against all defendants, Pastor Mathiot was condemned to eight months in prison (of which he would serve only six), Françoise Rapiné to three years while the Muslim was given a three-month suspended sentence corresponding to time already spent in detention but was sent to an internment camp.

The Sakiet incident and the arrest of Pastor Mathiot kept the debate about France's actions in Algeria very much alive in the Protestant community, as did efforts by the administration to promote further reform from above.

Some Protestant activists, meanwhile, joined forces with other radicals in urging a basic change in the government's policy towards Algeria. For more than two months during the spring of 1958, some 2,000 delegates from various left-wing organizations met at the Salle Pleyel in Paris for an *Assemblée nationale pour la paix en Algérie*. Two reports were submitted, one by Laurent Schwartz, the other by André Philip. Both urged recognition of Algeria's right to independence and recommended that this be accompanied by discussions designed to ensure close economic and cultural ties following the break. At the end of the lengthy session, a resolution was passed condemning government policy and urging the negotiation of Algerian independence to be followed by pledges of cooperation.[19]

The political crisis precipitated in May 1958 by the insurrection of Algeria's European minority and those in the army who shared their frustration had a decisive impact on the Algerian conflict. The rising triggered the collapse of the Fourth Republic and the emergence of a new regime in which a strengthened executive was better able to give firmness and consistency to national policy.

Long before the May crisis, French political commentators had expressed concern about the weak executive authority in the postwar constitution and the resultant lack of direction to national policy. At the end of January 1958, for their annual review of developments in the Maghreb, Algeria's Protestant study group, in a joint meeting with the council of the FPF, deplored "the impotence of Parliament as well as of the government not simply to execute but even more critically not to define a clear Algerian policy, thus testifying to a disquieting weakening of the state itself, something for which the nation as a whole must share responsibility."[20]

Following this meeting, with its prophetic sense of the imminent peril facing republican institutions, Pastor Marc Boegner, president of the FPF, relayed his impressions to a reporter from *Le Monde*. The leading figure in French Protestantism prefaced his remarks with a general reflection about the inner drama being experienced by Christians in dealing with a situation like that in Algeria: "Such a drama is frequent within the soul and conscience of the Christian who feels torn between his desire for Christian authenticity and the political positions which he feels he must adopt in the name of that same religion." The churches on whose behalf he spoke had condemned the use of torture by French troops as well as the disappearance and presumed abduction of Muslims and European dissidents. Finally, there was the long-term widening gulf between adherents of Christianity and Islam which called for serious reflection on all sides.[21]

As more observers attributed the nation's problems to the underlying weakness in the constitution, contributors to *Réforme* (like others) asked whether Charles de Gaulle might once again serve as France's "providential man." Late in March, Bernard Charbonneau noted that everyone "from Soustelle to Mauriac" was clamouring for the general's return; without it, internal conflicts and contradictions might lead to a totalitarian coup.[22]

One of the most perceptive commentaries both on the country's inherent constitutional weakness and on the internal divisions which were beginning to paralyze French socialism came from the Protestant Michel Rocard. As an *Inspecteur des finances* in 1958, already moving into the upper reaches of the republican mandarinate, Rocard could not openly comment on public affairs. Instead, writing under the nom de plume Jacques Malterre,

Rocard had for weeks before the May crisis been penning a series of articles on the steadily deteriorating political situation for *Cité nouvelle*.

On 1 May, two weeks after the fall of the Gaillard government, as the tensions and misunderstandings increased, Rocard pointed out that France was experiencing her eighteenth ministerial crisis since 1946. This ministerial instability, as Rocard saw it, was the symptom of a larger malady. It could only be cured if the fragile coalitions which had governed France since the Liberation were replaced by parties based on broad alliances, not narrow interest groups. Meanwhile, France's policy towards Algeria was alienating the Third World and might well force the United States (which had shown great forbearance) to become involved in what had so far been respected as a zone of exclusive French interest.[23]

By the spring of 1958 many French officers serving in Algeria began to wish for the overthrow of "The System" which was rumoured to be on the point of selling them out and suing for a negotiated peace. The undeclared war that half a million French soldiers were engaged in, to a large extent based on retaliation for guerrilla assaults and terrorist attacks, was peculiarly frustrating. The murder of three French soldiers on the eve of 13 May, perpetrated by the FLN in response to the army's execution of rebels, was one of the immediate causes of the insurrection.

A feeling of betrayal and abandonment in the European minority in Algeria also played a key role in the 13 May rising. As long as a "strong man" such as Soustelle or Lacoste was in charge, *colons* had some confidence that their interests were being protected. The departure of Lacoste just before the end of his mandate on the Saturday before the crisis broke, together with his refusal to disavow the anti-colonial pronouncements of his Socialist comrades and stay on to defend the cause of French Algeria, helped set the stage for the insurrection, especially when it was learned that the ministry about to be formed in Paris was to be headed by Pierre Pflimlin, rumoured to favour peace negotiations.

Although it is clear that there were restive elements both in the army and among *colons* in the spring of 1958, it is difficult to see the events of 13 May as the result of a conscious plot. In fact, a number of groups, often with very different agendas, intervened to try to capture and direct the mass energy that had been released. The *Union pour le salut et le renouveau de l'Algérie française*, founded eighteen months earlier by Soustelle, had attracted a number of distinguished clerics, academics and other intellectuals. Several other Algiers-based groups were involved in mobilizing opinion against the regime. Pierre Lagaillarde was head of the most important student union; Dr. Bernard Lefevre, a disciple of Charles Maurras, headed a small fascist faction; Alain de Sérigny was the publisher of the ultra-conservative *Echo d'Alger*; elements of the *Unités territoriales*, made up of reservists who formed a kind of national guard for the colony, were ready to defend Algeria to the end. For all these groups, the retention of Algeria as an integral part of France was paramount.

The immediate chain of events leading to the 13 May began on 15 April when news of the collapse of the Gaillard ministry, something which their hero Soustelle had helped to bring about, was enthusiastically received in Algiers. Rumours that Pierre Pflimlin might head a new cabinet and that he was well disposed towards negotiating with the FLN set in motion the process which led to the overthrow of the Fourth Republic. In the days that followed, devoted followers of de Gaulle including Léon Delbecque, a deputy of the *Républicains sociaux* party who acted as the general's unofficial agent in Algiers, began preparing to act in the event of the anticipated *crise de régime*.

One result of this Gaullist planning was the creation in Algiers of a *Comité de vigilance* designed to transform itself into a *Comité de Salut Public* when the Fourth Republic faced its death-agony. That they expected only in August.

On 11 May, newspaper publisher Alain de Sérigny (who had been a Pétain supporter during the war), signed an article (which Soustelle in France had approved beforehand) calling upon de Gaulle to step forward, head a new government and thereby save France's honour and her position in Algeria.

On the morning of 13 May, Léon Delbecque called together the *Comité de vigilance* and reminded its members that the key aim of that afternoon's demonstration was to prolong the rally until Soustelle arrived to be made head of an acting political directorate.

Shortly after 4 p.m. a huge crowd started assembling in front of the *Gouvernement Général* building. The rally then developed into a contest between champions of de Gaulle and partisans of the overthrow of the entire democratic and parliamentary system. Delbecque, the Gaullists' master strategist, would play a decisive role in orchestrating events in such a way that his hero prevailed.

As the crowd grew more restless, Lacoste's deputy, de Maisonneuve, asked his superiors in Paris whether he should give the order to shoot if and when there was an assault on the government building. In the end, this was averted when General Massu and Salan, with the approval of those in Paris, assumed responsibility for the regime and its local representatives. Massu, who was very reluctantly drawn into what was ultimately a political struggle, named himself president of the *Comité du salut public* while Paris yielded what amounted to plenipotentiary power in Algeria to Salan. Thus, ironically, two military men who had kept themselves aloof from the various plotters became the arbiters of the situation, contrary to what Delbecque and his companions had contrived.

Determined to prevail despite this setback, Delbecque announced to the crowd that he was the representative of Jacques Soustelle who would arrive imminently to champion the cause of French Algeria. Delbecque and friends had meanwhile prepared a telegram to the general which they pressed Massu into reading aloud from the balcony of the Government General. When Massu obliged and the crowd responded with shouts of "L'armée au pouvoir!" and "Vive de Gaulle!," the tide turned. The Gaullists, who had felt their hopes slip away, thus ended up winning the day.

Among observers of developments in Algeria during the May crisis was Tania Metzel who was in the middle of a second, four-month-long visit. During the dramatic events of the 13 May, Tania Metzel was staying with a colleague in Constantine, a pastor with a *pied-noir* background. They were at dinner when news of the events in Algiers came over the radio. The visitor lowered her head to hide her tears. Her hosts could not hide their jubilation. Later, however, easily reading her expression, they expressed the view that she was bound to find more members of the European community who would share her feelings back in Algiers. In fact, during a stopover at Philippeville on the way back, the chaplain was able to telephone a congenial fellow-pastor. "Finally, there's someone I can talk to!" she exclaimed. "Yes, finally! I'm in the same situation!" her colleague replied. It was not a good moment for European liberals.[24]

On 14 May, as news of Premier Pflimlin's confirmation reached the general population in Algiers, orders for a resumption of the general strike came from the extreme right.

On 15 May, General de Gaulle issued a press release making clear his willingness to assume power within the framework of republican legality. During the night of 15-16 May, the team which had plotted the general's return prepared for still another mass rally on the 16th, this time with the fullest possible participation of the Muslim population. To produce this result, word was spread that a new era was beginning in which all Algerians, whatever their culture or religion, would share the same rights and responsibilities as full-fledged citizens of France. The response was remarkable: some 30,000 Muslims, mobilized by the authorities for the occasion, joined 40,000 Europeans in the rally. The event was later hailed as clear evidence of a new-found *fraternisation* which would transform ethnic relations inside Algeria and link the territory even more intimately to a France which had rediscovered her liberating vocation.

Not surprisingly, interpretations of what actually occurred on the *16 mai* vary widely. That there was a deep loyalty to France among hundreds of thousands of Algerian Muslims cannot be contested. The massive purge visited upon those who stayed faithful to the tricolour after Algerian independence is devastating evidence of this. On the other side of the equation, the willingness of the *colons* to go beyond the rapturous communion of the *16 mai* and accept a genuine transformation in attitude towards Muslims and a sharing of power with the majority seems questionable, to say the least. It was one thing for an administrator such as Soustelle and for intellectuals back in Paris to signal their repudiation of the colonial past. It was quite another to expect the European minority to accept the full implications of majority rule with the obvious loss of status and security which it seemed bound to bring.

Memories of that remarkable day haunted Soustelle for the rest of his life. In 1973, a decade after the granting of Algeria's independence, the ex-governor reminisced about that moment of communion, deploring the oppression of Europeans and Muslims alike which had occurred under the new regime in Algiers, including the persecution of his old friend the francophile Muslim Si Bachir Ben Moussa. Soustelle was then living the life of a proscribed exile in his own country. He thought back even further to his days as a *normalien* when he had befriended young men from the Antilles, from Black Africa and from Indochina. It was shortly after the great Colonial Exposition of 1931, he recalled:

> We were at one and the same time conscious of being different (and proud of it) and yet deeply attached to one another. We were aware that we belonged to diverse human groups and cultures with different histories but also that we were part of a vast human community forged together by History. We shared a desire to purge that community, that empire, of all that was still tyrannous and oppressive; but it would have seemed stupid to us, even criminal, to dismember it. We agreed, didn't we, that all relationships of conqueror to conquered, of superior to inferior, all racist concepts, should be forever banished among our various peoples. We thought that colonies should be transformed into provinces, regions or states in a great multi-racial federation gravitating around the French Republic in a plurinational union with one single citizenship at the core of it in which Paris (and other capitals) would have shone like so many stars of different size and luminosity in the same galaxy.

At the end of this rhetorical flourish, Soustelle addressed himself directly to Si Bachir Ben Moussa, calling to mind the time when the Algerian society of which he was governor-general included Berbers ans well as Arabs, Europeans as well as Muslims, Christians as well as Jews. Again, *le 16 mai* is seen as the moment "when an immense wave of fraternity swept through the Forum," when all believed in a shared future. Nowadays, Soustelle added bitterly, all of France's colonies have been given over to the holocaust which resulted from the evil cult of "decolonization."[25]

By contrast with Soustelle, Pastor André Trocmé, who again found himself in Algiers in the spring of 1958 and was an eye-witness to the drama of the *16 mai*, took a rather cynical view of the same events. As the pastor saw it, the fraternization had been carefully stage-managed. The *Sections administratives urbaines*, groups of locally based *colons* whom Soustelle had helped to organize, together with young Muslims devoted to France (including former internees who had been released in return for pledges of allegiance to France), had trucked in a few hundred Muslims to create the appearance of fraternization; these same groups had put up banners and streamers long before the mass rally, again to help achieve the effect of "spontaneity." Trocmé did not hide his contempt for the quality of those Muslims dragooned to the scene:

> These men, scraped up in outlying shanty-towns, herded to the site by "shepherds in uniform" bused in by the truckload, were quite clearly from the lumpenproletariat and barely understood French. They gave no sign of enthusiasm; in fact, they did not actively participate. Apart from Dr. Si Cara, an eminence from Oran, there were no representatives of the educated class, Arab or Kabyle. With the exception of a few rather well-educated women and some veterans who sported their French army decorations, the demonstration could hardly be seen as a manifestation of conscious Muslim collaboration.[26]

Jan Czarnecki, writing in the 3 July issue of *Cité nouvelle*, supported Trocmé's cynical view. Very few Muslims, he wrote, had been deceived by the apparent sudden volte-face of Algeria's Europeans; the great majority of the youth wanted to be Algerian, not French.[27]

André Philip provided his own interpretation of the fraternization phenomenon in an interview published in the summer issue of *Le Semeur*. At the beginning of events, the veteran Socialist argued, the mass presence of Muslims in the manifestation had been "a game of bluff brilliantly organized by the psychological services of the army with the help of truckloads of paratroopers. Frightened by the *paras* and often without the proper papers, afraid of being arrested if they refused to participate, they had not only joined in the demonstration but even called out whatever slogans were relayed to them." Philip conceded that however artificially the Muslim involvement was engineered, it became in time "pseudo-sincere." After all, the blending of Muslims and Europeans into a shared community corresponded to a long-held dream, at least among the older generation. As a result, a quite impressive psychological shock had been administered, so strong that it affected members of the European community as well where it was at last being recognized that the simple application of the *loi-cadre* was no longer enough to bring peace to Algeria.[28]

A few weeks after the event, using the pseudonym Bernard Vollet, François Hauchecorne published an analysis of the army's use of psychological warfare with special focus on the way in which this technique had been employed to effect the apparently spontaneous expressions of fraternization on 13 and 16 May.[29] The mass demonstrations on and after 13 May were, as Hauchecorne saw it, a perfect illustration of this technique. Every street block in Algiers, every neighbourhood, every social group, had been systematically organized to respond in a manner which had produced the illusion of spontaneity. The Muslims had in fact been brought to the Forum in trucks or herded to the scene by military escorts. Once their presence was no longer politically useful, they had quickly deserted the scene.

What disturbed the librarian as much as developments in Algeria (grim as they were) was the thought that the Republic itself was in danger so long as psychological warfare was being pursued by the army. The technique being used by the military was by its very nature illiberal. Protestations of devotion to democratic values by those using strong-arm methods in Algeria were utterly hypocritical. "These modern-day sorcerers' apprentices, fully committed to the use of totalitarian techniques, are opening the way to fascism," he wrote "unless, in reaction to their efforts, they provoke the coming to power of Communists."

Not surprisingly, Hauchecorne's article in *Réforme* elicited a number of letters from conservative Protestant readers. "H.C.C." allowed that the methods described in the article might lead to fascism but insisted that France must defend herself against the FLN whose activities were just as likely to produce a totalitarian denouement of the Maoist type. "J. d'I." was in essential agreement, suggesting that two visions of human happiness were in conflict in Algeria and that the only way for France to engage in this battle was through effective psychological combat.

Responding to his critics, Hauchecorne declared: "For Christians at least, the whole question is precisely to show that there is another way, perhaps less efficacious in the eyes of the world, but in the end the only valid one."

Predictably, conservative Protestants took issue with those who dismissed *le 16 mai* as a contrived event. Philippe Brissaud, who would soon help found the newspaper *Tant qu'il fait jour* to express a point of view about France in Algeria which he felt was being marginalized in *Réforme*, hailed the 16 May experience in a suggestively titled editorial piece ("La grâce nous est offerte"). The spontaneous rising against the Fourth Republic had produced two welcome results, Brissault argued: the return to power of de Gaulle and the coming together of Muslims and Europeans. The two communities had sung the Marseillaise together in a thrilling expression of common allegiance. Even the Ultra faction had joined in the bonding which had occurred. Alain de Sérigny and others were now ready to accept the *collège unique*; Europeans were even giving up their seats on buses to Muslim fellow-passengers! It was a kind of miracle, a "providential" moment which the new regime in Paris and the army (which had always kept apart from Algeria's ethnic tensions) could exploit to help effect real political change.[30]

A month later, Brissault set forth in concrete terms the reforms needed to transform the mystical moment of *le 16 mai* into political reality: a massive increase in the literacy and general educational level of the Muslim masses; a radical improvement in the living standards of the majority who should be allowed access to public office; and a radical change in Algeria's social and institutional structure.[31]

The *Comité protestant d'études* for its part adopted an essentially positive view of *le 16 mai*. The "fraternization" at the Forum had no doubt been initially orchestrated by the army and the *Comité du salut public*; but, after all, "the use of force, as has all too often but quite truthfully been said, does inspire confidence in these people (the Muslims)" and those who had shown up had seemed enthusiastic enough. What was really significant, the committee reported, was that a new sense of dignity and a new hope for real equality had been engendered in the Muslim masses. Europeans at the rally had clearly been touched at the show of friendship and support given to the majority. The challenge ahead was to transform a purely emotional experience into a concrete reality with all the social and economic effort and sacrifice that that entailed.[32]

In the middle of the constitutional crisis precipitated by the *13 mai*, the editorial board of *Réforme* published a series of questions and answers coming out of a round-table discussion.[33] Was the existing regime worth defending in the name of *Algérie française*? No. Let the system die so that we may build a true republic, the staff replied. Was the *13 mai* a fascist plot? No. The demonstrators in Algiers had been no more fascist than those who marched subsequently in Paris and Lyon; and de Gaulle, whom they were summoning to power, was clearly not a fascist. Was Franco-Muslim reconciliation possible? Yes, with reservations. Those who had marched on 16 May seemed to testify to this possibility although much needed to be done to promote real change in the living conditions of the Algerian masses. In the end, the chief writers for *Réforme* agreed on two prerequisites for a sound Algerian policy: the nationalist rising must be stamped out and the *colons* must not be abandoned.

On 29 May, President Coty announced his intention to call upon Charles de Gaulle to form a new government. When the man who had spent the previous twelve years excoriating the Fourth Republic announced his acceptance and then made clear a few days later that his ministry would include such veteran politicians of the dying regime as Mollet and Pflimlin (but not the idol of the Ultras, Jacques Soustelle), Algeria's Europeans began to wonder what they had brought about through their insurrection a fortnight earlier.

The tension between de Gaulle and Soustelle which lay just under the surface throughout the crisis of May 1958 was based in part on their very different views of Algeria. For the former governor-general, *L'Algérie française* had become a shibboleth, a sacred cause; guaranteeing that the colony remained French by forcing the process of integration was an absolute priority. For de Gaulle, on the other hand, the Algerian question, whatever its intrinsic merit, was second to the larger issue of restoring French power and influence; if need be, the territory must be let go.

Following the investiture of de Gaulle as premier, Malterre/Rocard issued another admonition to the nation's Socialist leaders in the pages of *Cité nouvelle*. The collapse of the Fourth Republic had been due in part at least to the stubborn refusal of the Left to consider a structural revision of the constitutionally flawed Fourth Republic. Now, faced by the arrival in power of de Gaulle, they continued to invoke the threat of a non-existent fascism. Above all, it was irresponsible on the part of the Left to see the general's return as a manifestation of right-wing authoritarianism. Nothing in his writings or in his actions suggested the new premier's disdain for popular sovereignty. "De Gaulle is not the leader of a faction," Rocard wrote: "He does not represent fascism. He has been put in power less as a result of the military revolt than because of the impotence of the legal government to put it down.... In fact, the rumour has run the rounds that the general has liberal views about Algeria." [34]

André Philip was far less sanguine about de Gaulle's return to power than Rocard who would within a decade replace him as the leading Protestant personality in the French Socialist movement. The general, Philip pointed out to readers of *Le Semeur*, had come to power as a result of a military pronunciamento; he was not a contemporary politician but a figure out of the seventeenth century who felt a compulsive urge to change the course of history, all in the name of his sacred faith in *Notre-Dame-la-Nation*. There was every likelihood that, under de Gaulle's guidance, France would be transformed into a kind of liberal monarchy which might in turn give way to a fascist state. In the immediate circumstances, what was needed was the creation of anti-fascist watch committees. In the longer term, one could only hope for the emergence of a Gaullist-type party loyal to the Republic challenged by a strong opposition which brought together all the non-Communist forces of the Left.[35]

The editors of *Réforme* devoted much of the 7 June issue to comments about the investiture of Premier Charles de Gaulle.[36] The lead article signed *Réforme* began with a profession of the traditional Calvinist conviction about the essential unworthiness of the human species, then went on to suggest that, while Charles de Gaulle might well be the best hope for France in the current crisis, he should not be hailed as a "Saviour" capable of performing miracles. The Algerian question, the editors continued, was not one which could be solved in ideological terms. It was appropriate that the new ministry be made up not of ideologues but of experts such as ex-premier and finance minister Antoine Pinay and foreign affairs veteran Couve de Murville. It was particularly gratifying that de Gaulle had not let himself be surrounded by his own partisans, including Jacques Soustelle.

In mid-June, alarmed at the potential threat to the Republic posed by the committees of public safety which sprung up all over Algeria, Rocard urged Socialists to help guide de Gaulle ("who is not by himself a political force") along a truly democratic path.[37] A month after the investiture of de Gaulle, Pierre Bungener commented on the increased public support for the new premier and on the relaxation of the tensions which had brought France to the edge of civil war. We have been generous-minded but naive regarding Algeria, Bungener wrote, believing that nothing would be more precious to those living outside the metropolis than to absorb our customs and our culture. It was still worth dreaming that this generous attitude might inspire contemporary French men and women to build a fatherland without frontiers for all those who believed in "this gospel of racial fraternity and equal opportunity which de Gaulle spoke of in 1943."[38]

One of the immediate by-products of the *13 mai* was the launching of a new Protestant newspaper, *Tant qu'il fait jour*, in June. None of the contributors to the new paper came from the world of journalism, but all were solidly established on the Paris intellectual stage.[39] Roland Laudenbach was a gifted film writer who also served as director of the prestigious monthly periodical *La Table Ronde*. Like very few Protestants, he shared the monarchist faith of the right-wing nationalist Charles Maurras. Philippe Brissaud was a well-placed mandarin who had been named secretary-general of the *Institut de France*, one of the bastions of French intellectual life. Pastor Pierre Courthial of Passy provided the paper with its underlying moral and theological inspiration and direction.

As an orthodox Calvinist, Courthial based his political perspective on a deep belief in human depravity, a fundamental Christian tenet which, in his view, liberal Protestant theologians and politicians had thoughtlessly repudiated. The conservative pastor was also influenced by Calvin's argument, formulated during the turbulent sixteenth century when the Reformed were a beleaguered minority in France, that, when the sovereign has lost or betrayed its trust and authority, Christians are justified in turning to lower magistrates to restore the just governance of the state. If one came to regard the government of the Fourth (or for that matter the Fifth) Republic as having lost legitimacy, Courthial and other supporters of French Algeria would argue that the general councils of Algiers, Oran and Constantine could in a crisis declare themselves to be the proper custodians of French sovereignty, thereby replacing the regime in Paris.

Among the younger generation of those writing for *Tant qu'il fait jour* was a group of young Protestant theological students, led by Pierre Cochet who, as president of the *Cercle d'études des jeunes protestants français* (CEJPF) had decided to challenge the dominant influence among their peers of leftist pastors such as Georges Casalis. Contributors to the new paper insisted that they were not on the extreme right. All were conservative, nationalist and virulently anti-Communist. Many of them had been in the Resistance. While some were inspired by Maurras and sympathetic to the monarchist ideal, all felt marginalized by the mainstream Protestant organizations such as the *Fédé*, presided over by Jacques Maury, or by leading Protestant publications such as *Réforme*. No doubt over-dramatizing for effect, those who wrote for *Tant qu'il fait jour* argued that these influential bodies had been monopolized by partisans of the SFIO (or by its successors the PSA and PSU).

In a passionate lead article on page one of the first issue, the contributors to the new paper pledged themselves to defend the national honour and the cause of French Algeria. The text of this profession of faith was nothing if not grandiloquent: "In obedience to the Word of God, we honour the Nation in which God brought us to life and in which He made us His children responsible for the common weal both at home and abroad."[40]

Several contributors to the new paper had written for *Réforme* and, in an open letter to Albert Finet printed on Page One, Roland Laudenbach declared that he and his colleagues did not intend either to rival or to challenge the well-established Protestant weekly but rather to speak out more bluntly than they would be able to do under Finet's editorial direction. Addressing himself directly to Finet, Laudenbach declared: "You are essentially liberal and it is precisely this liberalism (or the direction that it takes in your columns) that does not suit us."

Albert Finet, replying to his challengers in the pages of *Réforme*, expressed sadness at this open break with former collaborators. Politics, the liberal pastor/editor went on to say, was not his profession nor that of his colleagues, except in the sense that no human activity is outside the frame of reference of God's Revelation through Jesus Christ which was neither Huguenot nor national. The presence of *Cité nouvelle*, a Protestant periodical well to the left of *Réforme* in addition to Laudenbach's new right-wing paper, was surely a cause for rejoicing since it guaranteed that all possible Protestant perspectives would be put before the public for its enlightenment.[41]

In this same first issue of *Tant qu'il fait jour*, Philippe Brissaud inserted an article on the Algerian conflict written before the *13 mai* but which he considered still relevant. The text begins with an analysis of what Brissaud believed to be the underlying causes of the 1954 insurrection: a group of pan-arabist agitators, driven by religious fanaticism and racial animosity, had planned the revolt which the Soviets had done their best to exploit. Algeria's Muslims had to a large extent joined the rebellion because of an uncontrolled population explosion resulting from the introduction of French medical improvements and Muslim cadres had participated in many cases because of frustration at lack of advancement within the administration. Other long-term causes included the failure of both Muslim and Europeans to appreciate each other's culture and the tendency of "poor whites" at the lower level of the civil service such as policemen and postal workers to harbour racial prejudice towards the majority.[42]

Brissaud's analysis amounted to a recapitulation of the theses which Jacques Soustelle had put forward while serving as Algeria's governor-general and which he continued to propagate subsequently in France. Soustelle was no doubt a subscriber to *Tant qu'il fait jour*; in any event, on 25 January 1961, the former governor-general addressed a letter to Brissaud expressing his gratitude to the conservative Protestant for having set the record straight on the complex circumstances which had led to the *13 mai*.[43]

On 4 June, just three days after his investiture, de Gaulle paid a visit to Algeria accompanied by the Socialist Max Lejeune, one of the settlers' *bêtes noires*. Conscious of the precarious nature of the coalition which had brought him to power, he reappointed Salan plenipotentiary representative of the Republic in Algeria while praising Soustelle (whose formal role and title remained unclear) as the soul of the 13 May rising. During his tour, de Gaulle avoided any explicit use of the politically charged term "integration." Only toward the very end of the visit, at Mostaganem on the coast near Oran, did he utter the words "Algérie française," the rallying-cry of European hardliners.

Not surprisingly, following de Gaulle's accession to the premiership, the minority which had struggled so hard to change the direction of the SFIO were outraged at what they perceived to be Mollet's collusion in the transfer of power to an authoritarian personality. Michel Rocard and others in the rising generation made their condemnation clear in an open letter on 3 June. Ten days later, Philip and other members of the minority demanded the holding of a special national convention of the SFIO by 15 July to review the party's general orientation and to consider the replacement of Mollet by Depreux. Philip took this occasion to renew his proposal for the creation of a broadly based coalition of the non-Communist left which would include Mendès France, Mitterand, and their supporters.

The internal crisis of the SFIO was brought to a head during the fiftieth national convention of the party held in the working-class suburb of Issy-les-Moulineaux near Paris between 11 and 14 September, just two weeks after the Yes vote in the referendum which approved the Gaullist constitution of the Fifth Republic.

Defending his own support for the Yes side before his fellow-delegates, Gaston Defferre argued that he and others who shared his views had not meant this support to signify a defense of the men behind the 13 May coup in Algiers whom he described as factious right-wing zealots. They had voted Yes because it was the clearest way to bring an end to the Algerian conflict; de Gaulle had made it clear than an endorsement of the new constitution would, among other things, allow for the unilateral withdrawal from the French Union by any of its members, something consistent with what had already been made clear in the Brazzaville declaration of 1944.[44] The motion which Defferre presented to the convention at the end of his intervention paralleled the resolution he had submitted at Toulouse in June 1957: military action should be pursued while negotiations were offered which would aim at finding a constitutional formula agreeable to both sides on the clear understanding that such a formula must include a clear pledge to guarantee the peaceful coexistence of Algeria's Muslims and Europeans.

While Defferre's forceful intervention helped secure a majority in support of the party leadership's backing of de Gaulle and the Yes vote, it did nothing to appease the minority. On 14 September, the last day of the convention, delegates from the minority faction met and formed the *Parti Socialiste autonome* (PSA). Basic disagreement over Algeria was only partly to blame for this dramatic schism: what was seen to be an overly bureaucratized and sclerotic leadership had created resentment and disaffection. The refusal to reintegrate André Philip into the party was denounced as a reflection of its generalized intellectual staleness, and finally, perhaps most tellingly, the complicity of Mollet and his associates in facilitating the transfer of power to de Gaulle and the fear that the general's return signified a real threat to republican institutions helped convince members of the minority that they had no option except to quit the party and find a new vehicle for the advancement of a genuinely Socialist agenda abroad as well as at home.

Not surprisingly, André Philip found a home in the PSA, and the Protestant Robert Verdier was chosen to be one of two adjutants to the new party's secretary-general, Edmond Depreux. The "conversion" of Mendès France was followed by other ideological and structural mergers, leading to the formation on 3 April 1960 of the *Parti Socialiste Unifié*. No doubt the excessive bureaucratization of the old SFIO might by itself have led to the restructuring of French social-democratic forces; but the Algerian question provided the catalyst which accelerated the process; and Protestant personalities who had been deeply troubled by events in Algeria played a key role both in the redefinition of doctrine and the renewal of leadership which opened a new chapter in French socialism beginning in the late 1950s.

During the late summer of 1958, while SFIO was undergoing intense self-scrutiny, French army units in Algeria were mobilized to propagate the gospel of fraternization and thereby to win support for the Yes option in the referendum on the constitution of the Fifth Republic which was to be held on 28 September.

The FLN reacted to this intensive campaign with a vigorous counter-offensive. Terrorist attacks were for the first time brought to continental France where Jacques Soustelle narrowly escaped an attempt on his life on 15 September. Two days later, in Cairo, representatives of the FLN announced the formation of a Provisional Government of the Algerian Republic (GPRA) under the presidency of Ferhat Abbas.

The referendum campaign divided contributors to the *Réforme* into two camps: Finet and Ellul favoured the Yes side while Roger Mehl and René

Courtin urged voters to write No on the ballot.[45] Finet observed that, since the army in Algeria would escort voters to the polls, the choice would really not be free. The inevitably favourable result of the referendum could not in any event be seen as endorsing integration.

The results of this vote turned out to be extraordinary. Four-fifths of the Algerian electorate participated (including Muslim women for the first time) and 96 percent of those who cast their ballots voted in favour of the new constitution which was enfranchising them.

André Trocmé meanwhile warned readers of *Cité nouvelle* of the fascist threat still emanating from Algiers. The situation of the *colons* there was similar to that of the French nobility before the Revolution, Trocmé wrote, equally ill-prepared to adapt to changing social and political circumstances. More important over the long term, it did not really matter what constitutional formula France devised, or what ideology she invoked, the African nations she had conquered were bound to break away from her sooner or later. The real question was whether France could reach a rapprochement with the formerly colonized, not through constitutional rearrangements or ideological formulae but through love.[46]

De Gaulle travelled again to Algeria early in October, announcing in the city that would carry its name, the Constantine Plan, a five-year programme to bring Muslims into the administration on both sides of the Mediterranean, to equalize wages, to distribute 250,000 hectares of land to Muslim farmers, to provide for the basic instruction of all Algerian children within a decade and, finally, to launch a vast enterprise of modernization based on industrial growth and the provision of proper housing. As a result of two-stage elections to the National Assembly held on 23 and 30 November, sixty-seven deputies were chosen to represent Algeria, forty-six of them Muslim, twenty-one European, all of them professing support for the principle of integration. Then, on 19 December, de Gaulle removed Salan as the plenipotentiary representative of the Republic in Algeria and dissolved the Committee of Public Safety which had orchestrated his accession to power. To restore civilian control, de Gaulle named Paul Delouvrier delegate-general of the government in Algiers and appointed General Maurice Challe his deputy in charge of military affairs. Two days later, on 21 December, Charles de Gaulle was chosen president of the Republic.

Following the landslide victory of the Gaullist forces in the fall election, contributors to *Tant qu'il fait jour* rejoiced. Philippe Brissaud denounced those who had tried during the election campaign to boost the cause of the Left by branding Soustelle as a fascist. By giving de Gaulle and Soustelle such an overwhelming mandate, Brissaud wrote, France had served notice to the world of her intention to survive as a great power.[47]

Throughout the fall of 1958, Finet continued to express modest hope for a peaceful solution to the Algerian conflict, taking comfort from the marginalization of the Committee of Public Safety and the Ultras as well as from de Gaulle's recognition of a distinct Algerian personality and his vision of a future Franco-Algerian community.[48] Writing to *Réforme*, "F.F.," on the other hand, was distressed that the FLN had boycotted the fall elections and that the European Liberals in Algeria had been unwilling to present themselves to the voters.[49] Pierre Bungener for his part speculated about the political future of Jacques Soustelle, a key member of the new UNR party. He suggested that, if given effective representation in the ministry, Soustelle would be bound to propose sacrifice and austerity while his many followers would assume that his presence in cabinet would guarantee a solution to the Algerian problem consonant with their own interests.[50]

Meanwhile, Soustelle was in the United States to represent France at the UN General Assembly. His presence had not gone unnoticed in the American press where, Jacques Poujol was delighted to report, he had been given a rather rude reception. *Time* magazine had characterized the Gaullist delegate as "an apprentice dictator, a supporter of single-party rule and a categorical opponent of the Algerian policy of de Gaulle." According to the magazine's reporter, de Gaulle had been thinking particularly of Soustelle when he forbade the use of his name during the recent French election campaign. Poujol went on to inform readers of *Cité nouvelle* that *Look* magazine had called him "the most dangerous man in France" and that Soustelle had tried to stop its distribution in France. In Poujol's opinion, the *Look* article had been well researched. It presented the ex-governor of Algeria as "a non-practising Protestant who has become the idol of the Catholic Right, an anti-Communist who was fond of Marxist terminology and analysis, and a man who, although timid and short-sighted as a child, had a brilliant mind. According to this view, Soustelle was a man who, during his sojourn in Mexico, had taught primitive tribes there to hate the United States and who, during his most recent political career, had brought down three successive French governments."[51]

Just prior to the Christmas festivities, *Réforme* published an unsigned letter from an army officer in Algeria who had been offering Muslims free medical service as well as guidance in sports activity and professional training. The officer deeply resented the idea propagated in metropolitan liberal circles that the kind of *encadrement* he was providing was fascistic. Like his colleagues, he was simply trying to transmit elementary lessons in civic behaviour to a population which might need centuries of practice to effect a full transition into the modern world!

The year during which events in Algeria had led to the fall of the Fourth Republic witnessed visits to the territory by four Protestants devoted to peace and Christian-Muslim reconciliation. Elisabeth Schmidt and Tania Metzel were the first female pastors of the Reformed church; Jean Carbonare was an engineer with deep pacifist convictions, and Jacques Beaumont committed CIMADE more fully to Algeria's Muslims. All would testify to the power of Protestant conscience when put to the test.

A few weeks before the *13 mai*, Pastor Elisabeth Schmidt, who had been consecrated in 1949 as the first female minister in the Reformed communion, had asked to be transferred from Sète on the Mediterranean coast to a parish in Algeria.[52] Through the next five years, until after the granting of Algerian independence, this pioneering spirit would preside over the small Protestant congregation in the city of Blida, fifty kilometres south-west of Algiers. The European minority there, most of it Catholic or agnostic, numbered perhaps 18,000, in an urban population of well over 100,000.

Elisabeth Schmidt was a quite exceptional person, not simply because she had broken new ground as France's first female pastor or because she had a highly sophisticated mind (she brought with her to the new posting copies of Calvin, Kierkegaard and Karl Barth) but because she made a passionate effort to reach out and understand not only her almost exclusively European congregation, but also the Muslims with whom she came in contact. Her memoirs offer a remarkably candid and lucid account of the tragic gulf a sensitive observer was bound to perceive between *colons* and Muslims during the last phase of the French regime in Algeria.[75] Pastor Schmidt's on-the-ground observations make it easy to understand why the hopes engendered by the *16 mai* were either the product of naive self-deception on the part of certain elements among the *colons* or, less attractively, the result of cynical manipulation.

From the beginning of her mission, Elisabeth Schmidt came to feel that she was in charge of "a European ghetto parish," almost entirely cut off from the surrounding Muslim population. Her *fatma* (or housekeeper) became something of a confidante, but disappointed the newcomer by not introducing her to the rest of the family.

On reflection, the pastor recognized that the Reformed church shared some responsibility for the singular lack of bridge-building between Christians and Muslims in the Maghreb. While French Protestants had developed an intense interest in missionary work in black Africa (she recalled quite vividly the enthusiasm shown by her grandparents for evangelical work in Madagascar), the *Société des missions de Paris* had sent no one into the field in Algeria.

Elisabeth Schmidt looked with envy as well as admiration at the two Protestant missionaries in Blida, both women like herself, one English, one Belgian, and both able to communicate with Algerian proselytes in their native language. And she was deeply distressed at the reluctant acceptance by her own congregation of the two Kabyle families converted to Christianity by these Methodist missionaries. Not surprisingly in these circumstances, Pastor Schmidt quickly began to question the relevance of her own communion not only to the people of Blida but to the future of Algeria in general.

The visit to Algeria by the leading figure in French Protestantism, Marc Boegner, in 1954, had clearly not brought any change in the essentially complacent outlook of the Reformed who lived in the territory; in general, Pastor Schmidt concluded, Algeria's Protestants treated with deep suspicion any initiatives inspired by their co-religionists in France. As Pastor Schmidt saw it, this indifference to the Muslim majority, lamentable in itself, made dialogue between the two societies oblique at best. What might have changed things for the better and made peaceful transformation possible was the existence of an autonomous Arab or Kabyle church.

Despite these negative feelings, Pastor Schmidt did her best to establish a link with local Muslims. Her most satisfying involvement came with the running of an *ouvroir* (workshop) connected to the parish church where she gave lessons in reading, sewing, child-care and hygiene to young Muslim women. In this little enclave of European influence, Schmidt was delighted to see small but symbolically significant changes in mentality. The seventy-odd girls entrusted to her care, together with the older women who acted as monitors, got into the habit of removing their veils once inside the workshop, transforming them into cushions, although they did so only after shuttering the windows on the street side in order not to be seen by their male counterparts!

Pastor Schmidt's contact with members of the European community in Blida often produced tension and frustration, especially when politics were discussed. She heard constant reference to the good life which preceded the 1954 rebellion, a life from which, it was clear, Arabs were excluded. Her parishioners regularly complained about the *progressiste* tone of the national synod's reflections and resolutions on the situation in Algeria. But when they tried lecturing her about the appropriate "patriotic" approach to the Algerian question, she responded by noting that her Alsatian grandparents had not hesitated to show their national credentials by opting for France after 1871.

Pastor Schmidt was regularly admonished not to trust Arabs who were good-for-nothings with a strong penchant for thievery. Pastor Chatoney, who greeted her on her arrival in the territory, had warned that, when talking about the situation in Algeria, she would be well advised to say nothing more radical than what she might have read in *Le Monde*.

Despite her dismay at the prejudice she found among her fellow-Europeans in Algeria, Elisabeth Schmidt came to understand and share the terrible insecurity in which they lived. She felt real compassion for the many isolated French women who taught school in remote areas. She sympathized with settlers in isolated parts of the territory who had no choice but to pay protection to the FLN to ensure their survival; and she came to recognize that the preferred victims of terrorists were precisely those liberal-minded Europeans like herself who were prepared to work for an understanding between the two communities which would make the cause of independence less seductive.

In many ways the most rewarding part of the pastor's service at Blida was the support she was able to give to emissaries of CIMADE who toured her region bringing aid to the suffering Arab population. She was also able on occasions to appeal to Protestant army officers in order that she might deliver food and drink to Muslim captives being held on property belonging to the *temple*.

As a Protestant chaplain who had spent so much time trying to console men and women behind bars on both sides of the Mediterranean, Elisabeth Schmidt's colleague Tania Metzel did not hesitate to pass the spring and summer of 1958 visiting French internment camps in Algeria, undeterred by the political tensions there.[53] The greeting she received was often chilly in the extreme. At one camp, which she visited in the company of the missionary Alfred Rolland, who spoke Arabic, she was met by a colonel whose eyes were murderously hostile but who preserved an impeccably proper form as he received her: "Ah, madame!" he began, "Our fellaghas interest you then? ... And my soldiers are of no concern to you?" In response, the chaplain tried to explain to the colonel that her function was not to serve as an accomplice to his prisoners but to offer solace to human beings, whatever their background, who might well have spiritual problems.

Inside the camp, Tania Metzel found men who were for the most part illiterate, who spoke only Arabic, and who were closely guarded by young French conscripts. Using Rolland as interpreter, she made herself the intermediary between captive and captor, asking each in turn about his family, helping Frenchmen and Muslims alike to break out of their separate solitude, perhaps even on occasion to overcome some of their reciprocal hostility.

On those occasions when Tania Metzel came across evidence of torture, the camp authorities seemed not to care, confident that no outside influence could limit their power over their prisoners or how they used it. Fortunately for those Muslims arrested in France itself, Tania Metzel with others had been able to ensure that, if and when transferred to Algeria, they would be spared the physical abuse which their comrades captured by the army so often endured.

Unlike Pastors Schmidt and Metzel, Carbonare's decision to become involved again in Algerian affairs was a direct result of de Gaulle's return to power.[54] When the general named Robert Buron public works minister in June 1958, the anti-colonial Catholic summoned Carbonare to Paris and asked if he would be willing to resume his earlier unofficial contacts with the FLN. When Carbonare agreed, he was briefed by de Gaulle's "point-man" on Algeria, Bernard Tricot. After greeting him with a curt "Bonjour, monsieur! Asseyez-vous! Je vous écoute," Tricot then said nothing further until the Protestant had outlined his impressions of Ferhat Abbas and other FLN leaders. Only at the end of Carbonare's remarks did Tricot speak again, in equally abrupt fashion: "Vous avez terminé ... Je vous remercie." Carbonare's reflections were no doubt at once conveyed to Premier de Gaulle.

Over the next four years, Carbonare made eight trips to the Tunis headquarters of the GPRA. His willingness to serve as intermediary between Paris and the Algerian government-in-exile was never in question, but the pacifist in Carbonare experienced a kind of moral malaise. He was after all, dealing with men on both sides who were committed to achieving their ends by violent means. The Protestant emissary had other scruples: he was concerned that his own deep yearning for peace might lead him to go beyond his informal mandate as the transmitter of messages and relay a too positive signal to one side from the other.

During these unofficial exchanges, Carbonare came to know and admire Ferhat Abbas in whom he saw a genuine, deep-rooted yearning for future Franco-Algerian understanding and cooperation. The one-time champion of integration appeared to his visitor like a wounded lover anxious to make up with his French suitor but pushed by younger nationalists, especially in the ALN, to avoid any appearance of reconciliation or affection.

Carbonare's personal pacifism was if anything intensified as the conflict became bloodier. In 1956, at the age of twenty-nine, he underwent a radical conversion experience which would guide much of his activity during the Algerian war and beyond. When Pastor Etienne Mathiot was jailed in Besançon early in 1958, Carbonare was the first person to write him a note, pointing out in comradely jest that the defiant pastor had been caught (as he deserved to be) by setting a trap for himself through his defiance of the law. While celebrating Mathiot's insubordination, Carbonare deplored members of his church's establishment, lay as well as clerical, who turned up at the parades of soldiers leaving for Algeria to bless men who had been trained to kill. Worst of all, there were pastors at these parades who told young recruits to fight without hatred although Christ had made it clear that even the expression of hatred in one's heart against another human being constituted defiance of God's word.

Like Carbonare, who was to become his close friend and collaborator in CIMADE, Jacques Beaumont had been concerned about Algeria since his appointment as secretary-general of the Protestant relief organization. Confronted by the enormous challenges posed by mass illiteracy, sub-standard housing and nourishment in Algeria, Beaumont and his colleagues spent some time feeling their way ("On naviguait" he explains) before deciding in February 1958 to open a small post in the *Clos Salembier* in the heart of the Muslim quarter in Algiers.

As in Marseilles, the team-workers who lived in the *Clos Salembier* offered a variety of services to the local population: food distribution, literacy programmes, and training in artisanal skills. The operation was from the beginning in the hands of a small group of forceful women: Denise Duboscq, Isabelle Peloux and, in some ways, most remarkable of all, Suzette Besançon, the physically diminutive widow of a well-known and much respected general who had served in Algeria. *La générale* was, as Beaumont puts it, "une force sociale de la nature," moving about the neighbourhood, befriending Muslim women, scolding a colonel who had been her husband's subordinate about the use of torture by the army and in various ways, testifying to the existence of another France.

Notes

1   REF, 20 February 1958.
2   Courrière, II, 195.
3   REF, 25 January 1958.
4   REF, 15 March 1958.
5   REF, 15 February 1958.
6   *France Observateur*, 6 March 1958.
7   Roser, "Discours interdits," CPED, Témoignages et documents #11 (April 1959).
8   REF, 22 March 1959.
9   JOC, 15 April 1958.
10 This account of Pastor Mathiot's involvement with Si Ali is based in part on conversations with Pastor Jacques Maury in Paris on 27 October 1994.
11 CN, 23 January 1958.
12 FPF, "Bureau de Presse et d'Information. Communiqué le 25 mars 1958."

13 CN, 20 March 1958.
14 Cited in CN, 20 March 1958.
15 Ibid.
16 TFJ, June 1958.
17 Cited in A. Nozière, *Algérie: Les chrétiens dans la guerre* (Paris: Editions Cana, 1979), pp. 178-179.
18 CN, 20 February 1958.
19 REF, 5 April 1958.
20 CPED. "Comité protestant d'études," 24-26 January 1958.
21 *Le Monde*, 31 January 1958.
22 REF, 29 March 1958.
23 CN, 1 May 1958.
24 This account of events derives from a taped conversation with Pastor Metzel on 29 October 1994.
25 Soustelle, *Lettre ouverte aux victimes de la décolonisation* (Paris: Albin Michel, 1973), p. 8; p. 10.
26 TJF, July 1958.
27 CN, 3 July 1958.
28 SEM, Summer 1958.
29 REF, 26 July 1958.
30 TFJ, July 1958.
31 TFJ, August/September 1958.
32 CPED, "Comité protestant d'études. Chronique d'Alger du 1er mars au 29 juin 1958."
33 REF, 24 May 1958.
34 CN, 19 June 1958.
35 SEM, Summer 1958.
36 REF, 7 June 1958.
37 CN, 19 June 1958.
38 REF, 5 July 1958.
39 Background information concerning the founders of *Tant qu'il fait jour* comes from an interview with Pastor Pierre Cochet taped in Passy on 28 October 1994.
40 TFJ, June 1958.
41 REF, 14 June 1958.
42 TFJ, June 1958.
43 TFJ, December 1961.
44 JOC, 12 September 1958.
45 REF, 13 September, 20 September, 27 September.
46 CN, 11 September 1958.
47 TFJ, November 1959.
48 REF, 18 October; 25 October; 1 November 1958.
49 REF, 15 November 1958.
50 REF, 6 December 1958.
51 CN, 4 December 1958.
52 Elisabeth Schmidt, *En ces temps de malheur. J'étais pasteur en Algérie 1958-1962*

(Paris: Cerf, 1976).

53   The account of Pastor Metzel's visit to Algeria is based on a taped conversation in Paris on 24 October 1994.

54   What follows is based on a taped interview with Jean Carbonare in New York on 2 October 1994.

Delegate-General Paul Delouvrier and Eric Westphal
(Courtesy Monsieur Eric Westphal)

CHAPTER SIX

1959—COMING TO THE RESCUE:
PROTESTANT RELIEF FOR UPROOTED MUSLIMS

As a result of the sweeping victory of his supporters in the legislative vote of the fall of 1958 and his own election as president in December, Charles de Gaulle was well placed at the beginning of 1959 to deal with the Algerian imbroglio which his own ambiguous pronouncements since the 13 May had done nothing to resolve.

Determined to keep personal control of the Algerian dossier, de Gaulle entrusted its day-to-day management to two confidential advisors: Public Works Minister Robert Buron, a liberal Catholic with a strong anti-colonialist perspective, and Bernard Tricot, a discreet and utterly devoted Gaullist who would act as conduit for confidential reports on developments across the Mediterranean.

The Protestant foreign minister, Maurice Couve de Murville, was not directly responsible for Algeria, which was technically still part of France. On this issue as on most others, there was, however, as he put it, "what amounted to a spontaneous, instinctual, meeting of minds between the president and his minister."[1] Couve de Murville shared his leader's antipathy to what they both saw as the hegemonic pretensions of Washington, made even less tolerable because they were accompanied by constant moralizing. In the new foreign minister's view, the United States had dominated French policy, domestic as well as foreign, since 1946, and American good offices following the Sakiet incident had not only compounded France's problems in the Maghreb but worsened relations between Paris and Washington.

Quite apart from the defensive posture France had found herself in thanks to the inept policies of the Fourth Republic, Couve felt that under her new leader the nation was bound to benefit from the liquidation of an overseas empire which had become an anachronism. In a world dominated by the superpowers, the arrival of many newly independent nations would provide a valuable counterweight.[2]

Michel Debré, who became prime minister on 9 January, 1959, and Jacques Soustelle (who was appointed *ministre délégué* to the new premier) posed a more complex problem. As outspoken partisans of French Algeria, they represented part of the complex coalition of forces which had helped de Gaulle come to power. In the end, Debré, however grudgingly, would submit to the president's decisions concerning Algeria, up to and including the Evian peace accord of 1962. Soustelle, on the other hand, twenty years after joining de Gaulle's Free French movement in wartime London, would break with him early in 1960 following the settlers' insurrection known as Barricade Week.

To handle the already difficult situation in Algeria and to restore civil control of an unruly military, President de Gaulle named Paul Delouvrier the government's delegate-general for Algeria. Born in 1914, Delouvrier grew up in a strict Catholic family. He had begun training for a civil service post in the *Inspection des finances* when the Second World War began. After a brief commitment to the Resistance at the war's end, he began a prestigious career as a high-level civil servant. In 1948, during a trip in the Constantine region of Algeria in the company of René Mayer, he concluded that integration of Arabo-Berber and European societies simply would not work, given the difference of language and religion and the lack of any sense of shared national identity.[3]

On 27 October 1958, Georges Pompidou, de Gaulle's *directeur du Cabinet,* sent Delouvrier on an exploratory mission to Algeria. He returned to Paris convinced of the inevitability of Algerian independence but hoping that before this occurred there would be a five-year grace period during which the *pieds-noirs* could be relocated.

When Delouvrier delivered his views concerning Algeria to de Gaulle on 24 November, the general heard him out without much comment. A few days later Delouvrier was named delegate-general to the territory. Over the next two years, as the situation became increasingly tense, he reported directly to Tricot and thus in effect to de Gaulle.

Given his personal convictions and the nature of his mandate, Paul Delouvrier found it difficult to establish easy relationships with members of the settler community. Fortunately, the delegate-general took with him a cabinet of close advisors who shared his general outlook. One of the most important of these was Eric Westphal, a twenty-nine-year-old Protestant whom the delegate-general had come to know and trust in Luxemburg where Westphal had worked for seven years as private secretary to Jean Monnet, one of the chief architects of postwar European unity. As soon as Westphal learned of Delouvrier's appointment, he had called to say: "Take me with you! You're going to be very lonely over there!" The delegate-general knew that the young Protestant took the Algerian situation to heart; as he put it years later to his biographer: "I had no choice but to accept this offer although I did not quite know what to do with (Westphal) since he did not belong to the civil service!"[4]

In the end, Delouvrier put Westphal in charge of the judicial portfolio in the cabinet which he put together before flying to Algiers. The reasons for this were obvious to him: "Westphal possessed the openness of mind which is typical of Protestants and he considered the independence of Algeria as inevitable, whether in the longer or shorter term."

Years later, Delouvrier reflected that Westphal had fully lived up to expectations. "He might have been only twenty-nine years of age but, thanks to his great force of character, he was one of the major sources of my awareness of what was going on. It was he who drew my attention to the army's use of excessive violence and torture and to the creation of internment camps."[5]

Delouvrier and his Protestant colleague travelled to Algiers together on 18 December 1958; they would return together on the same plane exactly two years later, on 18 December 1960. Westphal was full of enthusiasm for the task although, from the beginning, his frank and direct manner was to bring him into conflict with the military men who had so often abused their power.[6]

Delouvrier's "Justice Minister" had to deal with hundreds of cases of Muslims who had simply disappeared and whom he did his best to track down. There were endless instances of arbitrary condemnation to hard labour which he was able to rescind or attenuate. There were meetings with the government-appointed *Commission de Sauvegarde* which visited Algiers to examine abuses of military authority. Finally, there were the mushrooming *camps de regroupement* where conditions were such that any sensitive administrator would have to pause and take note.

Apart from these pressing issues, Westphal discovered that there were at least a dozen prison camps in Algeria housing about 25,000 men arrested by the army. A commission created to examine the dossiers of each Muslim detainee had not met for months. Westphal ordered the reviewing body to resume its sessions on a once-a-week basis. As a result, during the year that followed, some 20,000 dossiers were examined and roughly 15,000 prisoners released. Unfortunately, Westphal's good intentions were substantially undermined because the army maintained the pace of arbitrary arrest and confinement of Muslims so that the camps ended up with about the same number of captives at year's end.

During his two years in Algeria, Westphal received about fifteen letters a day concerning abuses by the military. His efforts to soften sentences or effect release of those arbitrarily arrested quickly made him the scourge of the army leadership. Officers such as General Massu considered Westphal a major irritant. In mess-hall conversation, they were often heard to say: "C'est lui qui nous emmerde!"

Like the delegate-general, Westphal saw little of the settler community.

As a Protestant and the son of Charles Westphal (who would soon replace Marc Boegner as president of the *Fédération Protestante de France*), Delouvrier's advisor occasionally met Pastor Capieu, a close friend of his father whom he regarded as "essentially a poet." Most *colons* whom he met tended to repeat well-worn shibboleths about the Muslims: "The Arabs only understand the language of force. These people are passive and need to be disciplined."

Cultural life in the European community had little to offer a man of Westphal's background. "Sun and sand," not cultivation of the mind, were the central pursuits of the *colons*, the young administrator observed, although there were rare exceptions such as Mme Henriette Lung, member of one of Algeria's wealthy vintner families. Reflecting on his two years in Algeria a generation later, Westphal estimated that perhaps 1,000 of the 900,000 settlers shared his liberal perspective and his taste for something beyond the philistine pastimes of a privileged colonial minority.

Apart from the service he performed for Delouvrier in the area of justice, Eric Westphal was able to reinforce the liberal tendencies within the Algerian administration of other progressive-minded Protestants such as Robert Poujol, prefect of Blida and Max Moulins, a close friend who was prefect in Constantine. Delouvrier's deputy also used his official status to support the work of Jacques Beaumont and CIMADE.

Reflecting on his two years' service in Algeria years later, Westphal concluded that he had done what lay within his means to make the grim life of the population there a little more tolerable. His own initiatives on behalf of Muslims made him extremely unpopular among the officer class but when after "Barricade Week" early in 1960, he was charged by Massu and others with stirring up popular unrest, Delouvrier was quick to cover him by taking overall responsibility for his actions. At the very end of his stay, the delegate-general insisted on assigning a bodyguard to protect him day and night. That Westphal came to see this protector as his potential assassin testifies to the kind of stress under which administrators with a liberal outlook lived during the last phase of the French regime in Algeria.

While Eric Westphal was doing his best to second Delouvrier's liberal policies, another young Protestant, Michel Rocard, was providing the delegate-general with the first clear picture of the relocation camps and a compelling argument that they be transformed. Having completed his studies at the *Ecole Nationale d'Administration* (ENA), he had been appointed to the prestigious *Inspection des Finances* and assigned to Algeria in line with a recently adopted policy which required all *énarques* (graduates of the ENA) to spend what amounted to a six-month internship there.

In the weeks that followed his arrival in Algiers in September 1958, Rocard busied himself with his formal duties,that is, the routine verification of the administration's financial records. During the travelling which these responsibilities entailed, he learned from an old friend, Jacques Bugnicourt, who was serving as an SAS officer, about the army's ruthless methods against the FLN, including large-scale forced transfers of population and the napalm bombing of areas from which Muslims had (in theory at least) been evacuated. The inspector of finances felt that he had no choice but to inform his superiors. As he reports in his memoirs: "Duty compelled me: the civil power had to be told of the actions being taken by an army which is no longer accountable." [7]

At this point in Rocard's tour of duty, Delouvrier arrived in Algiers and, through a well-placed friend who had access to the delegate-general, the inspector determined to reveal to the newcomer what he had learned. Delouvrier was outraged. Knowing, however, that the account would seem too outrageous to be believed unless it were meticulously authenticated, Delouvrier commissioned Rocard to make a further, more thorough, investigation and provide him with a confidential report.

Having been authorized to prepare a separate, technical, report by his superiors in the *Inspection des finances* (to whom he divulged nothing of his conversation with Delouvrier), Rocard proceeded to visit Algeria's relocation camps.

Rocard's observations during several weeks of touring these camps resulted in an official report which he describes as "precise, detailed and devastating" and which was forwarded to his superiors at the *Inspection des Finances* in Paris on 10 April. This report ("Sur l'évolution récente de la situation foncière en Algérie") began with an exposé of the legal and jurisdictional chaos concerning property rights in Algeria which had been created by the many overlapping and frequently contradictory pieces of legislation France had imposed on the territory since the conquest.[8] Most recently, as of 1956, Paris had done its best by decree to foster the development of small peasant proprietors without taking into account traditional property arrangements in the Maghreb.

The relocation of hundreds of thousands of Muslims in *camps de regroupement* (Rocard estimated that as many as one quarter of the rural population had been arbitrarily resettled) had clearly compounded the problem. Army men and SAS officers had done their best to turn these camps into viable village communities, often by arbitrary decision concerning property rights, but had sometimes established camps too far away from the arable land which might have made them self-sustaining. Experimental villages had been constructed but these required the presence of French army units or Muslim self-defence groups which were bound to be the target of the FLN.

Although he knew that a permanent solution to the complex problem he had exposed would have to await the war's end, Rocard recommended in the interim the creation (where the situation allowed it) of a vast network of agricultural cooperatives. Such structures would be in harmony with traditional communal methods of farming in Algeria (and with his own socialist views, Rocard might have added).

A second, confidential and semi-official, report was submitted directly to Paul Delouvrier whose private secretary typed out nine copies to be handed out to persons designated by the delegate-general. Delouvrier instructed Rocard to make sure that two of these reached the *Elysée*, the office of the president of the Republic.

The full text of Rocard's official (but confidential) report surfaced in *Le Monde* as well as in *France Observateur* in mid-April 1959.[9] The subsequent outcry brought Rocard to admit that he was the author and Prime Minister Debré, a consistent defender of French Algeria, to demand his resignation. It was only thanks to the intervention of Edmond Michelet, minister of justice, who admitted that the leak came from one of his subordinates, that Rocard's career as an *Inspecteur des finances* was not immediately aborted.[10]

The separate report which Rocard submitted to Delouvrier was based on a close scrutiny of fifteen of Algeria's many relocation camps, including those near Orléansville, Tiaret and Blida. All these camps had been created by army men with military strategy in mind; little or no attention had been paid to their economic viability. There were now approximately 1,000,000 souls living in these army-controlled resettlement zones. In some cases, there were plans to create permanent new towns where camps had been improvised; but these plans could not be implemented because no mechanism had been set in place to supervise their development. The SAS officers whom Rocard had interviewed were favourably disposed towards such long-term planning since it would make their role as social managers much easier.

One of the most serious problems posed by the establishment of the relocation camps, as Rocard saw it, was the social and economic dislocation faced by thousands of uprooted Muslim families; they were being subjected to "an inevitably considerable and sometimes total disconnection from their normal means of existence." Living conditions in the camps were critically insufficient; medical equipment was very limited, and sanitary arrangements were deplorable. There was a grim mortality rate: one child in every 1,000 died every second day and famine was a very real threat. At least 200,000 Muslims living in the camps had no resources and, as a result, they had become totally dependent on food distribution by the French army. This situation was particularly anguishing for male heads of households who suffered a serious loss of self-respect as a result.

While publication of his confidential report to Delouvrier caused Rocard some temporary embarrassment, including a three-hour dressing-down by his superiors, it brought the delegate-general to take action. Orders were given that no more *camps de regroupement* were to be opened without Delouvrier's express authorization and that conditions in all camps were to be radically improved. Taking up Rocard's advice, Delouvrier initiated a programme dubbed *Mille Villages* aimed at transforming the encampments into viable villages redesigned along traditional lines and equipped to function as agricultural cooperatives. The delegate-general made sure that 100,000,000 francs of state funds were committed to launch this programme of radical readaptation.

Jacques Beaumont had read Rocard's report in the 18 April issue of *Le Monde*. Like other readers, he was unaware that it had been produced by the Protestant *énarque*. In any event, he recommended it to all CIMADE volunteers as an eminently accurate and opportune analysis of the situation.[11] The situation in the camps which Rocard had brought so dramatically to the attention of the delegate-general had already begun to concern Jacques Beaumont and his CIMADE colleagues as well as a number of other Protestants then in Algeria, including Henriette Lung, representing the International Red Cross and Eric Westphal, part of Delouvrier's staff. Germaine Tillion, the ethnologist who had been part of Governor Soustelle's advisory council and who periodically returned to Algeria, met with Mme Lung and Westphal to consider what they might do to alleviate the misery of the thousands of Muslims living in the camps.

Early in May, Germaine Tillion urged a coordinated drive by all the relief agencies in Algeria to cope with what had become a major crisis. Beaumont agreed, suggesting that the best way to complement Delouvrier's plan to put the camps under strict civilian control and transform them into permanent villages would be to ask the leaders of France's three major religious denominations—Cardinal Feltin, Pastor Boegner and Rabbi Kaplan—to issue a joint appeal for food, clothing, and other supplies. Mme Tillion was convinced that only a coordinated Christian effort had any chance of acceptance, since it would be seen as devoid of self-interest or political calculation.

In response, the cardinal-archbishop of Paris, Monseigneur Feltin, joined the president of the FPF, Marc Boegner, in drafting a solemn appeal to the Christian community which condemned the policy of forcible relocation and asked for volunteers to provide medical and other forms of relief. On 26 May, Boegner and Cardinal Feltin's representative, Monseigneur Rodhain, director of *Secours catholique* (who had just returned from a visit to Algeria), gave a press conference at which the dean of French pastors declared of the arbitrary acts of the French army in Algeria that "all of France is guilty because she paid no attention to this problem."[12]

The problems created by the large-scale forced resettlement of Algerian Muslims were addressed again during the fifty-second national synod of the ERF which took place between 27 and 30 May. Responding to an appeal from the Algerian synod, the national body urged the faithful, and especially young people in Reformed congregations, to consider offering their services as medical, educational or missionary volunteers in these camps to help alleviate the suffering.[13]

For some dedicated Protestants, the goal of winning Muslim converts must proceed, whatever the situation on the battlefield, in the resettlement camps, or in the streets of Algiers. Professor Bichon, a member of the Algerian study group, in early February went so far as to argue in a report for his colleagues that Muslims were still open to missionary efforts, in part because their own spiritual and cultural structures were breaking down. This naive hope was shared by the superintendent of the Methodist church in North Africa, Pastor Aurbakken, who stressed the need to press ahead with evangelical activity despite the intensification of the war.[14] Representatives of CIMADE had a rather different perspective. Their day-to-day contact with Muslims living in the resettlement zones led them to conclude that the faith of the masses in Algeria was still their "centre of gravity" and that, unlike Europeans, they had little interest in ideologies based on belief in purely human values.

Concern for what was happening to hundreds of thousands of Muslims as a result of their forcible relocation was one of many moral preoccupations affecting the French Protestant community as the conflict in Algeria dragged on.

More and more young conscripts were obliged to spend part of their two-and-a-half year service in Algeria, and many of them wrote letters from the front to parents and pastors revealing their doubts about fighting a war of colonial oppression or a counter-revolutionary battle whose methods they deplored. Several key Protestant leaders decided to offer spiritual counsel. The *Alliance des Equipes unionistes de France* produced a pamphlet designed not only to give Protestant soldiers aid and comfort but also to assist interested Catholics.[15] The eight signatories included two well-known Protestant personalities, Jacques Maury, president of the *Fédé,* and his colleague

Dominique de Pury. A number of spiritual problems facing France's young men in uniform were addressed in this brochure. Some conscripts had developed a kind of moral indifference as a result of coming to feel contempt for both the *fellagha* they were fighting and the *Ultras* whom they were defending. Others may have succumbed to "the moral degradation which comes from boredom." A third group had become conscientious objectors and were suffering the consequences of that difficult option.

Above all, the authors of the pamphlet urged its readers to stay faithful to their conscience, particularly when involved in psychological warfare where their moral sense was shocked and offended. For the serious minded, truly reflective soldier, the text of the brochure was followed by citations from the Bible, the 1948 Declaration of the Rights of Man, and the 1949 Geneva Convention. Editorial comments drew the reader's attention to France's signature on the latter two documents and remarked that both the Bible and the evidence of history made clear that the "nation" was not an eternal political entity and that no Christian could regard its precepts or its structure as definitive. In letters addressed to the president of the Republic and to the prime minister, the authors of the pamphlet made clear that their intention was to provide spiritual counsel to young conscripts but not to take any position concerning the war itself.

In April, the radical Pastor Henri Roser, long associated with the pacifist cause, felt impelled to speak out against the military's increasing use of torture. How can we have come to this sad pass, he began rhetorically. What kind of neglect, or ignorance, or low moral sense has brought us to accept, like the Germans in the 1930s, what is going on within our own nation without voicing rage and indignation? It was especially appalling for those entrusted with teaching the nation's youth to read about the way our young soldiers are being seduced into acts of sadism by officers trained in brainwashing and psychological warfare. The proper course ahead, Roser concluded, was to ask pardon of the Muslims whom we have tortured. Just as important, France must abandon the ultra-nationalism which currently afflicted her. If such a shift in attitude brought with it the recognition of Algerian independence, "We would soon enough discover that France would gain thereby as much good will as we are now losing as a result of this war."[16]

Commenting on the defence which Pastor Roser and other radicals were making on behalf of conscientious objection as part of their absolute opposition to the war, a correspondent for *Tant qu'il fait jour* pointed out that a commission of Reformed pastors and laymen, chaired by Marc Boegner, had examined the subject a generation earlier during the rise of fascism and had voted on 9 April 1935 to recommend to the faithful that they accept the obligation to do military service.[17]

Municipal elections based on a single electoral college were held throughout Algeria on 19 and 26 April. The hope was that handing over responsibility to the majority at the local level would lead to emergence of a group of Muslims ready to share in the making of a new Algeria. Unfortunately from the liberal point of view, the FLN succeeded in limiting the impact of the vote by ordering a boycott of the vote.[18]

Liberal Protestant opinion in France, favourable to Delouvrier's reforms, was growing impatient at the refusal of the powers that be to accommodate to change. Four years into the Algerian conflict what troubled some contributors to *Réforme* was the unwillingness of the *colons* and much of the metropolitan political establishment to abandon shibboleths and slogans such as *integration* and *Algérie française* which were clearly no longer relevant or useful. For François Tendil, the continuing reference to integration was particularly provocative since those who used it clearly intended it to mean *assimilation* and thus to carry an unspoken message of racial superiority. The European minority had not experienced any real change of heart about the Muslims and was increasingly ready for an authoritarian solution to the conflict.[19]

Protestants within the Socialist Party resumed their debate over the government's Algerian policy during the national convention of the SFIO held between 9 and 12 July, 1959. Gaston Defferre was again attacked for the support he had given de Gaulle a year earlier and again defended the stand he had taken then. It was still true, the Socialist chieftain from Marseilles insisted, that the general was the only person able simultaneously to control the army and police and to guide public opinion in the right direction. Thanks to de Gaulle, civil war had been averted and the nation's civic spirit had clearly revived, making any repetition of the 13 May all but unthinkable. In the immediate circumstances, Defferre argued, de Gaulle needed Socialist backing to work towards an equitable resolution of the Algerian dilemma as much as the SFIO needed him to shore up republican institutions and values. If the party were to formulate a precise text on Algeria's future, de Gaulle would be obliged to give it serious consideration; it was the party's responsibility, then, to help guide the president as well as public opinion.[20]

In the end, it fell to Francis Leenhardt to present and defend the proposed outline of Algeria's constitutional future to which Defferre had referred. What must be recognized, Leenhardt continued, was that "an Algerian personality has clearly imposed itself...." This personality must be reflected in appropriate institutional ways including a guarantee of coexistence between Algeria's two distinct communities and of an "association étroite" between Algeria and France. To move the parties toward the negotiation of such a solution, the authors of the resolution presented by Leenhardt urged a renewal of the offer of a cease-fire which should be phrased in such a way that it did not imply capitulation by the FLN.[21]

The Leenhardt resolution passed decisively (3,358 votes versus 269 who backed a resolution by the hardliner Max Lejeune). Clearly the mood of the party had shifted, thanks in large measure to the Protestants Defferre and Leenhardt who had moved Socialist delegates away from the Mollet-Lacoste policy supported at earlier conventions.

Meanwhile, the *Parti Socialiste autonome* (PSA) continued to grow steadily in numbers and influence. For a full month (5 May - 7 June 1959), it sponsored a *Grande assemblée nationale* at the Salle Pleyel in Paris. Participants at this open-ended discussion included representatives of a number of groups which had come together to protest government policy concerning Algeria or to condemn human rights' abuses during the war. Professor Julien presented a formal report to the roughly 2,000 in attendance urging a negotiated solution to the Algerian dilemma. At the conclusion of the Assembly, a *Centre national de coordination* was created to lobby the government to this end.

While French domestic opinion was becoming increasingly exercised over developments in Algeria, the international pressures on France to seek a peaceful solution to the war grew apace throughout 1959. In mid-summer, the International Affairs Commission of the World Council of Churches urged France either to negotiate with the FLN or to seek outside mediation to help end the conflict. Albert Finet was upset at this initiative, confident that de Gaulle, through the vigorous reassertion of French authority and prestige, was fully capable of reconciling the recognition of an Algerian personality and the maintenance of a new Paris-centred political entity.[22]

A twenty-minute television address by de Gaulle on 16 September 1959 opened a radically new and in the end decisive phase of the struggle. The general proposed that, four years after a cease-fire which he invited the FLN to help put into effect, the Algerian population would be given an opportunity to choose their own political future. Self-determination might take any one of three forms: secession, *francisation* which would mean that all those living "between Dunkirk and Tamanrasset" would enjoy the same rights and responsibilities, or autonomy in association with France and accompanied by clear guarantees to the colony's cultural minorities.

The acknowledgement that Algeria might select independence and the avoidance of any reference to the term *Algérie française* in favour of the far less definite *francisation* provoked a keen sense of betrayal among those who had welcomed de Gaulle in May 1958 as the guarantor of a permanent French presence in the colony. Conservative members of the *Assemblée algérienne* formed a *Rassemblement pour l'Algérie française* and began lobbying on both sides of the Mediterranean for the replacement of the Debré government. Jacques Soustelle, in great distress, nevertheless remained in the cabinet, rationalizing this decision on the ground that one must gamble on the willingness of the Algerians to choose *francisation*.

Albert Finet called de Gaulle's bold offer to Algeria an "irreversible event" noting that the president had avoided referring either to independence or to integration in his speech. Instead, the head of state had relayed to the people of Algeria "the vocation of a liberal, humanistic, and emancipating France," not of an imperial power willing to retain the territory at any cost. Finet went on to praise the skilful way in which de Gaulle had pursued a long-term strategy which was only now becoming apparent to others. The result was that France's international position had been greatly enhanced and the French Left, which had never had the courage or foresight to propose Algerian self-determination, was now in disarray.[23]

By the fall of 1959, Finet had become an unconditional supporter of de Gaulle's Algerian strategy. On 24 October, he wrote: "I am tempted to write that this policy, which is generous in its essence and wise and prudent in its application, does not seem in any way different from one that is based on a Christian view of humanity and how it should be governed." In Finet's view, de Gaulle's strategy had not only restored France's international prestige and freedom of action; it had forestalled a repetition of the *13 mai*, leaving the nation at peace "since the army is loyal, the police obey, the government governs, and the people follow."[24]

Contributors to *Tant qu'il fait jour* were divided in their response to the president's 16 September speech, although their disappointment was unmistakable. Roland Laudenbach indicted de Gaulle for betraying the hopes engendered by the *13 mai* and its sequel. The general had followed a policy of conscious deceit and prevarication since then, even violating the constitution which had been designed in large part to embody his principles. "We are caught in the fog, in a world of imposture," he wrote. "Our victory (13 May) will simply have given the enemy a chance to broadcast its message openly in our schoolyards."[25] The newspaper's chief editor, Philippe Brissaud, suggested a more nuanced reading of de Gaulle's address. It was unthinkable, he argued, that the general would abandon Algeria. Such an abandonment would not only mean that he had repudiated a solemn pledge; it would surely end up provoking another *13 mai*! All was not yet lost, Brissaud reassured his readers, but everything must be done to promote *francisation*, the only acceptable option left open as a result of de Gaulle's speech.[26]

Pastor Pierre Cochet, then a student at the Protestant Faculty of Theology in Paris, recalls a debate over the implications of the general's offer with leftist friends including Pierre Encrevé, who was close to Michel Rocard, and Jean Baubérot who would become one of the leading historians of modern French Protestantism.[27] Cochet put the argument that, "under the cover of an abstract idealism, the right of a people to dispose of their own fate is often a retrograde ideology." An "Algerian Algeria," he predicted, might well turn into a fundamentalist Islamic state. As recently as the 1940s, he reminded his friends, the case for national self-determination had led the Croats to create a fascist entity with temporarily ominous consequences for its neighbours.

At the opposite end of the spectrum, writers for *Cité nouvelle* expressed equal frustration with the general's proposals. Raoul Crespin agreed that de Gaulle seemed to include independence among the possible solutions to the Algerian impasse, but the offer was not yet explicit enough. Jan Czarnecki was more sanguine. He argued that, by inviting the Algerian people to pronounce themselves on their future within four years of a cessation of hostilities, de Gaulle had in fact implicitly recognized their right to exist as a sovereign nation.[28]

While a serious rift had opened in the ranks of the government party following de Gaulle's 16 September speech, public attention was again being focused on the situation of the hundreds of thousands of Muslims struggling to survive in the resettlement camps. This renewed concern about the impact of the war on the civilians in Algeria was bound to undermine public support for the conflict even further.

The concern about the army's resettlement policy, expressed by Rocard to Delouvrier in April, had brought some remedial action concerning the camps, but half a year later, the problem was far from resolved. Following a two-week tour of these *camps de regroupement* during the last two weeks of October, Jacques Beaumont submitted a confidential report to Marc Boegner.[29] The secretary-general's evaluation of conditions in the camps was both critical and effective because of its balanced and thoroughly researched presentation. While noting the good intentions of many in the military, Beaumont was appalled at the circumstances in which hundreds of thousands of forcibly relocated Muslims were still living. Five months after Rocard's submission to the delegate-general, and long after Boegner and Cardinal Feltin had issued their joint appeal and after it had been decided that the civil authority would not approve creation of any new settlements, Beaumont reported that the number of sites had actually increased—from 1,000 to perhaps as many as 1,400 inside which some 1,200,000 people had been herded. Even more alarming, as many as 300,000 more men, women and children might be taken from their homes and added to the existing number before the winter was over.

From the military perspective, there were obvious advantages to these settlements. The army could keep a close eye on the civilian population and more easily patrol the area from which it had been evacuated. Even from the point of view of the Muslims themselves, there had been occasional benefits. Sleep, which had become a major problem in areas torn by conflict, was guaranteed inside the camps; medical assistance, food and schooling had been made available. While the FLN was clearly in contact with those inside the camps, the army had deprived the rebels of much of their logistical base.

While the massive relocation of population which had taken place would obviously not come to an end until the conflict was over, key members of the Algerian civil administration were asking themselves if the camps might not be made to serve a positive purpose. The secretary-general cited the case of Oued Harbill, where the civil and military authorities had cooperated and where, among other things, new housing had been built to allow for the seclusion of women according to Muslim custom (high walls, separate entrances and inner courtyards had been contrived out of former military structures). While there were cases of positive, even sensitive, application of the relocation policy, half of the centres which the army had created clearly had no future and were functioning at best as temporary shelters. The inhabitants of these sites depended entirely on social assistance which in theory at least provided basic food and clothing to people who had never been assured of these necessities.

Picking up a theme which Rocard had treated at length, Beaumont observed that in order that the relocation camps become viable over the long term, a series of obstacles must be overcome. Agrarian reform (which involved land confiscation) was a complex problem which tended to pit army officers against recalcitrant settlers. Of some 300,000 hectares currently under cultivation in the Orléansville department, for instance, 2,000 hectares had been appropriated but only 600 effectively redistributed to those dwelling in relocation centres!

Apart from delivering basic food and clothing, the administration needed to guarantee proper housing. As it was, at least one-fifth of those quartered in the camps were living in tents made of potato sacks or in situations where women were not segregated according to Arab custom. There was also a crying need for proper training in household management (something some SAS officers' wives had undertaken on their own) and for the delivery of minimal medical aid. Itinerant teams named by the delegate-general had started to make sure that basic services were provided. Meanwhile the Red Cross had sent out a number of female teams to establish basic medical and social assistance. It was worth stressing, Beaumont noted, that women alone were able to penetrate the interior of a Muslim household.

A massive displacement of population had resulted from the army's shift of strategy in 1957, but it was absurd to expect military men to cope with the socio-economic consequences, especially since, as a result of this operation, it had become clear that Algeria was "in a state of extreme under-colonization. Those dwelling in the countryside were still living in the biblical age or at best in the medieval period without our having realized it."

At this point in his report, Beaumont urged that an appeal for food for those in the camps be launched before the winter arrived; high-calorie items such as condensed milk, sugar, chocolate, cheese and oil would be especially welcome. Protestant youth groups had already agreed to participate; Sunday-schools as well as primary schools both public and private might be asked to join in; readers of *Réforme* and those who listened to religious broadcasts on radio might be canvassed as well.

The secretary-general of CIMADE hoped that, in addition to the kind of immediate action he was proposing to remedy a desperate situation, something could be done to provide the Muslim women in the camps with basic kitchen training. Some volunteers, he noted, were already attempting to meet this challenge, even learning to "think Muslim" so that their counsel would be easily received. CIMADE had plans to establish one or two teams of women volunteers who would apply themselves to the medical, social, educational, and even the artisanal, tasks which he had oulined. The establishment of a base at the Clos Salembier in the Muslim quarter of Algiers provided a model. Médéa or Orléansville were targeted as prospective new centres of CIMADE activity.

While the grim situation of those in the camps must have priority, Beaumont made a point of saying that the Christian minority in Algeria as well as France's soldiers there must not be forgotten. The secretary-general had seen army officers break down and weep because they did not have adequate medical supplies for their wounded. He understood the claustrophobic fear bordering on hysteria which had overcome members of the settler minority, often trapped inside cities, terrified to go outside the perimeter provided by paratroopers. Finally, he insisted, one must consider those few courageous civilians (Beaumont knew full well just how few they were) who were trying to rebuild a viable administration and "to undo the disastrous policies of which they, like the rest of us, have been guilty for so many years."

There was also, above and beyond the present horror, the secretary-general added, the long-term problem faced by a Muslim culture attempting to cope with modern technological civilization and its amoral underpinnings. "Our role as Christians," Beaumont wrote to Boegner, "is to assist these people, or at least those responsible individuals among them, who in turn will help guide their brothers to find the way to confront and master this technological world." Islam was ill-prepared for this confrontation and had in fact nothing relevant to say about it. Christians in Algeria were in the challenging position of being among the few people able to act as mediators.

In a supplemental text, the secretary-general of the CIMADE denounced the programme of psychological warfare used by the army during and after the resettlement process.[30] Beaumont had culled a good deal of information in this area from conversations with military and civil authorities as well as with Muslims. It became clear to him that, following the wholesale uprooting of population, there had been an intensive period of psychological reconditioning, beginning with three days of fasting, followed by five days of crude and revolting feeding, then a week of extravagant indulgence during which some Muslims told him they felt truly regaled. There followed two to three weeks of intensive re-education during which it was made clear that France was well-disposed to the Algerian people, that the rebels were bound to lose the war and that it was incumbent on those being treated by the army to join in the pacification programme by forming a local self-defence group. Beaumont suggested that this intensive psychological assault on a primitive population exposed to no previous contact with modern civilization was bound to be severely alienating. A Muslim who had joined the French army as a result of one of these sessions had talked to Beaumont at length about the need to battle communism but then, despite his "conversion," he had expressed great interest in the Socialist idea of land confiscation. Rather disquieting to those who put any faith in our soldiers' sophistication, Beaumont suggested.

The conclusion reached by Jacques Beaumont that the army's use of psychological warfare was not only immoral but ineffective was echoed during the same year by the eminent Protestant theologian and sociologist Jacques Ellul.[31] Ellul, who was director of the Centre for the Study of Propaganda at the University of Bordeaux, was also a friend of François Hauchecorne and Tania Metzel from whom he had received first-hand information about the techniques being used by the Fifth Bureau; he was thus admirably suited to examine the issue from a personal as well as scholarly point of view.

As a specialist in propaganda, Ellul was familiar with the teachings of Mao Tse-tung concerning brainwashing which the French army mistakenly assumed they might appropriate for use against the FLN. Mao's strategy, the Protestant social scientist observed, was to transform rather than destroy the mindset of the enemy through a subtle and if necessary prolonged process.

The communist leader's recommended technique was to begin by cutting the individual opponent off from his cultural roots, then to overwhelm him with a variety of stimuli and slogans to induce a new sense of collective consciousness and, finally, to subject him to group therapy which would exploit the feelings of guilt and remorse evoked by the preceding exercises and produce the desired psychological reorientation.

The Fifth Bureau, Ellul conceded, had done its best to transfer these techniques to the Algerian situation but without understanding that the most vital element in the Maoist strategy was the presence of an alternative ideology to implant in the mind of those brainwashed. In the face of the overwhelming pull of Algerian nationalism which had developed an all but irresistible momentum, the propagation of a counter-revolutionary ideology had little chance.

Ellul's denunciation of the army's use of psychological warfare was written in 1959 but not generally read until it appeared three years later in his masterful history of propaganda. Had it been published earlier, it no doubt would have reinforced the criticism of the Fifth Bureau's methods made by Beaumont in his report to Boegner. In any event, as a follow-up to his report on the camps, Beaumont asked Dr. Leslie Cooke of the Church World Service in Geneva to intervene with Americans to release surplus US food and other goods for distribution to those suffering in the camps in Algeria. Even before the present conflict, the secretary-general explained to Cooke in a letter, Algerians had lived, like the masses in India, in a situation of permanent undernourishment; the war, with its radical displacement of population, had rendered this situation even more severe, especially for women and children. Normally, government action would be appropriate to deal with such a crisis but the complex political tensions of the conflict made this impossible. There were clear assurances, however, that private aid would complement what the administration in Algiers (which supported CIMADE's initiative) was able to do under existing circumstances.[32]

Two months after Beaumont's appeal, Pastor Boegner as president of CIMADE addressed an even more urgent letter to Dr. Cooke.[33] Despite the best efforts of both civil and military authorities, Boegner reported, the situation in the camps had further deteriorated. Under the circumstances, Boegner concluded that the best solution was for CIMADE to undertake the food distribution directly rather than act under the supervision of the French civil authority. The leader of the French Protestant community concluded with a passionate declaration of spiritual commitment: "All the many and diverse contacts which CIMADE team-workers have had with Muslims convince us that we in France are living through a period in which Christians have a

special obligation to be present among our North African brothers...."
Boegner added that three veteran leaders of CIMADE—Suzanne de Dietrich,
Madeleine Barot and Jacques Beaumont—would be able to communicate this
same message directly to Cooke when they attended a forthcoming ecumenical
meeting at Spittal, Austria.

On 25 November, the FPF fully endorsed the emergency relief
measures suggested by CIMADE. At Christmas time, Boegner and Feltin,
again on behalf both of the Protestant relief agency and *Secours catholique*,
made a joint radio broadcast to launch "SOS Algérie," a special appeal for
continuing financial aid, food shipments and child sponsorships, to help
alleviate the grim conditions in the resettlement zones.

Phillippe Brissaud called on readers of *Tant qu'il fait jour* to respond
to Boegner's appeal. For the conservative editor, the motives for helping
Muslims forced into resettlement areas were mixed. Christian charity should
by itself bring French Protestants to help attenuate conditions in the camps, but
it was equally important to take whatever actions were necessary to keep
Algeria French and thus maintain control of an area vital to the strategic
defence of the West.[34]

Beaumont's on-the-scene report of conditions in the resettlement
camps and the subsequent renewed joint appeal by Cardinal Feltin and Pastor
Boegner resulted in launching a relief drive throughout the French Protestant
community. Newspaper ads and letters to church leaders at all levels brought
a flood of responses. The commitment of the Reformed synod of the Alpes-
Rhône region was typical.[35] Families in each parish were urged to furnish two
kilos of sugar, two bars of chocolate, and one can of condensed milk to be
gathered during Advent for transmission to CIMADE. Children attending
Sunday school were invited to bring a kilo of sugar and a can of condensed
milk on the last Sunday of the month to help provide basic nourishment to
Muslim children.

At the end of November, Soustelle travelled to New York to
participate in what had become the annual United Nations debate on Algeria.
After a session which began on 30 November and ended on 13 December, the
General Assembly passed on to other matters without adopting a clear
resolution. A Pakistani motion to begin debate on the issue of self-
determination for the Algerian people did not muster the requisite number of
votes thanks in large measure to the abstention of the United States. Again,
Soustelle's skilful maneuvering had helped stave off what was becoming an
all but irresistible pressure to force France to accept internationalization of the
Algerian question.

At year's end, J.-P. Lumire, writing in *Réforme*, expressed deep pessimism about developments in Algeria.[36] Muslim moderates were increasingly vulnerable and nervous. The less wealthy of the European community were tense about the future but lacked the means to relocate in France and hoped that they might at least be protected as the situation deteriorated. The army's willingness to subordinate its role to civil authority was problematic; some soldiers had taken the order to pacify Algeria as a mandate to conduct what amounted to a crusade against the rebels whom they identified as communist.

Notes

1 Maurice Couve de Murville, *Une politique étrangère, 1958-1968* (Paris: Plon, 1971), p. 9.

2 Ibid., p. 24.

3 Roselyne Chenu, *Paul Delouvrier ou la passion d'agir* (Paris: Seuil, 1994), pp. 169-170.

4 Ibid. p. 189.

5 Ibid.

6 The account which follows is based on a taped interview with Eric Westphal in Paris on 1 June 1994.

7 Michel Rocard, *Le coeur à l'ouvrage* (Paris: Odile Jacob, 1987), p. 30.

8 Michel Rocard, "Rapport sur l'évolution récente de la situation foncière en Algérie, 10 avril 1959," Ministère de l'Economie. Inspection générale des finances. Note #106. 59.

9 *Le Monde*, 18 April 1959.

10 Rocard, *Le coeur à l'ouvrage*, p. 31.

11 ACIM, Jacques Beaumont to CIMADE volunteers, 21 April 1959.

12 REF, 30 May 1959.

13 REF, 6 June 1959.

14 *Christianisme au XXe siècle*, 12 February 1959; LAP, March 1959.

15 CPED, *Aux jeunes appelés en Algérie* (Paris: Alliance des Equipes unionistes de France, 1959).

16 CPED, Henri Roser, "Discours interdits," in *Témoignages et documents*, April 1959.

17 TFJ, 6 January 1959.

18 REF, 25 April 1959.

19 REF, 13 June 1959.

20 OURS, "51ème congrès national SFIO, 9-12 juillet 1959," 20 July.

21 Ibid., 12 July 1959.

22 REF, 29 August 1959.

23 REF, 26 September 1959.

24 REF, 24 October 1959.

25 TFJ, September/October 1959.

26 Ibid.

27 These recollections, perhaps sharpened in hindsight, were relayed to the writer in a taped interview with Pastor Cochet in Passy on 28 October 1994.

28   CN, 1 October 1959.

29   ACIM, "Les regroupements en Algérie. Rapport présenté par J. Beaumont au président Marc Boegner à la suite de son voyage en Algérie 15-27 octobre 1959."

30   ACIM, Beaumont, "Regroupés et réforme agraire, 15 octobre 1959."

31   Jacques Ellul, "Autre exemple de l'inefficacité de la propagande: l'Algérie (1959)," in *Propagandes* (Paris: Armand Colin, 1962), pp. 303-327.

32   ACIM, Jacques Beaumont to Leslie Cooke, 16 May 1959.

33   ACIM, Marc Boegner to Leslie Cooke, 20 July 1959.

34   TFJ, 14 November 1959.

35   ACIM, "Pour les regroupés d'Algérie. Ordre du jour du synode Alpes-Rhône de l'Église Réformée de France, 15 novembre 1959."

36   REF, 26 December 1959.

Paul Ricoeur
(Courtesy Mme Janine Philibert)

Dorothée and Georges Casalis
(Courtesy Mme Casalis)

CHAPTER SEVEN

1960: THE MORAL BALANCE TILTS TO PEACE

The anger and frustration felt by Protestant partisans of French Algeria at de Gaulle's 16 September speech was shared not only by the usual right-wing *colons* but also by certain French army units doing battle with the FLN. In January 1960, a coalition of these disgruntled groups rebelled, challenging not only de Gaulle but the democratic base of the fledgling Fifth Republic. On 18 January a German newspaper published an interview given by General Massu in which he condemned de Gaulle for betraying the hopes placed in him in May 1958. That helped bring this new crisis to the boil. De Gaulle demanded Massu's immediate removal from Algiers and on the same day he made clear to three of Algeria's deputies in the National Assembly his conviction that integration (or by implication *francisation*) was a lost cause and that the colony's independence was inevitable.

The resulting explosion began on 24 January.The rebels planned to combine a general strike with a seizure of all critical nerve centres in Algeria in hopes of setting the stage for an assault on the regime in Paris. De Gaulle appears to have been badly shaken by this latest challenge, but he recovered his nerve and brought the rebellion to an end by appealing to the rank and file in Algeria over radio and television on 29 January.

Jean-Pierre Lumire, a liberal Protestant in Algiers who served as the regular correspondent of *Réforme*, offered the newspaper's readers a personal chronicle of the uprising which he attributed to a well thought through plot. At first he and other moderates had dismissed the insurrection as a farce, but it gathered momentum because of the inertia (or complicity) of certain elements of the army. Popular support for activists such as the student leader Pierre Lagaillarde came from the conviction of many *colons* that de Gaulle's promise of self-determination signified their abandonment. They had taken to the barricades to defend the status quo or, failing that, to promote the forcible integration of Algeria into France proper where they would become part of the dominant majority.[1]

Réforme devoted its entire 6 February issue to the rising. With more or less enthusiasm, all the contributors saw de Gaulle as more than ever the only person capable of leading France through this new crisis. Finet chided the Left for failing to recognize the general as "the republican and liberal aristocrat" he had always been.[2] Roger Mehl told Christians they must stop seeing all those in power as the enemy. Unless they offered support for the "empirically effective and juridically structured" use of power shown by de Gaulle, he urged, they might soon experience its more perverse, Latin American, equivalent. Jacques Ellul saw the insubordination of members of the officer class as a problem which had plagued the nation since the Revolution when the army and the nation were wrongly taken to be one and the same. In the present circumstances, it was vital that the army in Algeria be either dismissed or made to obey the civil authority.

Adopting a somewhat more nuanced position, Paul Adeline tried to get his readers to understand the "passionate exacerbation" of the *pieds noirs* who would be just as much a minority in continental France as they were in an independent Algeria; their resistance to forcible integration into an independent Algeria where they would be subject to a "pan-Islamic tyranny" was just as legitimate as the struggle being waged by Algerian nationalists.

Contributors to *Cité nouvelle* were understandably quick to rejoice at the collapse of the January insurrection. Jan Czarnecki remarked in the aftermath: "As of now, the myth of "fraternization" has had its day: that of French Algeria should fade away soon enough."[3] André Philip urged his fellow citizens to stand firm against insubordination in the army or face the prospect of seeing their nation become another Paraguay. Gilbert Allais thought it worth celebrating that, for the first time since 6 February 1956, the power to control events had returned from Algiers to Paris.

Among Pastor Elisabeth Schmidt's parishioners in Blida, news of the insurrection was greeted at first with spontaneous enthusiasm, even by the most thoughtful of her flock. Some anxiety followed as tensions continued to rise in Algiers. The pastor tried her best to persuade her congregation to admit that the European minority was using extreme provocation to get its way. In matters political, however, her parishioners took their cue from the news media controlled by the *colons* so they paid her little heed.[4]

During a cabinet meeting held to discuss the tumultuous events, the Debré government found itself seriously divided. Jacques Soustelle (whose responsibilities in the cabinet included the Sahara) made clear his sympathetic understanding of those who had taken up arms and with whom he felt the government should negotiate, while Couve de Murville joined those favouring severe punishment of the insurgents.

In the letter of resignation submitted to Debré following the cabinet meeting, Soustelle condemned the government's views on the Algerian issue. He declared bluntly: "having been in no way associated with the decisions just taken, I reject all responsibility for these decisions and am hereby resigning from the government." Debré, who had been internally torn by the uprising and its aftermath, rejected Soustelle's letter, but an angry exchange between the disillusioned minister and President de Gaulle brought Soustelle's resignation nevertheless and, with it, a definitive rupture between the Protestant-born defender of French Algeria and his one-time hero:

> After a last interview during which de Gaulle liquidated in 150 seconds a collaboration which had lasted 19 years and seven months, a communiqué issued by the Elysée (the presidential palace in Paris) announced that the President had "given his approbation" to my departure on the request of the prime minister.[5]

Despite the bitterness of this divorce between Charles de Gaulle and a devoted partner during two decades of political struggle, the general offered a fair, even generous, tribute to Soustelle in his memoirs.[6]

The state of emergency created by the January uprising brought de Gaulle to request and the National Assembly on 2 February to grant plenipotentiary power to resolve the Algerian crisis. Finet hailed the decision made by an overwhelming majority in the Assembly (441-75) to award the president powers that few of France's kings had enjoyed. He wrote: "One can hardly reproach this man for confusing himself with the nation, since it is the nation herself which is confirming him in this mystical belief!"[7]

Among the by-products of the government's triumph over the barricade rebels was the dissolution of the army's Fifth Bureau. Created in 1955 to handle education and information, the Bureau was in fact the army's instrument for waging psychological war.

The dissolution of the Fifth Bureau did not in fact mean the end of suffering for the Muslim masses. In late February *Réforme* published an update on the aid CIMADE was giving to victims of forcible resettlement in Algeria . There were now eighty-five centres distributing food and clothing, the paper reported.[8]

Pastor André Chatoney, president of the Algerian synod, voiced his own concerns about the relocation camps in a letter printed in *Algérie Protestante* in February 1960. He had joined Marc Boegner, and the prefect Robert Poujol, on a tour of one of these camps, built where there had been a tiny community of five or six houses. Now some 500 human beings were cramped together in horrifying conditions in dwellings which had only a tiny hole in the ceiling for ventilation. There was animal waste everywhere, and dried thistles and straw used to provide fuel for cooking. The one small sign of hope in all this desolation came from the initiative of CIMADE, in this and other camps.[9]

While supporters of CIMADE were doing their best to alleviate suffering in the Algerian camps, Pierre Bungener drew the attention of readers of *Réforme* to the grim conditions experienced by the Algerians who had been arbitrarily relocated to France on the grounds that they might be FLN sympathizers. They lived in a legal netherworld, Bungener explained, neither charged nor condemned. Most had of course lost their jobs and were living in these camps with neither wives nor resources. For some fourteen months, the minister of the interior had permitted visits by representatives of CIMADE, but these visits had been arbitrarily stopped for the last few weeks as a result of what Bungener hoped was a simple administrative error.[10]

Five years into the Algerian conflict, there were some 1,800 Algerian Muslims in French prisons, including Ben Bella and the four other FLN leaders abducted in 1956. Alarming reports of the psychological as well as physical conditions in which these men were held reached high-placed officials, including Simone Weil, then director of the national penitentiary system. Disturbed and concerned, Mme Weil commissioned Michel Philibert, a Protestant philosophy professor at the University of Grenoble, to study prison life and to report back with recommendations about its potential improvement.

Professor Philibert's report reached Mme Weil in 1960.[11] Thanks to Geneviève Anthonios de Gaulle, niece to the president of the Republic, it arrived on Bernard Tricot's desk and thus reached the head of state. The result would be a considerable amelioration of the conditions in which the Algerians were being kept.

Philibert remarked in his preface that the attitude of French public opinion was to a large extent responsible for the deplorable state of prison life. Apart from a widely shared indifference to the conditions in which men such as Ben Bella were forced to live, the prevailing attitude was hatred of the terrorist (presumed or real) and an absence of remorse for excesses committed by the authorities, a strong conviction of racial superiority vis-à-vis Arabs and Berbers, and a sense that the battle under way was between good and evil, one in which "virile force" was justified. The only just attitude, in Philibert's view, was one of "penitence which takes into account not only our crimes and errors but also those of our adversaries with whom we express our solidarity, shared responsibility and compassion even to instigators of violence." These considerations led the professor to insist that prisoners, Muslim terrorists among them, be treated without contempt, in fact with the kind of humility one should practice in the presence of men who were, potentially at least, capable of achieving moral superiority over the rest of us, using their time in prison to purge themselves spiritually (Philibert cited Oscar Wilde at this point).

Philibert's report clearly had an impact. As of 1960, Jacques

Beaumont was given increasingly easy access to Muslims in the five or six prisons where they were held, the biggest of which was at Larzac. During these visits, the secretary-general of CIMADE discussed penitentiary conditions with prison directors and engaged in dialogue with inmates, often agreeing to convey correspondence back and forth.

While CIMADE was doing its best to comfort Muslims incarcerated in France or herded together in camps in Algeria, some radical anti-war activists began to go beyond the law to protest the war.

In late February the French Intelligence Service (DST) uncovered the *Réseau Jeanson*, a network of intellectuals inspired by Sartre's collaborator Francis Jeanson to work on behalf of the FLN. Paul Adeline applauded. No doubt, the pastor suggested, those members of the network who were either neurotic or romantically involved with Algerian nationalists deserved a measure of compassion, but no sympathy should be shown those whose motives were political and who aimed at overthrowing the existing social order. Like the zealots of the 1790s, these "politicals" and their friends in the FLN believed that a lengthy war would advance the democratic cause. The nationalist passion which had engendered this myth during the French Revolution was just as abhorrent as the parallel expression on the Right. As Adeline put it:. "Maurras is on common ground here with Robespierre as is Lagaillarde with Jeanson."[12]

Revelations concerning *Jeune Résistance*, a second Paris-based organization devoted to supporting the FLN and operating out of the Protestant *Mission evangélique* in the 15th arrondissement outraged the editor of *Réforme*. Five young men and one young woman had been apprehended carrying 37,000,000 francs to a rendezvous with members of the Algerian National Front. Documents indicating the organization's past and future assassination plans were also found on their persons. The pastor of the church housing the mission had been unaware of the use made of the premises, and the pacifist cleric Henri Roser issued a special press release disavowing the actions of those arrested. Finet noted that, quite apart from the manifest abuse of the House of God which they had committed, the youthful zealots were totally misguided if they imagined that the best way to fight what they saw as the fascist policies of their own government was to aid and abet terrorism.[13]

The zealotry of *Jeune Résistance* and its willingness to abet violence was matched by the equally passionate but totally non-violent outlook of a group of intellectuals who took to the streets of Paris in the spring of 1960 to demonstrate against the war. A key organizer of these protests was Henri Roser. By the spring of 1960, as the pacifist pastor saw it, French public opinion was disconcerted about the conflict, looking for guidance:

Most importantly, a great many citizens were feeling deeply troubled. No doubt they were still flag-waving patriots (*patriotards*) and still somewhat nostalgic about the empire; but they were disturbed in their conscience when they saw North Africans being beaten up in their neighbourhoods and when they learned that the authorities had begun interning these men systematically without due process.[14]

In this situation, Roser was more than eager to respond to a proposal from Joseph Pyronnet, a Catholic philosophy professor, that a non-violent protest be organized by a number of peace-loving groups such as the International Movement of Reconciliation and the staff of *Témoignage Chrétien*. The first of these demonstrations was held on 30 April outside an internment camp erected near the fort at Vincennes on the eastern edge of Paris where more than 100 Algerians were being held. The night before, a small group met to make sure the protest would be totally pacific.

Although it had been decided in advance not to seek authorization for the march, the protesters were greeted by officers of the law when they showed up. There were some 600 demonstrators in all, including the distinguished Islamicist Louis Massignon and Paul Ricoeur. It had been agreed that Roser would end the silent protest with a brief address. When he had finished, the demonstrators pressed forward towards the barbed wire. The police then moved in to block their progress. To prevent their being dispersed before their mission was fulfilled, the protesters then sat on the ground, consciously borrowing a tactic from Martin Luther King and the American civil rights movement. The "sit-in" technique worked as planned. The police did not back off but arrested demonstrators, lifting them up to be hauled away to local police stations. Bystanders signalled their support as the priests and professors were dragged off the pavement, thrown into paddy-wagons and driven away.[15]

The first demonstration ended with the release of all the protesters after a few hours detention. This relative success was followed by the staging of a second demonstration in May, aimed like the first at two related problems—the arbitrary detention of Muslims and the dangers posed to civic liberties by such arbitrariness. This rally was at the Rond-Point at the foot of the Champs-Elysees from which it was planned to march on the offices of the Interior Ministry in the Place Beauveau. As director of this second protest, Roser was particularly concerned that the non-violent theme and style be preserved. As at Vincennes, the police, headed by Prefect Papon (who had collaborated in the rounding up of Jews for deportation from the Bordeaux area during the war), were waiting when the protesters arrived. Participants sat six to eight deep on the sidewalk, maintaining total silence, offering solemn witness to their opposition to the war. There were some 600 men and 400 women in attendance when officers of the law began dragging them, one by one, into the waiting paddy-wagons.[16]

The prisoners were driven off to an improvised holding area in rue du Faubourg Saint-Honoré where they were kept in large caged spaces pending individual interrogation by the fifty-odd policemen assigned to the task. In that pre-Vatican II era, Roser was gratified that the Catholic priests present rejoiced in the ecumenical nature of the rally. He was even more excited to learn that the young student standing near him waiting to be questioned was Pierre Joxe, a convert to Protestantism, and son of the man who would end up negotiating peace with the FLN at Evian two years later.

Roser was above all impressed that the large band of demonstrators had sustained their absolute commitment to non-violence throughout the day, acting, he thought, like members of a high tribunal representing humanity. There were veterans of the Resistance present as well as survivors of Buchenwald and Belsen-Bergen and, from the younger generation, a Communist who had shown up to express his outrage at a war which had transformed his conscript brother into a fascist.

Meanwhile, having prevailed over those who had defied him during Barricade Week, de Gaulle paid a second visit to the army's mess-halls in Algeria early in March. The president reassured the troops that France would not be dislodged from the land she had occupied for 130 years. At the same time, however, inventing another of those cryptic phrases by which he signalled a strategic as well as a purely semantic shift, the president referred on 4 March to the emergence following self-determination of "an Algerian Algeria linked to France."

Early in April, having tried to reassure the military at a time when he was contemplating a bold new political strategy, de Gaulle despatched one of his most devoted collaborators, the Protestant François Coulet, to keep a watchful eye on the army brass in Algeria. Coulet had studied at France's most prestigious schools (the *École Normale Supérieure* and the *École de Science politique*) before the war and had begun a career in the diplomatic service with a posting to Helsinki. The capitulation of 1940 so disgusted the Protestant diplomat that he resigned and began a long and tortuous journey which ended with his joining the Free French in the Middle East. Coulet's first meeting with General de Gaulle in Jerusalem on 7 April 1941 made him a convert for life. Soon afterwards, he became the president's *chef de cabinet*. After participating in the liberation of Corsica, Coulet played a key role in the assertion of French sovereignty in Normandy following D-Day; there he persuaded the military leaders of the invading Anglo-American forces that he could act as *commissaire* of the Republic at a time when de Gaulle's Provisional Government had not yet been formally recognized either by Washington or by London.

Following the Liberation, Coulet resumed his diplomatic career, serving with distinction, then returning to active duty in Algeria where for four years he headed an air commando unit. Throughout the postwar period, Coulet kept in contact with his hero, even buying a property not far from Colombey-les-deux-Églises. Following the general's return to power in June 1958, Coulet confided (prophetically, as it turned out) to his wife: "The return of de Gaulle means, from the point of view of the *pieds noirs*, the retention of their privileges while for the Muslims it means for sure the imminent conclusion of peace. Both groups are clearly mistaken."[17]

When de Gaulle visited Algeria immediately after his investiture as premier, he sought out the paratroop officer, proposing that Coulet yet again take on a special diplomatic mission. This time, the mission was to help Paul Delouvrier in the long term to prepare the ground for the acceptance of Algerian independence and in the short term to ensure effective implementation of de Gaulle's policies through the offices of the delegate-general.

Over the next few months Coulet flew back and forth between Paris, where he conferred with the government's Algerian "brain trust," and Algiers, where he acted as Delegate-General Delouvrier's chief political counsellor. All in all, de Gaulle's Protestant "spy" in Algiers played a critical but utterly unenviable role in the subsequent evolution of the Algerian drama.

Soon after taking up his new post, Coulet came to his own conclusion that the cause of French Algeria was already lost, partly because of the unyielding attitude of the *pieds-noirs*, partly because of the rigid outlook of the officers doing combat with the FLN. Not surprisingly, de Gaulle's special emissary found himself almost totally isolated, regarded as a traitor even by other Gaullists in or out of uniform.

The army's leaders at this stage were still counting on recruiting a substantial number of Muslims and the subsequent creation of a viable "Third Force" with whom a compromise short of independence might be arranged. For a while, this hope seemed plausible; despite an FLN boycott cantonal elections had brought more than half of the Muslim population to the polls. However, these same elections produced a harvest of votes among the European minority for partisans of Jean-Marie Le Pen.

Cautious optimism about the elections was shared by a small group of

Algerian Protestants who felt a common commitment to learn and teach more about Islam. In mid-May, they created a venue for contact between Muslims and Christians, *Le Centre Chrétien d'Études maghrébines* in Algiers.[18] The project had been under consideration for years, but its realization in 1960 at the height of the conflict seems particularly ironic. Pastor W. N. Heggoy was named the first full-time professor of what it was hoped would become a key centre of intellectual and spiritual communion. In October, Professor Bichon joined the tiny staff.

Between the arrival of Coulet in Algiers and the conclusion of peace between France and the FLN two years later, there were many tentative efforts to end hostilities. On 10 June there was a secret meeting in the Elysée Palace between President de Gaulle and a three-man delegation headed by Si Salah, the Kabyle in charge of the largest zone of ALN operations. Both parties ended up expressing the hope that the Provisional Government would respond favourably to the offer of a cease-fire and a guarantee of Algerian self-determination which the president undertook to make public.

The Council of the FPF welcomed the president's initiative. Albert Finet discounted the likelihood of a favourable outcome of this first attempt at direct negotiations, arguing that the Algerian delegation would come to these talks "with extreme prudence, sceptical, hypersensitive, full of suspicion, anticipating snubs and on the watch for traps."[19]

On 14 June, de Gaulle made his offer to the Provisional Government over national television. A preliminary meeting was held at Melun to discuss the modalities of a more formal negotiation session. When, on 29 June, after four days during which Ferhat Abbas, the head of the Algerian delegation, set forth a series of preconditions, de Gaulle declared the discussions at an end, thereby closing off all possibility of real negotiations. Ferhat Abbas reacted in kind: on 5 July, he made clear that, if independence were not conceded peaceably, it would be achieved by force of arms, however long the battle.

Contributors to *Cité nouvelle* welcomed de Gaulle's 14 June speech with its clear offer of self-determination and its no less categorical references to "the Algerian people" and "Algerian Algeria." We have clearly distanced ourselves from the *Algérie française* of the Ultras, Jan Czarnecki noted. Although negotiations between French and Algerian delegates at Melun had broken down at the end of June and although former supporters of de Gaulle such as Soustelle, Bidault, and Debré opposed the general's overtures, Czarnecki remained optimistic that a way out of the impasse could be found.[20]

As the peace process became a matter of public debate, the national synod of the ERF, meeting at Toulouse in June, reminded the Reformed community that "while the church is not qualified to arbitrate the political options of its members, it must not on the other hand seek to preserve internal peace by putting aside a proper reflection on the political issues which divide believers as much as non-believers." The role of the church, the delegates declared, was to seek reconciliation among the faithful and to offer a discerning opinion whenever a precise event brought it to make a particular judgment. To fulfil this latter role, the synod invited each parish to study the significance to the church of the current conflict in Algeria and to seek resolutions of that conflict compatible with God's teaching. The synod was mandated to stimulate these reflections at the local level.[21]

The editors of *Tant qu'il fait jour*, persistent critics of mainstream Protestant attitudes towards the war, denounced what they saw to be the unpatriotic outlook expressed at the national synod. "When given a choice between spiritual values and political realities," they asked their readers, "have we the right, in the name of an aberrant (but very fashionable) desire, to oppose, to undermine the nation which is in a sense our indispensable physical base?"[22]

Just as Algerian nationalists adopted an even more radical strategy following the Si Salah affair and the collapse of the Melun talks, the Ultras found new ways of expressing their unyielding commitment to French Algeria. De Gaulle's opening to the Provisional Government was followed by the creation of the *Front de l'Algérie française* (FAF) on 15 June. In short order, this omnibus organization attracted as many as 1,000,000 members, including more than 100,000 Muslims, to the great distress of Delegate-General Delouvrier.

Out of office since Barricade week, Jacques Soustelle fired a steady barrage of propaganda shots at the public throughout 1960, some of them direct, some oblique. All were aimed at defending French Algeria and damning the government's policy there. A *Centre d'information sur les problèmes de l'Algérie et du Sahara* had been created to serve as a propaganda base for Soustelle and his colleagues. In April, the Centre published *Algérie. Le chemin de la paix*, a forty-page tract by the ex-governor in which he returned to the leitmotif of his earlier reflections on the Algerian question. The rebellion of 1954 had been hatched in Cairo; the Muslim masses were overwhelmingly given to a "wait-and-see" attitude; integration, which had been seriously misunderstood, was still the best possible solution for all parties in the current conflict.[23]

Soustelle's increasing alienation from official government policy on Algeria was apparent in the public lecture he delivered on 2 June at the *Théâtre des Ambassadeurs* in Paris.[24] To meet the challenge posed by the intoxicating myth of Algerian national liberation, the former governor argued,

France must devise "an alternative myth charged with hope for the future." The strategic concept behind this myth ought to be tracing a Euro-African axis tying Paris through Algiers to the Sahara. Such a power link would have the added advantage of cutting across a potentially menacing pan-Arab east-west axis from Morocco to the Middle East. Soustelle's disaffection deepened following reports of a speech de Gaulle made in Normandy in mid-June. During it the president referred to the evolution of an "Algerian Algeria" and repeated his earlier proposal to the FLN that a cease-fire be reached, followed by a period of reconciliation and then an opportunity for all Algerians to choose their own future at the ballot-box. Soustelle's response to this was as bitter as it was incisive:

> Algerians will be free to choose, then, of course, but on condition that they do not choose French Algeria! For that matter, they will doubtless be offered (when the time comes) a magnificent statute for an Algerian Algeria united to France, although endowed with her own institutions, her own government, etc., etc. ... It will only remain for them to vote yes or no to this "Lebanese" text which will grant new guarantees on paper to compensate for those which will have disappeared in fact.[25]

While Soustelle was crusading for French Algeria, Protestant Socialists were urging their comrades to support de Gaulle's efforts to negotiate with the FLN. At the national convention of the SFIO at the end of June, Francis Leenhardt and Gaston Defferre insisted that they were not asking their comrades to give the president unconditional support, citing clear disagreement over de Gaulle's European policy and their opposition to the enormous powers conferred on the executive by the new constitution. For Leenhardt, the important consideration was that in the present circumstances, de Gaulle stood for a liberal resolution of the Algerian dilemma. On 16 September, de Gaulle had spoken of "self-determination" as the best way out of the impasse; he had also hinted at the possibility of partition to provide for those Europeans and Muslims who might not wish to live in an independent Algeria, thereby making a subtle threat that might bring the FLN to negotiate more reasonably.[26]

Defferre proposed a resolution urging that France engage in preliminary talks with the FLN about a cease-fire and the right of self-determination with the possibility of drawing up a provisional statute for Algeria to be submitted for ratification by the Algerian people (except for the Ultras). Without such prior discussion, there was a strong chance that the FLN might win any election that might be called. Although Defferre's motion won the support of 1,299 delegates, it failed to carry the day. Instead, a motion welcoming de Gaulle's invitation to resume negotiations and the subsequent positive response of the FLN prevailed with 1,876 votes. It was clear that, thanks in large measure to the case put by Protestant Socialists, the notion of retaining Algeria as an integral part of France had been abandoned by a substantial majority inside the SFIO.

While France's Socialists debated the wisdom of supporting de Gaulle's peace initiatives, the climactic point in the intellectual critique of the Algerian war came in the fall of 1960 with the publication of the "Manifesto of the 121" signed by a wide variety of celebrities from the world of arts, letters, and entertainment.[27]

Although the Debré government did its best to frustrate the efforts of the signatories, the text made its way easily enough into the public domain. The manifesto opened with an expression of support for the growing number of men and women who had chosen either not to participate in the Algerian conflict or to offer their support to the rebels. The battle was clearly a war of national liberation, yet, paradoxically, it was being waged by men whom the state still considered citizens of France. In a grim abuse of its authority, the regime had called up entire classes of conscripts to engage in what amounted to a police action against an oppressed people.

The Manifesto concluded with a ringing three-point profession of principles: (i) refusal to take up arms against the Algerian insurrection was clearly justified, (ii) acts of support or protection given those rebelling against colonial oppression were equally defensible, and (iii) the struggle of the Algerian people was playing a major role in the overthrow of colonialism and was thus the cause of free people all over the world.

Few Protestants are to be found among those who signed their names to the *Manifeste des 121*. The Africanist Théodore Monod, the art critic Marc Beigbeder and *Réforme's* Algerian correspondent Jan Czarnecki stand out as exceptions. Nonetheless the manifesto and, more especially, the concept of *insoumission* which it encouraged, produced reflection and debate within the Reformed community. After reflecting on what was implied in the Manifesto, Paul Riceour said in *Cité nouvelle* that he could not bring himself to counsel insubordination. The Algerian conflict was, he conceded, "an illegitimate war in which we are trying to prevent the Algerian people from constituting themselves in an independent state like all the other peoples of Africa."[28] However, as time passed, it had become clear that de Gaulle was less and less free to enter into effective negotiations with the FLN. In the meantime the Left seemed disappointingly frozen in inertia leaving the partisans of peace to face a rather special dilemma. Ricoeur argued that the point had not yet been reached where the state had lost all legitimacy; legal recourse was still open in France to those who opposed the war. France had not yet been confronted with the equivalent of the German crisis of 20 July 1944 when a number of officers had found it necessary to break their oath of allegiance to the Führer. In the present circumstances in France, neither acts of *insoumission* (which meant in practice desertion from the ranks outside of French jurisdiction or going underground in France, sometimes with the intention to support the FLN) nor direct support to the FLN were morally justifiable. Instead, the proper course of action was not to engage in acts which might only prolong the conflict but rather to try to detach both the government and public opinion from supporting the war.

The manifesto's invitation to military disobedience brought Jacques Ellul to reply with a series of provocative articles for *Réforme*.[29] These four essays went beyond the immediate issues of conscience as Ellul made a serious effort to review the larger problems faced by the Christian in response to war in general and to the demands of the modern state.

He began by suggesting that the current anti-war feeling was limited to Parisian intellectuals already ill-disposed to the regime and to young people with particularly sensitive temperaments. The issues these minorities were raising were not new, but they clearly merited serious debate. Moving to the philosophical core of the question, Ellul argued that, for Christians at least, there could be *no* just war. At the same time, however, followers of Christ must recognize that no state could survive which was not ready to use force to defend itself. War was the *ultima ratio* of the modern secular state, which was by nature agnostic. A permanent tension (if not an outright conflict) thus existed between the spiritual values taught by Jesus and the secular principles upon which the contemporary state must base its survival. These tensions sometimes produced grave battles of conscience within the Christian soul; the church had an obligation to shield and protect those of its members who refused to take up arms.

If there were no *just* wars for the Christian, Ellul pursued, there were clearly *legitimate* wars, wars fought for example to defend the integrity of the state and the rights of its citizenry. The intervention of the Belgian army to rescue Belgians under threat in the Congo, like the use of French troops to support the maintenance of the *patrimoine national* in Algeria, were cases in point; whereas the invasion of Cuba by the United States in 1898 or of Hungary by the Soviet Union in 1956 were clearly indefensible.

While there were fairly clear-cut distinctions to be drawn between legitimate and illegitimate action by the state, the individual Christian had only one means of justifying his refusal to bear arms. If the combat in which he was asked to engage obliged him to disobey God's law, that was always the higher imperative. Other reasons invoked for such disobedience were specious, including humanitarian concern, personal reflection, the interest of the working class, etc.

In the May/June issue of *Temps modernes* desertion had been defended as the politically appropriate action for the Left in the present situation. Against this Ellul argued that leftists saw the Algerian issue not as one of high principle but of political tactics. It was worth reminding these radicals, he wrote with bitter sarcasm, of the subtle word-play used by left-wing thinkers over the defence (or abandonment) of Danzig in 1939. French radicals opposed the war in Algeria because they harboured guilt-feelings about colonialism in general; their anguish about the use of torture was hypocritical since such vicious behaviour was typical of all wars.

Ellul went on to argue that those who were urging *insoumission* on France's young soldiers out of a desire to champion Algerian independence against the forces of oppression were equally naive. There was no guarantee that independence would bring liberty with it, especially given the rebels' passionate nationalism, a form of zealotry which the church had consistently condemned as a "corrosive element." Put even more bluntly, he said desertion signified committing oneself in effect to the FLN. In an even more devastating comment, the distinguished social scientist reminded his readers that there had been peace-minded French citizens supporting Italian nationalism in 1935, German nationalism in 1940, not to mention Russian nationalism more recently. Present-day desertion, then, meant "committing oneself to the war being waged by our enemy, and no Christian can give his support to such a passion." Those who had penned the present manifesto had yielded, then, to that most banal and pervasive of contemporary myths, nationalism, perversely transferring their faith to the Algerian incarnation of the myth because the French equivalent no longer inspired them to action, adventure and sacrifice.

Ellul's articles elicited a flurry of replies in *Réforme*. André Philip took exception to his sweeping indictment of nationalism. He argued that in the developing countries this collective sentiment reflected the will to create a fatherland above and beyond tribal entities, rather like the contemporary trend in Europe towards a transnational unity beyond traditional chauvinism. As for the immediate issue: "The issue of conscience is real; the question about *insoumission* is being asked and will be more frequently asked in the minds of our young people. We must face it head on and not mask it with exercises in intellectual prestidigitation."[30]

Not to be put down by this sally, Ellul replied in equally cutting fashion. He admired the committed Socialist for having spent forty years in politics and for having preserved "that ever-French illusion, that purity of faith, and that comforting optimism which are the attributes of those who have devoted themselves to the religion of Progress."[31]

The trial of the Jeanson network which took place in Paris in the fall of 1960 kept the public debate on *insoumission* alive. In the view of Jacques Pascal writing in *Réforme*, the group which had been charged had engaged in a criminal conspiracy involving forged papers as well as trafficking in arms and money with the FLN. The conspirators had justified their action on the ground that they had a right to defy a government waging an unjust war; in reality, they had collaborated with the enemies of France.[32]

In the lead article of an issue of *Réforme* devoted to the insubordination question, the editor, Finet, took strong exception to Pascal's argument. He pointed out that some of the current *insoumis* were genuinely horrified at the tortures they had been forced to witness and were refusing to be accomplices in its prolongation. On the other hand, Jeanson's dialectical argument, based on the need to fight with the FLN on the ground that the nationalist organization was struggling for liberty, was specious.[33]

The Manifesto of the 121 was met by a counter-attack from a group of 185 prominent nationalist personalities (including the Protestant scholar Pierre Grosclaude) who published their own manifesto in defense of French Algeria. Finet saw in both documents the reflection of a dangerously idolatrous mystique, a tendency to find absolute justice in one ideologically coherent position. "As a result of a fundamental spiritual disorder, neither can see in the opposite camp the face of his brother," he wrote.[34]

September brought with it a reminder that the United Nations General Assembly would soon again debate the Algerian issue. Pressure on France to define her aims more clearly and to open discussions with the FLN increased. During a 5 September press conference, de Gaulle included a new reference to Algeria's peculiar political personality and thus, by implication at least, recognition of the logical case that might be made for its independence. Predictably, Philippe Brissaud, writing in *Tant qu'il fait jour*, deplored de Gaulle's repeated use of the term "Algerian Algeria" as a thinly disguised concession of the territory's potential independence from France. Word-plays full of paradox such as this had made contradiction the very basis of Gaullist policy![35] But, as Roger Mehl saw it, the press conference revealed that the president's purpose was to orchestrate Algeria's irreversible movement towards independence in such a way that he became the architect of the new nation's freedom.[36]

As the international pressure for a change in France's Algeria policy continued to build, domestic preoccupation with the issue also intensified. In October, the French Reformed Church published a special booklet of reflections on the war and on the way it might be ended. These reflections were in part the product of discussions during the national synod in June and in part the result of subsequent debates at the parish level throughout France. Of all the texts which emerged from public discourse on the war, this remains one of the most succinct and thoughtful.[37]

The committee which drew up the brochure was made up of two pastors (Conord and Lauriol) and two laymen (Professor René Courtin and a lawyer, Maître Pascal). Among the wide variety of briefs considered during their reflections, one of the most forceful came from representatives of the *Alliance des Unionistes* which was anxious for guidelines to help them counsel the increasing number of young men opposed to the war. What had turned so many of their peers against the war, the *Alliance* representatives pointed out, were reports about the methods used by some French army units in Algeria. After six years, it was surely high time to expose the scandal of the war; the absence of free and open reflection on the subject had led to a kind of spiritual paralysis among the youth.

Beyond expressing their desire for explicit counselling guidelines, those mandated by the *Alliance* submitted recommendations which they hoped might help steer the nation towards peace. An appeal for mediation in the conflict through the World Council of Churches was suggested together with the insistence that in the end negotiation preceded by the recognition of Algeria's right to self-determination was the only route to peace.

The authors analyzed briefly the contemporary political situation in Algeria, conceding that "the Muslim majority, despite certain differences of race and language, appears to see itself as a distinct community, not to say nation."[38] Not surprisingly, a large proportion of Muslims, although not directly involved in the war, was clearly sympathetic to the FLN. Turning to the war itself and to the moral dilemmas it posed, the signatories of the brochure found clear evidence of terrorism by the FLN as well as of torture and forcible transfers of population by the army. The war had both retarded economic development in Algeria and cost French taxpayers a fortune. The nation was increasingly isolated diplomatically and demoralized internally. The army had intruded as never before in political affairs while those called to the colours were more and more ready to consider insubordination or desertion.

The pamphlet-writers offered a succinct, critical review of possible solutions. Integration, to be successful, required not only the massive consent of the Muslims but a willingness by the French public to pay what was necessary to raise Muslim living standards. Furthermore, if a special statute distinguishing Muslim society in Algeria did not accompany the drive for integration, it would bring about the secularization of that society and, beyond that, its total assimilation. Partition, the Irish solution, might work on the assumption that the Europeans living along the coastline would have adequate agricultural resources while the Muslims in the interior would be sustained by the substantial mineral wealth there. A federal arrangement along Swiss lines, with cantons reflecting ethnic differences, was no doubt possible. Finally there was the concept of a fully independent Algeria with or without links to France but clearly guaranteeing rights to the European minority.

The church had a number of special obligations, the authors added, including concern for the fate of Christian Arabs and Kabyles, and for full disclosure of aspects of the war which had been kept from the public, such as the Audin affair. Even more important over the long term was the search for spiritual understanding between Christians and Muslims. The report concluded by pointing to the peculiar problems faced by the young generation. Some had become conscientious objectors, adopting a position unfortunately not yet recognized in French law; the church must continue to press for a statute regulating civil service in lieu of military obligation. In its absence, those called up should declare their refusal to serve and take the consequences; the church would defend them. *Insoumission,* the writers of the pamphlet went on, could not be countenanced since the state had not yet reached the degree of perversion warranting such action.

Meanwhile, at the end of October, the French Protestant Federation came together for one of the general assemblies it held every five years. The Declaration on Algeria which the assembly adopted reflected·a radical shift of Protestant opinion concerning the conflict. This radicalization was due in large measure to a fundamental change in the Federation's representation and voting procedures. Up until 1960, general assemblies of the FPF had brought together representatives from the member churches together with a few foreign delegates, leaving unrepresented the wide variety of missions and volunteer associations which had sprung up alongside traditional ecclesiastical bodies and which had developed their own style and outlook, often better adapted to the changing socio-economic and cultural patterns of contemporary France. These associations included the Protestant Teachers' Federation, *Jeunes Femmes*, Sunday School societies, as well as the *Fédé* and CIMADE.

Access to the national council of the FPF by these bodies was bound to have a radicalizing impact. Men such as Jacques Maury, secretary-general of the *Fédé*, recently consecrated a pastor, and Jacques Beaumont, secretary-general of CIMADE, suddenly found themselves empowered to influence a body which had long been dominated by men of an older generation, less open to basic changes of orientation and commitment. The impact on this radical change of representation on the debate over Algeria was soon felt. The newly militant tone of the Montbéliard meeting was set early in the proceedings by Pastor Boegner, at one and the same time president of the FPF and of CIMADE. France's leading Protestant personality expressed the wish that "through the actions of CIMADE, our churches and their members, whatever their political options, are hearing a call from God to put themselves at the service of justice of which love, when carried to its limit, is the purest expression."[39]

Pastor Georges Casalis, the intellectual and spiritual mentor of many Protestants who came of age during the Algerian conflict, offered a bold, even defiant challenge to those preaching and teaching on both sides of the Mediterranean. In Algerian parishes particularly (some of which Casalis had come to know well from having spent a season as an exchange pastor in Algeria late in 1957), it was essential that the message transmitted to the congregation be in tune with changing circumstances, however ill-received this message might be. The notion that sermons should be strenuously apolitical was clearly not derived from the Gospel. The recent brochure on Algeria put out by the French Reformed Church was admirable in this regard although it came two years too late!

What the Federation must do, Casalis went on, even if it could not come up with a solution to the Algerian conflict, was to make clear to the faithful those solutions which had become unacceptable. Neither integration nor a decisive military victory was any longer a plausible option. What remained was the prospect of an autonomous Algeria whether or not linked federally to France, a formula which could only be arrived at through negotiation.

Thus far, Casalis noted, the church had used its moral authority to condemn certain specific abuses by France's armed forces in Algeria such as torture, summary execution of prisoners, or the forcible resettlement of civilians and their deliberately induced starvation. What was long overdue was a categorical denunciation of the war itself. Five or six grounds existed for such an action. The war could not be won, it had caused massive death and dislocation, perverted the state, undermined France's institutions of justice and police, and demoralized the nation's youth. The conflict had left all Africa open to communism and permanently jeopardized relations between Christianity and Islam. Above all, the war had never been a rational option. In short, there should be no question of trying to humanize or limit the conflict; it should simply be brought to an end.

What alarmed the radical pastor as much as anything else was the devastating impact of the war on France's youth. Anxiety about the very survival of the regime was such that young people were clearly prepared to do battle against the system, "preferring to join in the violence which liberates rather than in that which enslaves, taking action in the hope of bringing peace closer and thereby preserving future Franco-Algerian relations."[40]

Encouraged by Boegner and roused by Casalis, delegates to the General Assembly produced a "Declaration on Algeria." It went well beyond anything Protestant officialdom had thus far expressed concerning the war. The conflict had bitterly divided the nation, the delegates wrote. France was seriously alienated from the community of nations; the Christian witness of the European minority in Algeria had become increasingly difficult, and the state had suffered a serious loss of moral and juridical integrity which had in turn encouraged subversive enterprises. This recital of critical by-products of the conflict was followed by an expression of collective contrition: "We confess that our partisan passions, our passivity, our nationalism, our self-interest and our unconscious racism, have all played their part in creating a situation which now seems hopeless."[41]

In these grim circumstances, the faithful were urged to pray for all those civilians as well as military personnel who were caught up in the conflict. Pastor Boegner was mandated to seek an audience with President de Gaulle and the leaders of the Algerian nationalist cause, preferably in concert with the heads of the Catholic and Jewish communities, with a view to arranging a truce. Above all, the signers of the Declaration insisted, it was vital that negotiations be entered into without preconditions except for an understanding that an equitable statute for all communities living in Algeria be arrived at in advance.

In an obvious reference to the Manifesto of the 121, the Declaration made clear that fidelity to Christian principles did not dictate any particular course of action for those called to military service during the current conflict. However, the church "wished to make abundantly clear that any insubordination having as a consequence crossing the line of legality could only be justified in cases where there had been a fundamental perversion of the State." By implication the signatories clearly believed that the condition had not yet been reached.[42] Soldiers at the front, the text went on, as well as those waiting to be called up, should bear witness in front of their commanders as well as before those they might encounter in battle. They must never accept that those whom they fought be abused or degraded through moral or physical punishment nor must they become accomplices in such treatment. Any soldier offering legitimate resistance to orders of this kind was guaranteed the church's moral, material and legal aid. Those who felt they could only bear witness through conscientious objection were assured that the Federation would continue to press for a change in the law allowing for recognition of their position.

The Montbéliard "Declaration on Algeria" elicited a vigorous exchange of opinion within the Reformed community. Much of it, not surprisingly, came from men facing a military call-up. *Le Semeur* was the logical vehicle for Protestant students in this position. In the December 1960-January 1961 issue, A. Berthoud made clear his intention of responding to the call if and when it came. To begin with, it seemed to this young correspondent that it was far too simple to argue, as critics had done, that France had committed nothing but acts of folly or evil in Algeria. Berthoud added that, quite apart from the merits of the war, there was no evidence that insubordination (a tactic which he confessed to finding personally awkward to apply) would serve any useful purpose.[43]

"M.B.," writing in the same issue, was of opposite mind. His position was based on "Christian patriotism," a sense of solidarity with all his brothers everywhere in the world, utterly different from the nationalism or self-centredness which seemed to animate so many of his peers. Scripture might well justify taking up arms but only in the most extreme cases, such as that created by the tyranny of Hitler. Willingness to fight should be expressed existentially, based on particular circumstances. In the present case, "M.B." was ready to accept a uniform if called to the colours, but he would not serve in Algeria and was ready to pay whatever penalty disobedience brought.

While the French Protestant community debated the moral issues, tensions in Algeria continued to move towards the breaking point. Early in October, in their first direct attack on a member of the civil government, European terrorists planted a plastic bomb in front of the house of Eric Westphal, causing enormous material damage but leaving Delouvrier's Protestant counsellor unharmed. In an effort to defuse the rising polarization in the territory, Army Minister Pierre Messmer had on 22 September requested that General Salan quit Algeria. The former commander of France's military forces in Algeria, who was already sympathetic to the champions of *l'Algérie française*, reacted to his dismissal by accepting the leadership of this cause. Following a brief but highly provocative public denunciation of government policy at a Paris rally, attended by Georges Bidault and Jean-Marie Le Pen, Salan took refuge in Spain to continue the struggle there.

De Gaulle responded by articulating even more incisively his willingness to accept in advance a radical change in Algeria's constitutional status. In a television address on 4 November, the president spoke of an

Algerian Algeria which would have its own government and its own laws and institutions and would become "an Algerian republic." This phrase had not been in his original text but was improvised in front of the television cameras. To many of his listeners, it seemed to signal a concession to one of the main demands of the GPRA.

Writing from Algiers, J.-P. Lumire observed that the notion of an "Algerian Algeria" was gaining ground even among the *colons*, most of whom were clearly willing to stay on whatever the future of the territory while Muslim masses were losing their trust in the president.[44] André Philip rejoiced that de Gaulle had moved reconciliation forward by using the term *Algérie Algérienne* with its clear implication of ultimate political independence, but the veteran Socialist regretted the general's rejection of any direct dialogue with the FLN. Philip suggested that the Algerian Liberation Front was in roughly the same position as its Gaullist predecessor in 1942. At that time the Americans had refused to recognize Free France, preferring to train their own French cadres in Virginia to serve as their surrogate administrators in liberated France. De Gaulle should recognize and respect in the FLN what Roosevelt had denied to *La France libre* and move ahead to negotiate with an organization that just as legitimately reflected dominant Algerian opinion as Free France had done years earlier. Of course, guarantees for the European minority should be included in any negotiating agenda.[45]

While liberal and leftish Protestants welcomed the new boldness of de Gaulle's proposals about Algeria's future, the military hierarchy there was far less receptive. Delegate-General Delouvrier decided that he could no longer stay on in a post which he had not accepted in order to promote an Algerian republic no longer attached to France. To replace Delouvrier, the president turned to Louis Joxe who had rallied to him in Algiers in 1942. Unlike his predecessor who had been responsible to Prime Minister Debré, Joxe was named *Ministre d'Etat chargé des Affaires algériennes*, bound to report directly to the president of the Republic.

De Gaulle followed up his provocative radio address with a four-day visit to Algeria which began on 9 December. Coulet had warned the general that the trip was risky in the extreme, given the almost universal hostility towards him in the army. The *Front de l'Algérie française* greeted de Gaulle's arrival with a call for a general strike, hoping that the fury generated by his visit might ignite conflict between the forces of order and the *pieds noirs* and, ultimately, a series of revolts culminating in the overthrow of the regime. In a lightning-fast tour, de Gaulle ignored hostile European demonstrators and made a point of greeting Muslims who responded by crying out the phrase "*Algérie algérienne.*" Then, while the president was off in Kabylia, a crowd of excited Muslims, convinced that the future was theirs, went wild inside the Muslim quarter of Algiers, displaying the FLN flag. French paratroops responded with fire. For the next two days the city was plunged into a brief but vicious civil war which left 112 Muslims and eight Europeans dead. Apprised of these tragic developments, de Gaulle congratulated his recent appointees for having prevented further chaos and urged them to press on with the forthcoming referendum on self-determination.

Like his fellow-Protestant Coulet, Jacques Beaumont had anticipated the explosion of anger in the settler community. He could not, however, have foreseen that European demonstrators would begin their rioting against the visit on 9 December in front of the CIMADE hostel in Algiers. Despite the obvious danger, Beaumont decided to escort the two female team-workers (Denise Duboscq and Pierrette Faivre) back within the little enclave where they would remain as witnesses while the battle raged all around them.[46]

Two days after the first violent skirmish, a dense crowd of Muslims who had been provoked by rifle-shots fired from the second floor of a nearby building, started their own demonstration, chanting *"Algérie algérienne,"* then, as their numbers grew, they began shouting *"Algérie musulmane,"* terrifying the Europeans in the neighbourhood.

Beaumont reported that this verbally aggressive crowd was selective in its physical assaults, targeting the shops of Europeans who had shown them contempt. Horrible acts of violence occurred. Two Muslims were incinerated in a baker's oven; others had their throats slit by fellow-Arabs in what appeared to be a settling of accounts.

Reporting on these grim events, the secretary-general reassured his correspondents that the work of CIMADE had resumed on the morning after the battle. Psychological wounds, however, still needed attending to: sixty-five Europeans had sought refuge in the nearby Red Cross kindergarten and were refusing to return to their homes. Discussions were under way to give them a degree of security if they left.

Faith inspired optimism in Beaumont over the long haul. He perceived hopeful signs even in the midst of conflict. The two team-workers who had stayed inside the hostel during hostilities had testified to a reinforced friendship between Muslims and CIMADE personnel. Finally, there was anecdotal but touching evidence of Christian-Muslim reconciliation. While the Clos Salembier district was all but cut off by the army, Fatmah, a Muslim woman who had become part of the CIMADE community, was lying in hospital with a broken arm, without news and concerned that she would no longer be welcome there. Team-workers had asked Pastor Capieu to break through the security cordon around the medical building and reassure her.

When Beaumont ran across Fatmah three days afterwards, she told him that she had not stopped praying for her daughters (the female team-workers) and her son (Philippe Jordan, a Reformed lay theologian who had arranged Pastor Capieu's access to the hospital). They were, all three, clearly the children God had found for her. To which the secretary-general replied: "What you are really telling me, Fatmah, is that this is what God has given to all of us at Christmas time."

The tragic killings of early December drew world-wide attention to Algeria at a time when the UN was again about to discuss the territory. Ferhat Abbas prepared the terrain by speaking out against the "genocide" being visited upon his people while Krim Belkacem, grand strategist of FLN diplomacy, exploited the grim news to mobilize sympathy for the nationalist cause in New York.

De Gaulle's response was to order a boycott of the sessions dealing with Algeria in the General Assembly. This action was based in part on his supreme contempt for the world organization and in part on the conviction that France had nothing to gain from rhetorical battles with leaders of the Third World and their Communist backers. In October Jacques Soustelle had formed his own parliamentary bloc (the *Regroupement national*) to mobilize opinion against de Gaulle's recognition of an "Algerian Algeria" and had subsequently been denied both access to the publicly controlled media and the right to travel to Algeria. De Gaulle's boycott led Soustelle to set off on a propaganda tour of the United States presenting the case for French Algeria and against the FLN as a band of terrorists.

In the end, the political commission of the General Assembly adopted a resolution drafted by twenty-three African and Asian nations and edited by one of Krim's colleagues, M'Hamed Yazid. It recognized the right of the Algerian people to self-determination and independence and insisted on the need for a just framework in which this right could be exercised. A separate paragraph stressed the responsibility incumbent on the world body to guarantee such a framework through a UN-supervised referendum. This last paragraph passed the political committee but failed to win a majority in the General Assembly. A modified version which "recommended" rather than "decided" on the UN involvement, missed the requisite two-thirds majority by a single vote. Had the United States joined the majority, the vote would have carried the day, but Washington's policy at this stage was based on the assumption that de Gaulle had a strong chance of producing de-colonization on his own without outside meddling.

Towards the year's end, Beaumont submitted a number of reports on his organization's activities to benefactors of CIMADE in Europe and the

United States as well as to Reformed synods in Algeria and France.[47] There were now seventeen team-workers in the field, providing a wide variety of socio-economic, educational and medical services to Muslims throughout the territory. Food imports from Protestant churches in Europe and North America had accelerated substantially since the beginning of the year: some one hundred tonnes of food supplies per month were now being distributed. But with the approach of winter, Beaumont made a special appeal for layettes, shoes, warm clothing, cheese, chocolate and soap as well as for raw materials for the artisans whom CIMADE was supporting in the camps.

CIMADE had opened a hostel (*foyer*) at Sidi-Naamane, one of the resettlement camps which Delouvrier wished to see transformed into a model village. As of March, two team-workers, both of whom were qualified nurses, had opened up a dispensary there as well as a makeshift hospital capable of handling up to 2,000 patients.

An even more ambitious project had been launched at Médéa where by mid-year a group of itinerant team-workers had helped some sixty Muslim families learn or retrieve a variety of artisanal skills such as weaving or pottery. Not only had this exercise resulted in a new sense of dignity for those involved; their handicrafts had been distributed by CIMADE to Reformed churches in Algeria and France and sold at specially organized parish exhibits.

Médéa benefited from a second, even more vital commitment by CIMADE. The war had raged all around the city bringing with it an epidemic of tuberculosis, particularly devastating for infants and children. The arrival of two remarkable Protestant women would help save the younger generation of Muslims and provide the basis for modern medical treatment in an independent Algeria.

One of these women was Mireille Desrez who volunteered for service in Algeria after hearing an appeal for help in her parish church.[48] Mlle Desrez had been a Protestant girl guide (*éclaireuse unioniste*) and had received Red Cross nursing training. Although a woman of Socialist conviction, she saw her commitment to CIMADE in Algeria as that of a *"chrétienne engagée"* who was also motivated by a sense of civic responsibility.

Before leaving for Algeria, Mireille Desrez spent some time at the *Club des jeunes algériens* in Paris, familiarizing herself with the mindset of those across the Mediterranean. In Algiers, she was met by Pastor Chatoney and by Professor Bichon and his wife. While she found the Bichons politically conservative (*pieds noirs de droite*) in time she came to admire their Christian forbearance in the face of young CIMADE team-workers freshly arrived from France all too anxious to visit their leftish opinions on those they encountered.

After two weeks of training, Mlle Desrez left Algiers for Médéa in May 1960. Some 70,000 *regroupés* whose villages had been torched by the army were gathered there. The area around Médéa was still in fact being contested by the FLN and the French military. It would be hard to imagine a more vulnerable situation for an uprooted rural population which, apart from a loss of sense of belonging, was suffering from the tuberculosis epidemic Mireille Desrez and her and her co-worker Hélène Pons were set on containing.

Happily for the Protestant team-workers, the political and psychological environment turned out to be anything but hostile. Officers on both sides of the conflict soon came to an understanding that neither would interfere with the installation of CIMADE's relief operation. The local sub-prefect Robert Poujol, a fellow-Protestant, was fully sympathetic to what his co-religionists planned to do and provided political cover when it was needed. Even more important, the only hospital in the area, a military facility able to deal with tubercular cases, was directed by a medical officer, Dr. Jean Guillermand, who put his Hippocratic oath above any obligation to the French army command.

The Quaker-style attitude of dispensing compassion to whoever needed it in the middle of a war zone meant that Mireille Desrez and Hélène Pons, with Dr. Guillermand's help, ended up treating not only tubercular Muslim children but wounded *fellagha*. In fact embattled partisans from both sides felt free to talk openly within the confines of the CIMADE hostel. Some, Mlle Desrez admits, were inevitably FLN spies; others just as ineluctably supporters of the OAS. Many were young French conscripts horrified by the brutality of the war. Dropping in at the Protestant relief centre afforded them a chance, however brief, to recover their sanity.

Not surprisingly, the devotion of the Protestant nurses to the Muslim children endeared them to parents and families. In time they were able, with the help of three Muslim women, to begin training in basic household management each afternoon. While in Médéa, Mireille Desrez and Hélène Pons lived in Muslim public housing and made regular contact with their neighbours. Inevitably, this enraged certain Ultras in Médéa who took it to signify sympathy for the FLN on the part of CIMADE. Sub-prefect Poujol, whose support for CIMADE was steadfast, was concerned that such rumours might become a major handicap. To deflect this possibility, he suggested that one of CIMADE's key workers, Isabelle Peloux, visit the detention centre at Berrouaghia where a number of European Ultras as well as Muslims were held. The suggestion was eagerly taken up. Thanks to the intervention of Eric Westphal, Jacques Beaumont and Mlle Peloux travelled to Berrouaghia. There they found some 250 men, including thirty Europeans arrested on the eve of one of de Gaulle's visits, as well as right-wing students and others who had simply been apprehended for being on the street at the wrong place or time. Beaumont and Peloux did their best to comfort and reassure the internees and afterwards contacted as many relatives as possible. Beaumont felt these contacts helped establish the political neutrality of CIMADE and offered Isabelle Peloux an increased opportunity to meet and teach Muslim women in their own households.

The situation remained extraordinarily tense, the secretary-general of CIMADE reported in November, adding that any team-workers experiencing panic or loss of nerve had been advised to take a leave of absence in France. Given the particularly trying circumstances in which team-workers now had to function, Beaumont added, it would be especially helpful if young people from Algeria's European minority would commit themselves to participate in the relief work. Fortunately for CIMADE, one very dynamic *pied noir* had in fact joined the team that fall. Bernard Picinbono, the prominent settler's son who had been radicalized by the burning of the family property, had offered his services during the summer of 1960 as guide and instructor to a group of young volunteers on their way to serve the organization in Algeria. Much impressed, Beaumont invited Picinbono to join the committee in charge of CIMADE's Algerian operation in order to provide a much needed critical evaluation from the settlers' point of view. Picinbono's wife Beatrice, daughter of Pastor Henri Capieu, joined him in that task. Through the next few years, even beyond Algerian independence, the young Protestant couple filled this role admirably.

One of the most graphic accounts of the relief organization's work in 1960 was written in unpublished diary form by Captain Eoche-Duval, chief of the SAS in the Médéa department where Robert Poujol served as sub-prefect.[49] Poujol proposed to him that a team of CIMADE workers be invited to help set up medical facilities in Sidi-Naamane. The team in question was made up of two women who had served as volunteer nurses in Germany, East Europe and Palestine. Marguerite Cruse was from a prominent Protestant family in Bordeaux; Ita Stelma was a young Dutch woman with boundless energy. Eoche-Duval worried at first about the international quality of the prospective newcomers. Recognizing, however, that the existing paramedical services provided by *harkiettes* (Muslim nursing aides) was totally inadequate and that Sidi Naamane had to rely for proper hospital services on Algiers which was a good 200 kilometres away, he yielded.

The two women arrived shortly afterwards, bringing their own prefabricated cabin and establishing themselves in an olive grove near the huge camp-city. A little later, a Dr. Gonin arrived from Paris, taking a month's leave from his flourishing practice to supervise the building of a small dispensary and to train the local women in basic hygiene. From then on, as Captain Eoche-Duval describes it, the history of CIMADE at Sidi-Naamane merged with that of his own SAS operation. As Eoche-Duval puts it concerning these modest but resolute local efforts: "we were reconstructing a whole small world with wisdom and determination. We kept telling ourselves that this new world would be Algerian, something which in our eyes was no longer out of focus with our own hopes."

The year 1960 also saw the arrival in Algeria of a young, politically sensitive pastor, Bernard Roussel, who took over the parish of Tizi-Ouzou Minerville, which included a huge area to the east and south of Algiers, a territory Roussel described as imperial.[50] Born in Marseilles, Roussel grew up in a postwar France that experienced a long series of colonial crises. Relatives and friends told him about the rebellion in Madagascar at the war's end and about its cruel repression. As an adolescent at the time of the Indochina war, the young Roussel supported his nation's determination to retain this imperial foothold in Southeast Asia. Then, in 1960, exempted from military service on physical grounds, Roussel came to Algeria as a newly ordained and recently married pastor. The two years he spent in the territory (where his brothers served in the army), left him emotionally as well as physically exhausted.

The parishioners whom Roussel met in Tizi-Ouzou were mostly people of modest means facing terrible pressures from all sides—FLN, OAS, the army and the wealthy settler community. The relatively small number of well-to-do *colons* had in most cases acquired property in France and were thus assured against catastrophe. The prevailing view in the congregation was that no accommodation with the Muslims was possible. During his first meeting with the presbyterial council the new pastor enquired about Muslim prisoners being kept in local wine-cellars. The effect was stunning: total silence. Afterwards, one elder drew Roussel aside and urged him not to get involved in such matters, adding that such an effort would be fruitless.

Roussel soon learned that two of his parishioners were active members of the OAS and that two other families gave shelter to partisans of the right-wing organization. On the other hand, there was the liberal upper-class Mermier family which owned substantial farm property near Algiers and who by themselves contributed four-fifths of the parish's budget! André Mermier was a champion of a radical reform programme which would have included the immediate grant of equal rights to Muslims, the gradual transfer of political power to the majority, and the creation of vast agricultural cooperatives jointly operated by Muslims and Europeans. This liberal outlook made Mermier the target not only of the OAS but even more of the FLN which was determined to subvert all attempts at reform.

His responsibilities took Bernard Roussel on a regular basis up through the high plateau east and south of Algiers to visit what had once been a series of prosperous farm communities. The settlers had come from the Hautes-Alpes department following the nineteenth-century famine there or from Alsace following the German annexation in 1871. Many had left for France at the time of the Sétif disturbances in 1945; those who remained felt a visceral attachment to the land. Roussel understood this passion and knew that few in France recognized or appreciated it. He knew, too, that this land had been seized from Arab tribes and that the memory of this dispossession played a key role in the current conflict. While travelling around his parish, Roussel often stopped over at the Rolland Mission at Tizi-Ouzou. He was much impressed by the local missionary Roby Bois who used experiments in cooperative farming as a means of bringing Muslims and Christians together.

From the beginning, the new pastor tried his best to understand the mindset of the various groups inside Algeria's Protestant community. He had a number of rewarding conversations with the president of the Algerian synod, Pastor Chatoney (whose memoirs he began to record years later as part of a never finished effort to put together an account of the experiences of the last generation of that community in Algeria). Chatoney told Roussel about the antisemitic rioting he had seen in 1936. He reminded his young colleague that many members of the European minority had fought with the Free French in Italy and in France in 1944 and felt they should be recognized as partners in liberation, not reactionary *colons*.

Arriving at a time when the OAS was beginning its ruthless campaign to keep Algeria French, Roussel did his best to sympathize with those holding diametrically opposed opinions. When he heard army officers defending the use of torture, he remembered listening to accounts of the slitting of settlers' throats at the beginning of the insurrection. Yet he also learned that some young settlers had joined the FLN. Roussel confesses to having experienced some of this ambiguity himself. He had been forbidden to visit the marginally orthodox Georges Tartar, pastor of Boufarik, who campaigned to convert Muslims, developed a syncretic theology designed to bring Christians and Muslims together, and passionately supported the fraternization policy that he saw to be the political complement of this process. Nonetheless, Roussel admired this spiritually eccentric confrere and condemned his own church for failing to use Tartar's creative energy. At the same time, Roussel felt admiration for Protestants who sheltered FLN supporters and was highly critical of military chaplains who seemed all too anxious to defend the army even when it abused its authority.

What frustrated Roussel above all during his stay in Algeria was the refusal of his co-religionists to face up to their internal divisions and debate them openly instead of sacrificing spiritual openness and truth in the name of church unity. Nor was the pastor of Hussein-Bey impressed by efforts at reconciliation made by Marc Boegner during what he dismissed as show visits to Algeria during the latter stages of the war.

Notes

1 REF, 20 February 1960.

2 REF, 6 February 1960.

3 CN, 4 February 1960.

4 Schmidt, *En ces temps de malheur*, p. 102.

5 Soustelle, *Vingt-huit années de gaullisme* (Paris: La Table Ronde, 1968), pp. 187-188.

6 Charles de Gaulle, *Mémoires d'espoir* in *L'esprit de la Ve République* (Paris: Plon, 1994), p. 73.

7 REF, 13 February 1960.

8 REF, 27 February 1960.

9 LAP, February 1960.

10 REF, 2 April 1960.

11 Michel Philibert, "Pour une doctrine pénitentiaire," RCS, March/April 1960, pp. 145-154.

12 REF, 5 March 1960.

13 REF, 18 June 1960.

14 Henri Roser, "Manifestations pour l'Algérie à partir de 1960," (Paris: Cahiers de la Reconciliation, June 1977), p. 21.

15 Ibid., p. 23.

16 Ibid., p. 25.

17 François Coulet, *Vertu des temps difficiles* (Paris: Plon, 1967).

18 *Foi and Vie* (May/June 1963), p. 139.

19 REF, 25 June 1960.

20 CN, 7 July 1960.

21 *Plan d'étude sur l'Église et le problème algérien à l'usage de l'Église Reformée de France* (Paris: Conseil National de l'ERF, 1960), Preface, p. 3.

22 TFJ, June 1960.

23 Soustelle, *Le chemin de la paix* (Paris: Centre d'information sur les problèmes de l'Algérie de du Sahara, 1960), p. 39.

24 Soustelle, *Après l'échec du sommet: l'Algérie et l'Ouest. Conférence prononcée par Jacques Soustelle, ancien ministre délégué auprès du Premier Ministre, le jeudi 2 juin 1960 au Théâtre des Ambassadeurs sous les auspices des Conférences des Ambassadeurs* (Paris: Imprimerie de la Presse, 1960).

25 Soustelle, *L'Algérie à la normande* (Paris: Vérités sur l'Algérie et le Sahara, 15 juillet 1960), p. 1.

26 OURS, "52eme congrès national SFIO," 1 July.

27 *Le Monde*, 6 September 1960.

28 CN, 22 September 1960.

29 REF, 6 August, 20 August, 27 August, 3 September 1960.

30 REF, 17 September 1960.

31 REF, 15 October 1960.

32 REF, 24 September 1960.

33 REF, 1 October 1960.

34 REF, 15 October 1960.

35 TFJ, September/October 1960.

36 REF, 17 September 1960.

37 *Plan d'étude sur l'Église et le problème algérien à l'usage de l'Église Réformée de France* (Paris: Conseil National de l'Église Réformée de France, October 1960).

38 Ibid., p. 7.

39 "Rapport du président Marc Boegner," in *Actes de la Xeme Assemblée générale du Protestantisme Français, Foi et Vie*,January/February 1961, p. 23.

40 Georges Casalis, "Les tâches d'avenir des Églises Protestantes en France," Ibid., p. 89.

41 "Déclaration sur l'Algérie," Ibid., p. 133.

42 Ibid., p. 134.

43 SEM, December 1960/January 1961.

44 Ref, 5 November 1960.

45 CN, 24 November 1960.

46 ACIM, Jacques Beaumont to Conseil de la CIMADE, 21 December 1960.

47 ACIM. "A year of CIMADE work in Algeria. Report given at the synod of the French Reformed Church in Algeria, November 1960," English version forwarded to World Council of Churches in Geneva.

48 What follows concerning Mireille Desrez's activities is based on a taped conversation with her in Paris on 27 October 1994.

49 ACIM, "Extraits d'un projet d'ouvrage non-publié redigé par le capitaine Eoche-Duval, chef de SAS dans le département de Médéa, signé Limoges le 4 mai 1981."

50 The account of Pastor Roussel's experiences in Algeria is based on a taped interview in Paris on 27 May 1994.

Elisabeth Schmidt
(Courtesy Dr. Simone Schmidt)

CHAPTER EIGHT

1961: PUTTING PEACEMAKERS TO THE TEST

To prepare the largest possible majority for the "yes" vote in the 8 January 1961 referendum in Algeria, the territory's tiny group of European liberals worked hand-in-hand with Muslims as well as with de Gaulle's agents Morin and the Protestant Coulet.

On the eve of the referendum, two team-workers at the Clos Salembier hostel in Algiers, Denise Duboscq and Pierrette Faivre, wrote to Jacques Beaumont and the CIMADE executive in Paris.[1] They had stayed inside their quarters during the December rioting in their district, they reported, doing their best to maintain a strictly neutral attitude as Muslim and European crowds fought in the streets outside. Afterwards, when they asked what had provoked the cries of "Algérie musulmane!" and "FLN vaincra!," their Muslim friends had told them they had listened too long to European students crying out "Algérie française!" by day and night.

The street fighting of December had clearly widened the gulf between Algeria's two communities, the women went on to report. For most Muslims, the referendum was too late in coming; substantial abstentions were thus expected; if the youth were intoxicated, it was because the franchise had at last been granted them. The Europeans, meanwhile, were in a bitter and equally volatile mood.

Regular contributors to *Réforme* revealed their voting intentions as the referendum deadline approached. Roger Mehl indicated his reluctant commitment to the "yes" side;[2] André Philip, true to his reputation as a free if somewhat cantankerous spirit, rejected both "yes" and "no" options, indicating that, to gain his affirmative vote, de Gaulle would have to offer a specific negotiating position on Algeria before 8 January or at least to release Ben Bella and punish the paratroopers who had fired on Muslim demonstrators in Algiers in December.[3]

René Courtin, who was at the time presiding over the French chapter of the *Mouvement européen*, was resolutely committed to the "no" campaign. He was challenged in this by the Protestant diplomat René Massigli who had resigned from the Vichy administration to serve de Gaulle and Free France during the war. Massigli suggested that Courtin's opposition was motivated by a refusal to accept the idea of Algerian self-determination. A massive "yes" vote, in Massigli's view, would end FLN speculation about France's intentions and allow the president to move towards a liberal, pragmatic, solution in

Algeria while containing both Ultras and extreme Algerian nationalists.[4]

In explaining his decision to vote "yes," editor Finet conceded to the readers of *Réforme* that he was influenced in part by the tradition of his Huguenot forebears. As a Christian, he would cast his ballot in favour of maintaining peaceful relations between Algeria's two communities even in the face of evidence that the myth of fraternization was now dead. Tragically, 9,000,000 Muslims had once longed to be fully French only to discover that this passion was not reciprocated. Meanwhile the zeal to remain French among Algeria's Europeans was, alas, based on nothing more than the impulse of their chromosomes! Unfortunately, French and Algerian nationalisms were now both driven by visceral feeling. Only de Gaulle seemed capable of inspiring in both groups a commitment to rise above the passions that divided them.

Elie-Georges Berreby, a *pied-noir* who had contributed a number of articles to *Réforme* during the conflict, took exception to the tendency of the French press to characterize the European community as uniformly committed either to the Ultra or the *activistes'* cause when in fact so many were, like himself, supporters of the kind of genuine integration proposed by Maurice Viollette in 1935. As Berreby saw it, the indigenous population of Algeria which had heretofore had no fatherland of its own had been seeking to be part of France. If denied this option, it would surely find its own *patrie*.

Like others on both ends of the political spectrum, Jacques Soustelle denounced the referendum as a thinly disguised plebiscite which de Gaulle was bound to win, not because of the merit of the question put before the electorate but because the president had threatened to resign if the "yes" side did not win.[5]

When it was announced, the anticipated massive victory for the "yes" in metropolitan France was balanced by an overwhelming rejection on the part of the *pieds-noirs*; and a "yes" vote by Algeria's Muslims was in large measure cancelled out by substantial abstentions in response to an FLN boycott.

The co-editors of *Tant qu'il fait jour* were understandably bitter at the referendum result. Philippe Brissaud suggested that the victory of the "yes" left everyone confused and disoriented. The Muslim majority was now uncertain about where France was headed. The European minority was in anguish and the army was deeply divided. The "providential opportunity" opened up in May 1958 had been squandered. What lay ahead was the prospect of a totalitarian regime in Algeria accompanied by the kind of "Great Fear" which had swept over France in 1789.[6]

Jacques Soustelle pointed out that, although Gaullists saw the triumph of the "yes" side as a vindication of the president's Algerian policy, only 39.14 percent of those voting in the territory had supported the affirmative option and the "no" had prevailed in all of Algeria's urban centres.[7]

Following the referendum and in anticipation of what they assumed to be de Gaulle's intention to "liquidate" the Algerian problem by granting the territory its independence, the Ultra elements, led by Jean-Jacques Susini and Pierre Lagaillarde and linked to Salan in Spain, came together to form the *Organization armée secrète* (OAS). Its sole purpose was to coordinate military and civilian efforts on both sides of the Mediterranean to keep Algeria French. Tracts signed OAS began to circulate at the end of February 1961.

Tensions were immediately heightened. The leadership of French army units in Algeria, increasingly restless at what they saw to be a hopeless battle and therefore more and more vulnerable to OAS propaganda, were purged. The recommendation had come from François Coulet, one of the few intimates of de Gaulle able to suggest such action and to name names. In proposing as Salan's replacement the former commando leader General Gambiez, Coulet confided to his hero: "Do you know, *mon général*, why you don't want Gambier? ... Because he was a partisan of French Algeria. But I, too, was for French Algeria, *mon général*. ... And I, too, Coulet. I was once for French Algeria too! de Gaulle replied."[8]

Meeting in the wake of the 8 January referendum, the Algerian Protestant study group offered its full support to immediate negotiations with the FLN. It urged Christians in Algeria to take the lead in furthering collaboration with the Muslim majority in shaping the territory's future. Such clear signals would help isolate those Europeans who were intractably opposed to Algerian independence. They would also make the possibility of a military coup or of civil war far less likely.

While pressing the case for peace through negotiation, the study group suggested that third-party intervention might help prevent a mass exodus of the European minority. Multinational rather than purely French aid would be required to help Algerian reconstruction including French and Algerian exploitation of the promising energy resources in the Sahara.

This bold declaration of principle was signed by a remarkable group of Protestant luminaries, not all of whom were on the Left: Henri Burgelin, René Courtin, Georges Casalis, Jacques Maury, André Philip, Etienne Trocmé and Maurice Voge.[9]

Taking an even more radical tack, beginning in mid-February Jan Czarnecki published a series of articles in *Cité nouvelle*, praising in advance the new Algeria which would follow independence. He foresaw an Algeria at once Muslim and secular in which women would achieve equality with men and in which the new nation, through enlightened agricultural reform, would move peaceably to socialism. Czarnecki conceded that this glowing future would be balanced by the grim fate of most "poor whites" who would no doubt lose everything in the transition to independence.[10]

As the prospect of negotiations grew closer amid rumours of the FLN's blueprint for an independent Algeria, Jacques Soustelle published an alarming scenario of an Algeria under a GPRA government. Ethnic groups would be treated differently according to a hierarchically designed scheme; it would grant rights and privileges on a flexible scale with Jews, seen by the nationalists as traitors to the Arab world, granted absolutely no guaranteed rights.[11]

Rumours of diplomatic moves brought champions of French Algeria to meet twice-weekly in Paris to frustrate what they saw as de Gaulle's readiness to abandon their cause. Jacques Soustelle, Robert Lacoste, Max Lejeune, and Georges Bidault were joined in these talks by former generals Maurice Challe and André Zeller. The military men involved were motivated in part at least by a sense of obligation to the 200,000 Muslims who had worn French uniforms.

An effective challenge depended on the willingness of French army units in Algeria to join their officers in defying the president. The possibility of just such a mutinous disposition was provoked by the government's proclamation of a unilateral truce in the field. Although not made public until June, the government's intentions were clear, creating a dramatically altered set of circumstances. The FLN was reinvigorated, thousands of *harkis* (Muslim auxiliary troops) deserted, and French army morale plummeted.

In this situation, a conspiracy became a significant reality. The general's "eyes and ears" in Algiers, François Coulet, warned the president that a serious challenge to the regime was in the offing. Throughout March, "the soviet of Colonels" (Colonels Argout, Lecheroy and Godard) was created and plans for a putsch made more concrete. When, on 31 March, it was announced that the scheduled preliminary talks between Paris and the FLN had been put off, the plotters decided to move.

The immediate cause of the insurrection was a public pronouncement on Algeria made by President de Gaulle on 11 April which was designed to revive the chance of negotiation. At a press conference, the general declared that "France has no interest in maintaining under her law and dependency an Algeria which chooses another road." He said he was personally convinced that Algerians would opt to be part of a sovereign state and then he added provocatively that whatever others might think in the matter, decolonization was in France's as well as Algeria's interest

Jacques Soustelle dismissed the president's 11 April press conference with utter contempt. France was now showing herself as neither good, nor great, nor generous.[12] The editors of *Tant qu'il fait jour*, in which this piece appeared, added an even more biting comment: "One can't help leaping up in protest after hearing so many impressive lies, offered as usual with the same majestic self-assurance."

The president's declaration brought General Challe (who had until then hesitated to commit himself) to decide to use the full power of the French military to crush the FLN. He saw this as a clearly manageable assignment which would be followed by the welcome recall of 200,000 troops. Such a redeployment he thought would surely win metropolitan support for the conspiracy. The plotters took for granted, quite wrongly as it turned out, that the rank-and-file would remain passive as the putsch took place.

The subversive operation was launched on 21 April and achieved an apparently immediate and total success. Within twenty-four hours, the strategic core of Algiers was seized and many of de Gaulle's key civil and military aides were arrested or otherwise neutralized. The triumphant plotters proclaimed that those who had betrayed French Algeria would be tried for crimes against the state. The overall collapse of support for legitimate authority on which the conspirators had counted did not occur, however; the air and naval commanders remained loyal to the regime, as did the civil administration in Algiers.

De Gaulle's reaction was swift. Louis Joxe and General Olié, chief of the general staff, were despatched to the scene. Joxe carried with him plenipotentiary authority to act in the name of the state while Olié was instructed to replace Gambier as commander-in-chief, Algeria.

In Algiers, the OAS ruled the streets. They released right-wing extremists who had been jailed, created an armed militia, and made their own list of those to be arrested, including François Coulet and the executive of the *Association de soutien au général de Gaulle*.

Returning to Paris on 23 April, Joxe reported immediately to de Gaulle. After describing the divisions within the officer class in Algeria and the rising tensions between professional soldiers and conscripts, he reassured the president of the unwavering loyalty of the civil administration and its willingness to help frustrate the conspiracy.

That same evening, appearing in full-dress uniform, the president of the Republic addressed metropolitan France by television and the army in

Algeria by radio. He denounced the putsch and ridiculed its leaders. They comprised a quartet of aging generals whose competence was limited and who were out of touch with the mood of the nation. Their reckless enterprise had risked undermining the state and compromising France's international prestige as well as her role in Africa's future. The rebels would be duly punished, de Gaulle promised. Soldiers serving under their command were instructed to obey none of their insubordinate officers' commands. For the moment, however, panic took hold of Paris as the capital awaited an attack by troops loyal to the rebels. Volunteers mobilized across the city to do battle to save the Republic. The government decreed a state of emergency early that same day. Furthermore, on 24 April, Article 16 of the Constitution was invoked, which allowed for the arrest and detention of those suspected of subversive activity.

On the same day, five representatives of the *Fédé* including Jacques Maury met in emergency session and drafted a text of unconditional support to de Gaulle, asking the president what they might do to help defend the Republic. This initiative provoked criticism from a few student groups. Some felt that the Protestant student federation should remain strictly apolitical. Others were worried that giving de Gaulle a free hand to deal with the insurgents during the crisis might imply a willingness to sacrifice the interests of the European minority in Algeria.[13]

In Algiers, the rebel generals, joined by Salan who had arrived from Madrid, issued a revolutionary manifesto, ordering the mobilization of eight classes of *pieds-noirs* and urging the citizenry at large to take up arms in defense of French Algeria. Happily for the regime, the support the mutineers had hoped to generate did not materialize.

Within four days of its inception the insurrection was over. François Coulet reoccupied his office in the Government-General building and phoned Paris to announce that the putsch had been defeated. The relentless campaign to liquidate the OAS and its supporters led to hundreds of arrests, often followed by consignment to detention camps. Following the failed putsch, these men and their families were, temporarily at least, in some jeopardy.

In May, to provide the detainees and their relatives with spiritual as well as financial support, a group of conservative academics founded the *Secours populaire par l'Entraide et la Solidarité* (SPES). Several hundred well-known professors joined this ad hoc relief organization including two right-wing Protestants: Pierre Grosclaude and René Courtin, as well as Georgette Soustelle, the Catholic wife of the former governor of Algeria and an ethnologist in her own right. SPES published an appeal on behalf of the detainees in the right-wing weekly press as well as in several mainstream dailies. By the end of November, some 25,000,000 francs had been collected and distributed to those being held and to their families.

Not surprisingly, the appeal puzzled a number of potential Protestant donors. A Mme Seidenbinder from the Ardèche department wrote to Jacques Beaumont for advice. The secretary-general urged her to reject the appeal. Today's so-called victims had little call upon our conscience, he wrote, given the much greater suffering they had inflicted on Algerians for the last seven years. CIMADE was ready as always to offer help in particularly needy cases, but most of the internees were undoubtedly receiving sufficient funds from anonymous donors, quite apart from the current appeal. Beaumont added that those who now seemed so preoccupied with the plight of these activists had shown no concern for the massive numbers of refugees flooding into France from Algeria for whom CIMADE was trying to organize both relief and integration into a different culture.[14]

In the wake of the failed putsch, *Réforme* devoted its entire 29 April issue to the event. Under the general heading, "After the madness in Algeria, let's keep our heads!," five prominent Protestant intellectuals and a soldier turned army chaplain offered their reflections. The weekly's editor, Albert Finet, expressed some compassion for the officers who had staged the revolt, some of whom he knew personally. However, they had clearly committed themselves to a lost cause and one which had no justification. Even more seriously, had they triumphed, they would have paved the way for a fascist coup against the Republic. This in turn would have put responsible leaders of opinion in France in the same position faced by honourable German army officers in June 1944, bound by conscience to engage in revolt.[15]

Jacques Ellul agreed that the rebels, by initiating civil conflict, had committed the ultimate political sin. Fortunately, their lack of political acumen prevented their success. As usual, Ellul deplored the deleterious impact of propaganda on the events. France still had a long way to go before attaining the political maturity needed to cope with such crises.

Roland Helminger, a soldier turned chaplain, reported that the young soldiers with whom he had spoken during the crisis had shown an almost universal lack of zeal for the war and were experiencing a profound sense of abandonment. Charles Westphal, the newly selected successor to Marc Boegner as president of the FPF, came to the same conclusion after a visit to Algeria in June. Everyone in the territory felt betrayed or abandoned by metropolitan France.[16]

Jacques Soustelle's public support of the putsch resulted in an arrest order. He fled to Switzerland. There he wrote *L'Espérance trahie*, a bitter indictment of de Gaulle's Algerian policy, presented as a betrayal of the commitment the president had given the *colons* and army men who had brought him to power three years earlier.

The failed putsch of April 1961 produced further tension and alienation between Pastor Elisabeth Schmidt and her congregation in Blida. As the minister saw it, the mindset of her flock had long since been inalterably affected by "the weight of habit, the lack of information and the absence of spiritual connection with the continental French Protestant community or, for that matter, with the rest of the world."[17] Towards the end of 1960, Pastor Schmidt became even more seriously alarmed by the openly expressed hatred for the government in Paris and the candidly voiced desire to see de Gaulle killed. She felt particularly concerned about the outlook of children brought up in this atmosphere and invested a lot of time in the catechizing of teenagers to resist the virulent, frequently racist, propaganda to which they were exposed.

On 22 April, the date the insurrection began, Elisabeth Schmidt took comfort from a discussion with two fellow-Protestants, Bosc, the sub-prefect of Blida, and Poujol, secretary-general of the Médéa prefecture. All three had participated in the Resistance and their shared memories helped strengthen their prayers that the army in their area would stay loyal to de Gaulle.

On the following day, a Sunday, Pastor Schmidt preached a sermon on the words of Matthew 10:28 ("And fear not them that kill the body, but are not able to kill the soul; but rather fear him which is able to destroy both soul and body in hell"). The younger members of the congregation were incensed at what they perceived as an indictment of Challe and his colleagues and left the church. Many of them were later to return, somewhat embarrassed at their own instinctive reaction.

When it became clear that the putsch had failed, the pastor gave credit to the disproportionate number of strategically placed Protestant officials throughout Algeria who had helped ensure its defeat. "People sometimes criticize the Protestant tendency to be rigorous," she wrote in her memoirs. "During periods of extreme gravity, this rigour means that compromise and ambiguity have been rejected and that firm courage prevails. De Gaulle knew this since, during this terrible crisis in Algiers, he was able to count on thirteen Protestant prefects or sub-prefects!"[18] Following the defeat of Challe and his colleagues, Pastor Schmidt visited the detention centres where the rebels were being held. She was quick to note that wherever she went, the once close rapport between the *colons* and the army had turned into mutual antipathy. The small crowd which gathered for the annual Bastille Day celebration in mid-July 1961 was sullen and resentful, a grim harbinger of what was to come.

Between 18 and 21 May, less than a month after the failed putsch, the

SFIO held its annual national convention. Gaston Defferre again urged the party to maintain its vigilant support of de Gaulle on the Algerian question while subjecting the president to appropriate critical scrutiny on all other aspects of his policy. In his most recent pronouncement de Gaulle had talked explicitly about independence for Algeria, something Defferre had not supported earlier. These differences apart, what was becoming increasingly clear (and something which Defferre had long been recommending) was the need for direct negotiations with the GPRA.[19]

Like Defferre, Francis Leenhardt disparaged the views of party members who saw Charles de Gaulle as "a Caesar disposing of supreme power and bent on emptying the Republic of all substance...." We may indeed be living in a *télécratie*, Leenhardt conceded, but those who railed against de Gaulle's use of the extraordinary constitutional powers were not feeling so secure against future putschists that they would wish to see the executive deprived of emergency powers. Comrades needed to remind themselves of the "stubbornly liberal orientation of General de Gaulle and of his determination to decolonize," attitudes made abundantly clear in his speech of 4 November 1960. In fact, Leenhardt suggested, were it not for de Gaulle, France would still be fighting colonial wars in thirteen former African colonies![20]

Like the SFIO, the directors of CIMADE felt the need to reflect on the changed circumstances created by the abortive putsch. At the end of May, the executive committee travelled to Algiers for a three-day discussion with team-workers there. The dialogue ranged from immediate practical problems to reflections on the moral and spiritual challenges which had brought volunteers to Algeria in the first place.[21]

Marguerite Cruse, the nurse who had helped open the dispensary at Sidi-Naamane, stressed the need not to focus on the denunciation of wrongdoing such as torture by French army units. What was needed was an expression of spiritual solidarity with those who had inflicted as well as endured torture. They must never forget that, as Europeans, they must bear their share of responsibility for the injustices at the root of the current conflict. When Muslims told CIMADE workers, as was often the case, that they were "good" French men and women by contrast with their compatriots, they must make clear that all were "accomplices in the sins of the world" (*solidaires du péché de ce monde*).

Finally, the meeting turned to the obvious question given the early likelihood of Algerian independence. Did it make sense to continue simply coping with local crises? Or should CIMADE not turn much of its energies to helping in the long-term reconstruction of a society badly battered by seven years of conflict and a full century of underdevelopment?

Meanwhile, order having been restored in Algeria, de Gaulle had signalled his interest in reopening a dialogue with the FLN. During an 8 May press conference, the president talked of the future relationship between France and Algeria as an "association," a term used in the 1958 constitution to reflect the transformation of former imperial-colonial links. Albert Finet commented that the use of this term in advance of the resumption of talks with the FLN both undermined de Gaulle's bargaining power and offered little or no comfort to the already troubled *colons*. If only the head of state could remember that he was just an ordinary Christian like the rest of us, the editor wrote, he might have shown more compassion and conveyed more hope.[22]

Two weeks later, Finet was more charitable: de Gaulle's decision to declare a unilateral truce on the eve of the Evian meeting was a "generous act" which clearly expressed the president's "will to untie the knot of misunderstanding, bitterness and hatred" which had made dialogue thus far so difficult.[23]

One occasional contributor to *Réforme* felt quite nervous about the coming negotiations. Gérard Israël was concerned about the FLN's definition of the Algerian people. There were clear differences, to begin with, inside the Muslim population; the Kabyles were radically different from Arabs in culture, for instance. The best way of resolving the problem posed by this cultural heterogeneity would be for both parties to agree that Algeria be defined as a secular and democratic state, something which again brought to the fore the need to separate Islamic from secular authority.[24]

On 10 May, the GPRA announced that negotiations with representatives of the French government would begin at Evian ten days later. There the two most vexing problems turned out to be the disposition of the Sahara region and the fate of Algeria's European community. The failure to agree on these and other key issues exasperated de Gaulle who decided at the beginning of June to suspend the talks.

In their zealotry at this stage, some members of the OAS such as Susini conceived of the creation of a separate European state within the existing boundaries of Algeria, a kind of North African apartheid. On 5 July, the FLN organized a peaceful demonstration in Algiers against this partition proposal. The results established conclusively that the city's Muslim population had been won over to the nationalist cause.

French army units now began to depart, many of them full of embittered soldiers who felt that their combat had been in vain. The pacification programme which had at one point seemed so close to success was abandoned and only local combat with the FLN was sustained.

By the end of June, the situation in Algeria, especially in those urban areas with European population concentrations, was deteriorating rapidly. As Jean-Pierre Lumire reported in *Réforme*,[25] OAS partisans were operating, Maoist style, like fish in water within the European community, most of whose young people were *activistes*. Tracts promising severe retribution for any *colons* planning to leave had created an atmosphere of extraordinary intimidation. On the other hand, there was a sudden rush to take courses in Arabic, especially among the less privileged, those with less opportunity to flee. For their part, Muslims were meeting more and more openly to discuss the future. Those whom the authorities had released as a goodwill gesture were showing up at FLN rallies, helping to revive the nationalist organization which had been losing support.

On 4 July, meanwhile, the representatives of the French government and the FLN who had remained in or near Evian agreed that it would be opportune to renew their efforts. On 20 July, Joxe and his colleagues met Krim and the other members of the FLN negotiating team at Lugrin in the mountains above Evian. There were three key issues in contention at Lugrin: the disposition of the Sahara region, the rights of the *pieds-noirs*, and the right of the GPRA to speak for Algeria at large. In the end, none of these issues was resolved and both delegations returned to their superiors for further consultation.

The intermittent and unrewarding efforts to negotiate with the FLN exasperated Protestant defenders of French Algeria. In the June/July issue of *Tant qu'il fait jour*, Philippe Brissaud condemned the "utterly mad path" of de Gaulle's Algerian policy. In part because of this madness, he argued, the Gaullist interlude would surely go down in the records as even worse than the successive ministries of the little lamented Fourth Republic! The head of state was now openly violating Article 16 of the constitution he had helped inspire, resorting to plebescitary dictatorship and "direct democracy" to stay in power. He said special tribunals headed by the general's own appointees were acting outside the written law and with no regard for the Algerian courts and that France's soldiers were being asked to choose between obedience and dishonour. Finally, negotiations were under way between officials of the French state and rebels who were meanwhile engaging in acts of terror.[26]

Writing from Algiers, correspondent Lumire reported a serious deterioration in the situation in August. Members of the *Délégation spéciale* sent to replace the municipal councillors in Algeria had been attacked with plastic bomb devices. Army units were thoroughly demoralized and there was a universal sense of impotence throughout the European civil community. Evidence of panic among the *colons* became clear when Jean Noël, the commissioner charged with overseeing repatriation plans, was overwhelmed by the numbers of men and women he interviewed. The commissioner was particularly frustrated because there were no adequate arrangements in France to resettle those who were to be repatriated.[27]

On 5 August, Louis Joxe, while on a visit to Algiers, was greeted with particular defiance by the OAS which broke into the local radio and television network to invite Algerians to oppose the policy of abandonment which, they alleged, de Gaulle and his agents were promoting. "Ni valise ni cercueil, la patrie et le fusil!" ("Neither suitcase nor shroud! For the fatherland, gun in hand!") cried General Gardy, inspector-general of the Foreign Legion and Salan's delegate in the OAS network.

On 8 September, de Gaulle narrowly missed being assassinated by an OAS squad at the Petit-Clamart in suburban Paris. That evening, Philippe Brissaud, editor of *Tant qu'il fait jour*, was arrested for presumed complicity in the plot. His colleagues declared that, if they were seen as accomplices in the effort to save French Algeria, they would accept such a charge with pride. This provocative stance evoked a furious retort from Roger Mehl, a sociologist who wrote in *Réforme*:

> The recourse to plastic bombs signifies very clearly that certain people in France, as in Algeria, no longer believe in a dialogue either with their government or with their fellow-citizens ... and that, from now on, they count only on panic and terror to influence the course of history in a way which they find acceptable.[28]

S. Montcladi, responding to this letter (which *Tant qu'il fait jour* reprinted), reminded Mehl that it had been de Gaulle who had cut off all communication concerning Algeria through strict government control of the media. This arbitrary interruption of the free and open exchange of information might not excuse the recourse to plastic bombs, but it surely helped explain it.[29]

Released from prison after a six-week detention, an unrepentant Brissaud resumed his indictment of Gaullist policy:

> A system which rewards, consecrates and legitimizes violence by raising the leaders of assassination squads to the dignity of diplomats and government officials, clearly has nothing but disdain for the irrefutable demands of those Algerians who wish only to remain French in the land of their birth.[30]

Brissaud followed up this indictment with an explanation to his readers. He had been arrested because, without his knowledge or consent, he had been chosen as a letter-drop (*boîte aux lettres*) by an organization (OAS) to which he had never belonged.

On 27 September, at a time when France's negotiations with Algerian nationalists were again at an impasse and OAS terrorism was reaching a new intensity, the SFIO summoned an extraordinary national council meeting at Puteaux. Gaston Defferre delivered a harsh verdict concerning de Gaulle's negotiating methods. He warned that, if an accord with the FLN were not soon reached, republican institutions might again be in jeopardy. France's official dealings with Algeria's nationalists were dangerously vacillating, the veteran Socialist argued. Paris tended to refuse outright one day what it was ready a fortnight later to yield. Concessions were being made to the GPRA without reciprocal commitments. There was now a real concern about the fate of the European minority who were no longer designated *Français d'Algérie* but simply *Algériens d'origine européenne*. He thought this clearly reflected a decision to diminish their status as well as their security.

Defferre's outrage over the brutal methods being used by the OAS boiled over during this same address. In a rare outburst, the Protestant Socialist suggested that the party insist that members of the European terrorist organization be "shot, guillotined, or hanged, I'm not sure which would be the best means."[31]

Leenhardt, just returned from Algeria, reported that the army had clearly triumphed in the field. The major current problem was that the European minority was ready to scream in protest at any suggestion of withdrawing any of the 400,000 troops based there; Leenhardt added that it would certainly be unconscionable under existing circumstances to leave the *colons* without adequate protection. Tragically, the administration in Algeria was cut off from the two rival terrorist networks (OAS and FLN) and had virtually no contact even with members of the European community still living there.

Beyond the immediate crisis, Leenhardt foresaw the very real possibility of a *congolisation* of the situation in Algeria and of the simultaneous emergence of fascism in France itself. Given these dangers, he urged his comrades to help organize a *Comité de vigilance républicaine* in every department. Should de Gaulle for one reason or another disappear, they must help form a provisional government to defend the Republic while the president's successor was being elected.

By September, the OAS had driven civil as well as military authorities from Algiers. The official administration (which included Robert Poujol and

André Mermier) took refuge in the nearby Rocher-Noir, an impregnable fortress from which General Ailleret issued a declaration of war against the illicit organization. In November, Salan became the effective leader of the OAS, giving it new prestige and offers of support from a number of eminent metropolitan. These included not only Jean-Marie Le Pen and Georges Bidault but even colleagues of Guy Mollet and Valéry Giscard d'Estaing. A group known as the *Comité de Vincennes* brought together Jacques Soustelle, Robert Lacoste, Georges Bidault, ex-premier Bourgès-Maunoury, Le Pen and Leon Delbècque to sustain Salan's efforts on behalf of French Algeria. Later, on 22 November, it was dissolved for subversive activities.

On 1 November, the anniversary of the 1954 uprising, when an explosive series of popular demonstrations on behalf of the FLN throughout Algeria was anticipated, a discreet understanding was reached at Constantine between the French authorities and the rebel organization in order to prevent the situation from getting out of hand.[32] The intermediaries in arranging this agreement were Protestant. Jean Carbonare, the recently arrived representative in Constantine of CIMADE and the promoter of an ambitious local reforestation programme, put the general secretary of the local prefecture (another Protestant by the name of Massendès) in touch with Si Bachir, a one-time medical student who was in charge of FLN political and military operations in the area. Two secret meetings were held between Massendès and Si Bachir in the apartment of the local Reformed pastor, Moussiegt, who urged moderation on both. In the end, a compromise was reached whereby the FLN would be permitted to have its demonstration provided that it followed a relatively unprovocative itinerary and that it did not display the nationalist flag until the parade had reached a certain part of the city. The resistance of FLN radicals and the local French army commander was overcome and the demonstration went off without a hitch.

Jean Carbonare, the key figure in this mediation, had arrived in the eastern Algerian city that summer. His experience with Muslims from the Constantine area had begun years earlier when he did his best to improve the living conditions of men from the region working in and near Besançon. In Constantine, where he attached himself to the local Methodist church led by the American pastor Aurbakken, he was impressed by the relief work being done by CIMADE and disturbed that this was clearly establishing a morally disadvantageous relationship between Christian donors and Muslim recipients. This unhealthy relationship became particularly unlovely when Muslims who gathered to receive food started bloody disputes to see who could get the most. Jacques Beaumont gave Carbonare carte blanche to remedy the situation. What resulted was a creative improvisation with long-term happy consequences for Algeria. Carbonare launched a reforestation project (*chantier de reboisage*) based on distribution of food in return for labour.[33] At Belkitane, to the southeast of Constantine, Muslims were given a pick and shovel and directed to the planting of masses of seedlings in an area where mature trees would help substantially in the defense of the soil against the encroaching desert. Ten days work earned each labourer a month's supply of food for a family of five. With the aid of substantial funds from the American Methodist Church and with the support of a number of American Mennonite volunteers known as "Pax Boys," the project was soon a going concern.

The Belkitane project quickly mushroomed. Before long, some 3,000 Muslims were engaged in tree-planting, many of them sporting a cap with the CIMADE logo. From the beginning, Carbonare was determined that this reforestation scheme be seen as complementary to the reforming aims of the Delouvrier administration in Algiers. In fact, the pacifist deputy of Beaumont was anxious that the government be given full credit for whatever creative steps CIMADE was able to take. When he received a shipment of farm tractors provided by the English relief agency OXFAM, Carbonare asked that a government official be present to receive the machines and then transmit the keys to those who would be using the equipment. The administration, as he saw it, should be "validated" when such forward-looking action was taken; when the government was lax, on the other hand, it should be challenged by groups such as CIMADE.

Carbonare stayed in Constantine through the grim months leading to the peace talks at Evian and afterwards. He respected the good intentions of many of the SAS officers he met who were trying their best to bring progressive changes to Muslim communities.

In Paris, meanwhile, the government was increasingly concerned that resuming the Lugrin talks would be disadvantageous as long as the OAS controlled much of European Algeria. In order to reverse this psychological disadvantage as well as to encourage the possibility of long term ethnic coexistence in Algeria, a group known as the *Mouvement pour la Communauté* (soon to be rebaptized *Mouvement pour la Coopération*) was created. On 13 November, this newly founded organization plastered posters on the walls of Algeria's major cities with slogans of hope including: "Ni la valise ni le cercueil, mais la coopération" (literally: "Neither suitcase nor casket but cooperation").

The wall posters had a dramatic impact. For the moment, the psychological initiative seemed to pass from the OAS to the partisans of peaceful coexistence. In the end, however, those who had championed this cause with slogans had no choice but to engage in real combat with Salan's men. Ironically, out of this heroic commitment to ethnic harmony came something far from liberal—the creation by the government in Paris of a corps of professionally trained counter-terrorists, nicknamed "Les Barbouzes," whose purpose was to liquidate the OAS but whose methods rivalled those of their target. The battle for Algeria began to take on a desperately murderous quality. The triangular combat among OAS, FLN and *barbouzes* threatened a whirlwind of violence which could end only in anarchy.

As the *barbouzes* applied their own ruthless methods, including torture, in an effort to stamp out the OAS, General Salan, the head of the outlawed organization, sent letters of protest to France's leading newspaper editors. Albert Finet, on behalf of *Réforme*, could not refrain from irony. "One might note that, in M. Salan's case, the rebel has forgotten the general who, together with his colleagues, denied all responsibility in the case of a certain Alleg, a certain Audin, and a certain Djamila Boupacha (a young Muslim killed by the French army").[34]

Paul Adeline, who had lived for much of his life in Algeria, was less categorical. He condemned those "pious metropolitan apostles" who denounced the OAS without acknowledging that, like the FLN, its supporters had recourse to violence in what they sincerely believed to be the cause of freedom. Adeline perceived the OAS as simply a fragment of a Europe-wide right-wing conspiracy which had its origin in the ideological battles which followed the French Revolution and which included survivors of Nazi Germany currently working as special agents in Nasser's Egypt.[35]

The ethical concerns which had troubled a number of French Protestants since the beginning of the conflict found increasingly anguished expression during 1961. The question of conscientious objection, for instance, continued to preoccupy some of them into the sixth year of the war. A series of court cases in Toulouse, Lille and Metz in 1961 led to prison terms for Catholic as well as Protestant soldiers who refused to serve in Algeria. The normal punishment meted out for refusal to bear arms was a two-year term—although there were instances where fifteen years imprisonment was deemed necessary.

Georges Richard-Morand reminded readers of *Réforme* in March 1961 that, ever since 1928, the French Protestant Federation had been requesting the government to introduce legislation allowing for a form of civic service for those unwilling to bear arms. Such legislation was on the statute books of most modern democracies. The correspondent noted that a bill authorizing such an arrangement had been submitted to the National Assembly in 1952 and deplored the failure of successive ministries to take it up.[36]

Richard-Morand addressed the same issue in September following the distribution of pamphlets supporting the right of objectors. The leaflet distributors, calling themselves "a peace brigade," were a mixed group of young people, Catholic, agnostic, and Protestant . They had held a three-day fast on international ground in front of the UNESCO building on the right bank of the Seine. Among activities which the young protesters were willing to undertake in lieu of military action was the integration back into civilian life of the *harkis* (Muslim volunteers in the French army). Following their protest, the demonstrators were hauled off to the local police station.[37]

The champions of conscientious objection did not allow the issue to die. They formed an organization known as *Action civique non-violente* which was backed by more than 200 well-known personalities. When their pamphlets were seen as inciting those already in uniform to desert, four representatives of the *Action civique* were brought to trial at Carpentras in the south of France on 22 November.

Pastor André Trocmé spoke grandiloquently on behalf of the defendants:

> They were attempting to imitate Christ.... Their action, seen today as reprehensible, will be regarded as virtuous tomorrow.... Together with several other pastors of the Reformed Church, I have signed "*L'appel aux jeunes*" which was the basis of the incriminating charge; so all of us should also be pursued.[38]

Reporting on the case, the correspondent of *Réforme* remarked that the presiding judge was eminently fair. In the absence of a law explicitly defining the actions of the group of protesters as illegal, the verdict exculpating the accused was not hard for him to reach.[39]

In October 1961, the council of the FPF met to review the worsening situation of the European community in Algeria. Protestants living in Algeria were urged to persevere in their Christian witness by staying. At the same time, members of metropolitan congregations were exhorted to offer a fraternal welcome to those who felt compelled to flee. Above all, an effort must be made to find jobs and housing for those who were uprooted.[40]

While Protestant officialdom began to shift its thoughts towards the moral and spiritual challenges which peace would bring, the army's psychological warfare remained a constant if not obsessive preoccupation of a number of concerned Protestants. In the fall issue of *Christianisme social*, Michel Philibert, a professor of philosophy at the University of Grenoble, published a thoughtful essay on the theme.[41]

The professor's essay ultimately derived from a resolution passed by the Algerian Reformed synod in December 1958 urging that a full scholarly analysis of the relationship between Christianity and Marxism be undertaken with special attention to the challenge posed to Christians by the Maoist concept of revolutionary warfare. Philibert begins by reminding his readers of the gulf between the French nation and its armed forces which opened in 1940 and was widened in Indochina when "the nation committed itself to peace while committing the army to war...." This tension between France and her military had increased even more as a result of the Algerian conflict, during which "the government had plunged both army and nation into a war which it has neither proclaimed nor explained nor effectively conducted because it has not thought it out."[42]

Successive ministries had not understood that, among other causes, the rebellion of 1954 had had its origin in the humiliation of a proud people fed up with being deceived by false promises and electoral fraud, wounded both in flesh and spirit by the terrible repression following Sétif. The same ministries had denied integration when the Muslims demanded it and then insisted on it when it was no longer timely. They had clouded over the army's methods, tolerating torture, summary executions, destruction of vital resources and displacement of population. At the same time they proceeded apace with efforts to modernize, fraternize and uplift, not even recognizing the contradictions between one set of policies and the other. This discredited the nation's intentions and discouraged those who were trying in disinterested ways to bring about reform. All of this had forced the army to improvise its own strategy and then to invent a justification for its implementation.

The veterans of Vietnam had correctly understood that the FLN was using Mao's methods. They were seriously mistaken, however, in their assumption that the rebellion of 1954 had been masterminded in Peking or Moscow as part of a world-wide conspiracy. Quite apart from this error, it was psychologically far more exalting for these men to situate the Algerian war in this abstract Marxist framework than to regard it as a rearguard action designed to preserve a retrograde European minority in its privileges and illusions.

The consequences of these misperceptions, Philibert pursued, had been serious from the military perspective. They had also failed in terms of the recourse to propaganda. Mao had taught that military victory was worthless without a psychological conversion in the population but the zealotry of French efforts at political re-education with all its accompanying brutality and injustice had proved to be unavailing. Meanwhile the contention that the war in Algeria was a battle against communism had neutralized (when it had not silenced) public opinion. Those who had ventured to raise their voices against torture (including the highest-ranking ecclesiastical authorities) had been vilified as traitors. In the end, because of the traumatic rift between army and nation, France had teetered on the brink of civil war. Partisans of desertion on the one hand and of coup d'états on the other had risked tearing the nation apart.

Happily, Philibert observed, the loyalty of the rank and file and the clear support of French public opinion for Algeria's self-determination had averted internecine conflict, for the moment at least. But it was vital in the professor's view that the dialogue between army and nation resume. The churches had a clear obligation in this regard since they were agents of reconciliation and well suited to urge an end to mutual vilification by *insoumis* and *activistes* and by all other groups which had consumed so much of the nation's energies in fratricidal debate.

Professor Philibert's focus was on the perverse and ineffectual application of Maoist tactics in a counter-revolutionary cause. In the fall of 1961, French Protestants and their fellow-citizens alike were brought face to face with another facet of this vicious dialectic. That was when the FLN brought its terrorist tactics to France and the Paris police responded against the roughly 400,000 Algerians then living in the *métropole*, roughly half of them in the Paris area.

On 15 March, Jacques Beaumont sent a confidential memorandum to Marc Boegner detailing evidence of police torture of forty-two Muslims.[43] In some cases, relatives had written to describe arbitrary arrests and subsequent beating; in other instances, there were medical diagnoses of trauma. The secretary-general of CIMADE indicated that the officers of the law, under the direction of Prefect of Police Maurice Papon were using a wide variety of tortures to extract confessions from alleged FLN sympathizers in a campaign to destroy the Front's French network. *Harkis* (who, as volunteer auxiliary soldiers fighting alongside the army in Algeria had every reason to hate and be hated by partisans of the Liberation Front) were being used to assist in this repressive activity following an absurdly inadequate two-week training period. Recently, a number of Algerians had disappeared from their living quarters without a trace. There had been cases of suicide, no doubt brought on by the methods employed by Papon and his men.

Beaumont suggested two responses to this officially sanctioned brutality. The auxiliary police force made up of *harkis* should be disbanded and interpreters added to the regular constabulary and public attention should be drawn to the officially sanctioned use of torture against people who were, after all, French citizens.

To deal with the immediate pressure put on its own relief work by the police harassment of Algerians, CIMADE created a special North African Service in February. Étienne Keller and Jacqueline Peyron were put in charge of this operation which included welcoming injured Muslims at headquarters, paying visits to the *centre de triage* at Vincennes where Algerians were interrogated, and comforting families of those arrested.

In August and September, sixteen Paris policemen were killed by FLN terrorists in Paris and forty-five others wounded. Police retaliation was swift and grim. Jacqueline Peyron wrote Pastor Boegner on 9 October detailing new cases of gratuitous attacks on unarmed Algerians, declaring: "It seems useless to try to intervene on behalf of these Muslims at the present time given the feelings of hatred and vengefulness which prevail at the Prefecture of Police and the Interior Ministry at all levels."[44] Algerians were not of course entirely without support apart from CIMADE and other relief agencies. Legal help was available from a fairly wide variety of sources. Among the most dedicated of these was Jean-Jacques de Félice, scion of a family which had given France a number of distinguished pastors and historians. He was committed to doing what he could, not just as a Protestant but as vice-president of the *Ligue des Droits de l'Homme* and as a convinced advocate of de-colonization. De Félice was deeply affected by the murder of a Muslim friend and colleague Ould Aoudia. He paid regular visits to the notorious prison at Fresnes on the outskirts of Paris where many Muslims were detained and travelled frequently to Algeria to talk to men condemned to death. Like Etienne Mathiot, whom he had defended in 1958, de Félice was convinced that the only solution to the conflict and to the injustice which had provoked it, was through the practice of absolute non-violence: "As believers we felt intimately linked to the tortured, the condemned, the prisoners and the pursued; but our ideas kept us at a distance from those who saw in "liberating" violence the solution to all injustices."[45]

The tensions in Paris between police and Algerians came to a head after 3 October when Papon imposed a discriminatory curfew. Algerians were forbidden to circulate publicly between 8 p.m. and 5:30 a.m. except with special authorization; they were urged to move about singly rather than in groups and cafés catering to Muslims were ordered to close at 7 p.m.

To protest, the French Federation of the FLN organized a peaceful demonstration for the evening of 17 October. Some 30,000 responded, streaming down towards the *grands boulevards*, the major arteries of downtown Paris, from outlying working class suburbs early in the evening of the appointed day.

Soon after the march started, the police radio announced that ten policemen had been killed at the Rond-Point of the Défense, a complex of

high-rise buildings recently built out along the western axis of the Champs-
Elysées. In fact, ten policemen had been wounded and none killed in the many
melees which followed but this provocative news-flash produced what turned
out to be a night-long carnage. Assisted by *harki* auxiliaries, the police moved
in on bands of marchers at various points throughout Paris, shooting,
strangling, and drowning 200 unarmed demonstrators. Fifty alone were shot
in cold blood in the courtyard of the Prefecture of Police. Bodies tossed into
the Seine showed up over the next several days. Some 11,000 demonstrators
were arrested and carried off to the *centre de triage* where their papers were
burned or confiscated. Thousands of those arrested were deported to Algeria
and the notorious resettlement camps controlled by the army.

The official casualty list reporting three dead and sixty-four wounded
and 11,538 arrested was later amended to concede that 140 had in fact been
killed. According to FLN calculations, some 200 had been murdered and 400
others had disappeared.[46]

On 20 October, the council of CIMADE came together to discuss the
massacre and to consider how best to respond to it. Jacques Beaumont wrote
at the time to one of his colleagues: "I leave unspoken the human, social and
family implications of the 17 October in order to try to think ahead to those
consequences which will affect our hopes for cooperation and reconciliation
which now, more than ever, will require a miracle."[47] Following the council
meeting, Marc Boegner wrote to Papon, requesting a freer and fuller access for
CIMADE to the detention centre at Vincennes and other holding areas.[48]

Having decided that, given its own reputation as biased in favour of the
FLN, it would be impolitic to make a public protest against the police, the
council of CIMADE wrote urging President Westphal of the FPF to issue a
press release, if possible in concert with the cardinal-archbishop of Paris and
the city's chief rabbi. The executive of the relief organization also exhorted
the *Fédé* and the *Alliance des Equipes unionistes* to join in denouncing police
repression.

In response, the FPF issued a press release on 27 October declaring
that, however revolting the FLN terrorist attacks had been, the inhuman
treatment to which Algerian demonstrators had been subjected had provoked
widespread indignation and anguish. Westphal had meanwhile expressed
these feelings directly to Papon on 14 November. The response of the prefect
of police was predictably terse: Papon made a point of chiding the leader of the
Protestant churches for not having come forward earlier when FLN terrorists
were killing his men.[49]

On 23 October the CIMADE council, meeting with what was in some
ways its counterpart, the Catholic *Mission de Fraternité*, helped turn the

protest at Papon's initiative into an expression of ecumenical solidarity. Together, the two bodies went so far as to declare that "the government is in the process of favouring the development of fascism in the population."[50] Three days later, Papon forbade holding a meeting called to denounce violence and racism and promote peace.

At the end of the month, Justice Minister Roger Frey, under considerable pressure, agreed to the naming of a parliamentary committee to look into the events of 17 October. Nothing came of this investigation, which ended up without passing judgment on the police action.

Bernard Tricot, who was in President de Gaulle's confidence with regard to Algeria, was more sympathetic. He received Philippe Jordan of CIMADE following the launching of a hunger strike by Muslim prisoners in Paris and Lyon. Jordan reported that the physical condition of many of the prisoners was deteriorating rapidly and that every effort should be made to end the strike and to stop the discriminatory treatment against those being held in jail solely for political reasons, treatment which had helped to precipitate the strike. Tricot promised to do what he could.

Under these circumstances, CIMADE had no choice but to proceed as best it could to console and comfort. The trust shown the organization by Muslims was, if anything, reinforced in this grim situation. Algerian detainees in the camp at Larzac forwarded to Boegner early in November a description of the "concentration camp atmosphere" in which they were held.[51]

If CIMADE was outraged by the police treatment of Muslims on 17 October, right-wing Protestants were equally upset at the judgement handed down to an officer of the Foreign Legion who had just been condemned to ten years in prison for his role in the failed officers' putsch.[52]

Even in this last apocalyptic stage of the war, the challenge of evangelizing Muslims remained a priority for some Protestants at least. Alfred Rolland of the Tizi-Ouzou mission wrote to Jacques Beaumont late in May, asking for an exchange of views with representatives of CIMADE. If such a dialogue were arranged, the Methodist was anxious to present the traditional missionary perspective.[53]

Beaumont took half a year to reply. There was nothing, he reported to Rolland, to indicate that either the Reformed or the Methodist church was anxious to press forward on the missionary front, for the time being at least. Speaking for his own organization, Beaumont stressed the need for prior dialogue and shared reflections with Muslims, something which was likely to reveal more common ground than was normally presumed to exist between the two faiths and to clarify what true divergences there were between Christianity and Islam. In any event, Beaumont noted, his forthcoming visit to Algiers would be too brief to allow for an extended discussion with Rolland. Perhaps the dialogue might best be put off until March 1962 when, God willing, several members of the CIMADE's executive committee would be in Algiers.[54]

Among the many preoccupations which kept Beaumont from giving Alfred Rolland's request quick consideration was his concern about the morale of his team-workers whose physical situation was increasingly perilous. In November, the secretary-general wrote to Pastor Elisabeth Schmidt in Blida, asking if she would assume responsibility for maintaining close contact with the men and women working for CIMADE in her area, particularly at Médéa. The many difficulties these volunteers were facing in a situation of rising tensions put them under enormous pressure. While letters from Paris headquarters might offer some comfort, direct and fairly regular contact with a pastor would be infinitely more rewarding.[55]

What sometimes seemed to be the bias of CIMADE towards helping Muslims while remaining largely indifferent to the increasing plight of Algeria's European minority, angered a number of settlers. In an effort to set the record straight, Pastor J.-P. Haas, chaplain to a French army division fighting in south-central Algeria, wrote to one of these distressed settlers in November to say that, from his personal experience, the Protestant relief teams had been anything but "unilateral"; they offered aid and comfort to all those in need, European as well as Muslim.[56]

At the end of November, thirty-eight students from the Protestant Faculty of Theology in Paris wrote to the Paris regional synod condemning the OAS and the right-wing deputy Jean-Marie Le Pen who had defended the terrorist organization at a public meeting on 8 November, thereby inciting civil disorder. S. Montcladi, in response, cited nine other theology students who had signed a separate petition protesting violence whatever its ideological origin and adding his own comment that while the FLN had been engaged in terrorism for seven years, the OAS activity had only lasted six months.[57]

Most journalists who wrote for *Tant qu'il fait jour* had welcomed de Gaulle's return to power in 1958 and taken his pronouncements in the spring of that year as a solemn pledge to defend French Algeria. The president's subsequent shifts were seen by these writers as a consummate act of betrayal. By 1961 their rage at him boiled over. Reflecting on the 13 May, Jacques Oberlin no longer saw it as the triumph of Charles de Gaulle but rather as the victory of the people of Algiers against the world-wide forces of communism which the president had subsequently thrown away. Arrogant French intellectuals (Roger Mehl and Jacques Ellul were cited) had helped prolong the conflict with their anti-militarism while greedy financial interests with an eye on the wealth in the Sahara had joined them in prolonging the conflict for their own benefit.[58]

No one was more passionately determined to revise the history of the 13 May than Jacques Soustelle. In a lengthy letter to Philippe Brissaud which began with a tribute to the conservative editor for helping to fight the progressivist "gangrene" which had infected so many Protestant commentators on the Algerian issue, the ex-governor sought to correct the impression that he had been part of a plot to effect de Gaulle's return to power. This clarification apart, Soustelle had to agree that, like Lacoste and the army leaders in Algeria, he had sincerely believed that de Gaulle would save the territory for France, a tragic error of judgment but not one for which he bore responsibility. In an editorial footnote, Brissaud confessed that he too had been taken in by de Gaulle in 1958, in fact even as late as after the general's 16 September 1959 speech. Only in the spring of 1960 had he come to understand the deceitful methods and subversive intentions of the head of state.[59]

In the same issue, Philippe Brissaud spoke of a new rebellion in Algeria, this time involving Europeans and Muslims ready to fight to remain part of France. The French government's failure to analyze the root causes of discontent in the territory had led to many errors over the years, beginning with the tragic bombardment of the Sétif rioters in 1945 and culminating in the desperate insurrections of 1960 and 1961. The spectre of fascism conjured up by leftists was real enough but it was as much present in the regime's repressive methods as it was in the OAS. France was already experiencing "a de facto fascism under the cloak of republicanism," as Brissaud saw it.

In the months between the collapse of talks at Lugrin and efforts to reopen the dialogue in the fall, de Gaulle considered various tactics still available to him in the Algerian situation. After much reflection, the president ended up making another major concession to the FLN: on 5 September over the protest of Debré, he decided to recognize the Sahara as an integral part of Algeria. This bizarre negotiating ploy, news of which soon reached the GPRA, exasperated Joxe who exclaimed to intimates on hearing the news: "The general's playing poker with a fully revealed hand!"

Three days after his speech conceding the Sahara, de Gaulle narrowly escaped an attempt on his life by the OAS. While de Gaulle, at great risk to himself, had been moving toward renewed negotiations, the FLN had both changed its leadership and its bargaining strategy. Those who had come to the Front from the UDMA, including Ferhat Abbas and Dr. Francis, were charged with responsibility for the failed talks at Evian and Lugrin. They were replaced by more radical personalities such as Saad Dahlab, Ben Khedda, and

M'Hmed Yazid.

By October, secret conversations between the French and Algerians had resumed. During December 1961 and January 1962, a series of notes was exchanged between Paris and the GPRA. Even more significantly, Louis Joxe and the FLN delegate Saad Dahlab met twice during this period in a villa on Lake Maggiore to review their respective positions.

At year's end, in a letter from Algiers titled gloomily "Waiting for Godot," Jean-Pierre Lumire wrote that de Gaulle had cut himself off from everyone and from reality. The situation looked quite hopeless on both sides of the Mediterranean.[60]

Notes

1   ACIM, Denise Duboscq and Pierrette Faivre to Jacques Beaumont, 2 January 1961.
2   REF, 24 December 1960.
3   REF, 31 December 1960.
4   REF, 7 January 1961.
5   Soustelle, *Vingt-huit ans de gaullisme*, p. 199.
6   TFJ, January 1961.
7   Soustelle, *Vingt-huit ans de gaullisme*, p. 201.
8   Cited in Courrière, II, 760.
9   CN, 2 February 1961.
10 CN, 16 February 1961.
11 Soustelle, *Vingt-huit ans de gaullisme*, p. 252.
12 TFJ, April 1961.
13 SEM, June 1961.
14 ACIM, Jacques Beaumont to Mme Seidenbinder, 21 February 1961.
15 REF, 29 April 1961.
16 REF, 10 June 1961.
17 Schmidt, p. 110.
18 Ibid., p. 126.
19 OURS, "53eme congrès national SFIO," 19 May 1961.
20 Ibid., 20 May 1961.
21 ACIM, "Rencontre Equipe de Direction/Equipes Algérie, 30 mai-1 juin 1961."
22 REF, 13 May 1961.
23 REF, 27 May 1961.
24 REF, 8 April 1961.
25 REF, 1 July 1961.
26 TFJ, June/July 1961.
27 REF, 6 August 1961.
28 REF, 9 September 1961.
29 TFJ, August/September 1961.
30 TFJ, October/November 1961.

31 OURS, "Conseil national extraordinaire, SFIO, 27 septembre 1961."

32 An account of the way this potential explosion was averted is offered in Courrière, II, 962-965.

33 Jean Carbonare relayed the story of his involvement in Algeria to the writer in a taped interview in New York on 2 October 1994.

34 REF, 30 September 1961.

35 REF, 14 October 1961.

36 REF, 15 April 1961.

37 REF, 30 September 1961.

38 CN, 7 December 1961.

39 REF, 2 December 1961.

40 FPF. "Algérie. Message aux Églises, 19 octobre 1961."

41 Michel Philibert, "Petite suite sur la guerre révolutionnaire," RCS, July-September 1961, pp. 475-510.

42 Ibid., p. 490.

43 ACIM, Jacques Beaumont to Marc Boegner, 15 March 1961.

44 ACIM, Jacqueline Peyron to Marc Boegner, 9 October 1961.

45 Jean-Jacques de Félice, "Une solidarité vécue," in *Cimade-Information*, August/September 1991, p. 15.

46 For a critical review of the statistics here, see Françoise Jeanty, "Les faits," in ibid.

47 Cited in Arlette Domon, "Le combat dans les prisons," ibid., p.12.

48 A.C.I.M., Marc Boegner to Prefect Papon, 20 October 1960.

49 ACIM, "Communiqué de la préfecture de police, 27 octobre 1961."

50 ACIM, "Communiqué pour l'A.F.P.," 26 October 1961.

51 ACIM, "Les assignés de Larzac" to Jacques Beaumont, 6 November 1961.

52 TFJ, October/November 1961.

53 ACIM, Alfred Rolland to Jacques Beaumont, 30 May 1961.

54 ACIM, Jacques Beaumont to Alfred Rolland, 9 November 1961.

55 ACIM, Jacques Beaumont to Elisabeth Schmidt, 20 November 1961.

56 ACIM, Pastor J.-P. Haas to Jacques Beaumont, 23 November 1961.

57 TFJ, December 1961.

58 TFJ, October/November 1961.

59 TFJ, December 1961.

60 REF, 30 December 1961.

Max-Alain Chevallier and son
(Courtesy Mme Marjolaine Chevallier)

Georges Tartar
(Courtesy Georges Tartar)

CHAPTER NINE

1962: THE SPIRITUAL COST OF A PROBLEMATIC PEACE

In January 1962, nine months after fleeing France to escape arrest, Jacques Soustelle finished *L'espérance trahie*, a powerful polemic that served both as apologia for the ex-governor's consistent defense of French Algeria and indictment of what he saw as Charles de Gaulle's betrayal of the promise made to those who had brought him back to power in 1958. The book was published in the spring, just as the seven-and-a-half-year war was winding down.[1]

As had so often been the case during his long political career, Soustelle invoked his Protestant origin and upbringing as essential sources of what he presented as a conscience-driven devotion to French Algeria and an equally lively moral resistance to the authoritarian streak in de Gaulle:

> By background and upbringing I belong to the humble Cevenol folk who profess the Reformed faith. Throughout my childhood I listened as my elders celebrated the memory of these stubborn mountain people, fiercely attached to their beliefs, who dared to defy the most powerful of our kings (Louis XIV). Forced to live in the wilderness, Bible in one hand, sword in the other, pitching camp around their inspired prophets, they endured hunger, exhausting marches, prison, slavery aboard the king's galleys, the hangman's noose, death by fire; or they went into exile in protest against the injustice of the Revocation of the Edict of Nantes. The state might break them; it could never make them bend. I grew up admiring these heroes. A woman on my mother's side of the family died a prisoner behind the thick stone walls of the Tour de Constance near the spot where one of her companions, Marie Durand, had inscribed the word "Resist." These images of a bygone day as well as memories of a less remote past when my great-grandfather was one of the Republican leaders in Nîmes during the Revolutionary period (a highly unpopular role to assume then in our part of France) contributed, together with my native temperament, to alienate me forever from the notion that any temporal ruler, no matter how august, should decide in sovereign fashion what his subjects should believe or accept.[2]

The first part of Soustelle's impassioned tract is taken up with defending his actions as Algeria's chief administrator. In justification of what he insisted was a consistently progressive policy, the ex-governor cited

223

correspondence with Premier Mollet as well as decrees he had issued promoting full-scale integration of the Muslim population and efforts he had made to persuade the European minority to accept a single electoral college. He had won the Europeans around to his progressive views, Soustelle argued and, following the end of his mandate, de Gaulle had praised him for the books he had written in defence of French Algeria.

The president's attitude towards him and the policies he espoused had changed, however, following de Gaulle's return to power in June 1958. Ignoring Soustelle's advice and marginalizing him in the cabinet, de Gaulle had thrown away the real opportunity afforded by the insurrection of the *13 mai* to transform Algeria into "an enclave of fraternity" between Europeans and Africans.

The most serious charge he laid against Charles de Gaulle was that his Algerian policy was in the final analysis based on ethnic prejudice, a disdain for Muslims and a dismissal of Algeria's Europeans as "restless and agitated subjects whose Mediterranean and southern souls, part Spanish, part Arab, he could never as a man of the North either appreciate or understand."

Just as damning was Soustelle's indictment of the president for violating the principles of the Fifth Republic he had helped to articulate. De Gaulle had not only recklessly invoked Article 16 of the constitution to eliminate open criticism of his disastrous Algerian policy; he had in fact created a virtual dictatorship: "We are living now in an authoritarian, personal monarchy, a dictatorship whose fascistic arbitrariness is limited only by the anarchy which its very excesses has produced."[3]

In the same month as Soustelle's indictment of de Gaulle, three French officers were accused of torturing a young Muslim woman caught distributing FLN propaganda in France who had subsequently died while being transported to hospital. During their trial by military tribunal at Reuilly near Paris overwhelming evidence of their culpability was produced, but the three men were acquitted. Albert Finet was astounded and dismayed at the verdict and the moral lapse it implied. He went on to observe that, all things considered, the Fifth Republic did not yet carry the Sign of the Beast; in fact, because it had preserved basic civic freedom during a time of high crisis, the regime was deserving of popular support.[4]

Not surprisingly, the judgment in this case offered by those writing for *Tant qu'il fait jour* differed substantially from that of Finet. When the government appealed the acquittal of the three officers, Philippe Wilfried commented, parodying the radical pastor Casalis, that those who fought for *L'Algérie française* had opted for "the violence which liberates against that which oppresses."[5]

Meeting on 26-27 January, the synod of the ERF for the Paris region urged its members to live with the divisions within its ranks but issued a warning to those (including members of the OAS) whose militant anti-communism had led them to rationalize the use of violence. In the current political climate, delegates to the synod added, it was imperative to restore the moral authority of the state.[6]

In February as rumours circulated concerning renewed negotiations between Paris and the FLN, the OAS opened a series of attacks on metropolitan France, thereby destroying whatever sympathy it still enjoyed there, except in extreme right-wing circles. This blunder, coupled to the willingness of the European minority in Algeria to indulge in what seemed like politically suicidal adventures, reinforced de Gaulle's resolve to prepare for the definitive abandonment of France's Algerian departments.

If de Gaulle was being conditioned to move towards peace by the rapidly deteriorating situation in Algeria, so too was the GPRA. Agreement was reached to begin negotiations on 11 February in the tiny municipality of Les Rousses in the Jura mountains. The French delegation was again headed by Louis Joxe. Following blunt telephone directives from de Gaulle to Joxe on 18 February, a number of key issues were quickly resolved. It was agreed that France would have a full year in which to reduce her army in Algeria to 80,000 men, then three more years to complete her military evacuation. Bases in the Sahara could be used for five years and Mers-el-Kébir near Oran kept under lease for fifteen years.

At 5 a.m. on 19 February, the two negotiating teams reached agreement in principle. Two days later, de Gaulle called the cabinet together to review the results. Couve de Murville, one of the most cautious of the president's counsellors, expressed a prophetic concern about the possibility that Algeria might soon live under a thoroughly revolutionary and totalitarian regime with which Paris might have a hard time cooperating.

Following announcement of the accord and that it was to be ratified within forty-eight hours, Albert Finet observed that France's last colonial conflict had now ended, adding: "I cannot declare this to be a defeat. I would like very much to see it as a new dawn. But, in my desire to remain honest, I hesitate to decide." Above all, the editor of *Réforme* hoped that the end of the war would bring a victory over France's inner demons.[7]

In the same issue, Paul Adeline expressed a more sombre view. Part of the war's tragedy had been the sense of abandonment experienced by the *pieds-noirs* for whom de Gaulle felt little or no sympathy. The president had no doubt tolerated the fascist OAS simply to bring the FLN to the bargaining table, disregarding the long-term suffering which the European minority was bound to undergo as a result of the secret terrorist organization's activities.

In mid-February, the executive committee of CIMADE discussed how to deal with what was now a dangerously unstable situation in Algeria. The directives emerging from this discussion and relayed to Philippe Jordan were clear and bold. Team-workers should stay in place and avoid at all cost the impression that they might desert or abandon their mission.[8] Members of the executive would travel to Algeria to share the perils and challenges of the trying weeks ahead.

Although Beaumont who had received death threats from the OAS was unable to make such a trip, Peter Dyck, on behalf of the American Mennonite Central Committee, paid a week-long visit to Algeria on the eve of the cease-fire. In the big cities, first in Oran and then in Constantine, the visitor noted the apparently absolute power of the OAS. As he put it in his report to the MCC:

> There is no question in my mind that today the OAS is the real problem in Algeria. Two French soldiers from Strasbourg who visited CIMADE team-workers and with whom we lunched reported that it was not unusual to hear a Muslim say that he would rather have real Frenchmen in Algeria than the "Black Feet."

In the countryside, things were very different, Dyck reported. There, the FLN was present everywhere. The visitor added that, as far as he could tell, "from the FLN we have nothing to fear." Interestingly enough, the Mennonite went on to observe, "the Algerian leaders, including Muslim FLN chiefs, not only speak French but think French. They could not possibly be as close to any other nation as they are to France." Even more important from Dyck's point of view, "the FLN know about CIMADE and our work and we have good reason to believe that they approve of it and, after independence, will want us to continue."

During his brief but highly charged visit, Dyck managed to visit several CIMADE projects, including those at Médéa, Sidi-Naamane and Constantine. Although generally pleased with what he saw, the visitor was disturbed about the devastatingly depressing passivity in the Muslim population:

> Not only do they lack all the basic skills required but also the initiative. They simply sit around and wait.... They wait for the rains to stop. They wait for Ramadan to end. They wait for the cease-fire. They wait for peace.... They just wait. But this is part

of the sickness of Islam and one of the striking differences between Mohammedanism and Christianity.[9]

Following this lightning tour, Dyck met Jacques Beaumont at Orly airport to discuss future collaboration between the MCC and CIMADE (which would continue to give Mennonite volunteers apprenticeship training). Both agreed that, in the changed circumstances of an independent Algeria, they and other Protestant churches should merge to create "a united Christian witness in a Muslim world."

While Dyck was visiting Algeria, grim news of the continuing havoc being wrought by the OAS reached Paris. Other bad news was that there had been no signal from Tunis that the peace accord reached at Les Rousses would be ratified. Under these circumstances, de Gaulle gave Joxe more latitude to bargain not on vital but on secondary issues should the negotiating teams need to come together again. In the end, Krim and others won out over the hardliners in the GPRA, and agreement was reached to reconvene the two negotiating teams at Evian.

On 11 March, as the final round of negotiations opened, Joxe exhorted both teams to press rapidly ahead. Then, after an intense twelve-day dialogue, the three French delegates signed their names to the ninety-three-page document which came to be known as the Evian accords. Joxe and his colleagues had good reason to see the terms as a reasonable compromise, the result of patient but forceful bargaining. French troops were to remain in exclusive control of Algeria until its people had exercised their right to self-determination while the National Liberation Army would remain outside the territory until that date. The vote on self-determination must occur within three to six months of the cease-fire, on a date fixed by the High Commissioner who would be named by the French government and would carry the full authority of the Republic. The referendum would offer the people of Algeria a choice between three clearly defined options: status as a French department, independence accompanied by a complete break with France, or independence together with an agreement that the two then separate states would be bound by a pact of cooperation.

The European minority for which Joxe and his fellow-delegates had lobbied hard was granted the right to hold dual nationality for a three-year period after which those enjoying such status must choose between becoming Algerian citizens or accepting the status of foreign residents with special privileges. The European community would also enjoy explicit representation in the Algerian Assembly in proportion to its numbers; and, in Algiers and Oran, both the president and vice-president of the municipal council would be chosen from within that community. An *Association de sauvegarde* would be created, bringing together all French citizens to protect their rights. Those wishing to leave the new state could take with them their property or the proceeds of its sale.

French rights in the Sahara were safeguarded—in the short term at least. For a six-year period, companies based in the metropolis would have the right to issue research and exploration permits there, and French army bases in the area could be used for five years after the cease-fire. Algeria, it was agreed, would remain in the franc zone and Paris would pursue implementation of the Constantine Plan. In parallel fashion, France would continue its active cultural investment in Algeria, supporting the schools and lycées she had founded.

De Gaulle counter-signed the Evian accords on 18 March. The cease-fire took place the following day at noon.

Réforme's editor had no difficulty in deciding between the politics of peace reflected in the diplomacy of Joxe and the politics of subversion represented by Salan. Following the signing of the accords, Finet praised the intelligence and tenacity of Louis Joxe. Nevertheless, the editor felt obliged to note that thousands of his fellow-citizens felt shattered, even terrified, at what lay ahead of them. Someone needed to express solidarity and compassion with them. More than anything else, what might jeopardize the lot of these *pieds-noirs* was the perverted zealotry of the OAS leaders who had invoked the Gospel to justify their terrorism. In the aftermath of such a distortion of the faith, it was hard to imagine peaceful reconciliation between Christians and Muslims. The tracts distributed by the OAS with their specious appeal to the Christian conscience were full of the kind of unctuous and sophistical reasoning which Pascal had condemned in the Jesuits. Their invocation of the Lord was the worst kind of *tartufferie*. The attempt to co-opt Christian teachings to shield nefarious exercises was reminiscent of Paul Reynaud's very public attendance at mass at the time of the 1940 armistice or of the Nazis' efforts to suborn Christians to support their evil designs during the Third Reich.[10]

Jean-Pierre Roux, reporting to *Réforme* from Evian, saw the terms of the accord as potentially very hopeful. The remarks of Ben Khedda that Algeria's Europeans had no need to fear retribution from the majority and that France could now resume her creative dialogue with the Third World were surely signals of a welcome new attitude.[11]

Not surprisingly, news of the 18 March accord was also welcomed in the pages of *Cité nouvelle*. In jubilation at the terms reached in Evian, Czarnecki observed that, given the way in which Muslims had until recently been described rather disparagingly as *indigènes*, the FLN was being generous in the terms it had agreed to, offering a three-year period of grace to the *colons* during which they could choose to retain the Algerian citizenship they were now granted or to opt for France.[12]

The outrage in the pages of *Tant qu'il fait jour* was as great as the joy in the liberal Protestant press. The Catholic historian Raoul Girardet, writing a guest column clearly aimed at Protestant subscribers, talked of a new Revocation of the Edict of Nantes like that which had proscribed the Huguenots three centuries earlier. This time, however, it was designed to deny French nationality to the entire European minority in Algeria.[13] Philippe Brissaud, meanwhile, furious at a newspaper photo showing FLN "terrorists" posing as statesmen beside Louis Joxe, saw the outcome of the Evian talks as a "horrifying St. Bartholomew's Day" during which the leaders of a newly independent Algeria would exterminate all those, European and Muslim alike, who did not share their faith.

When the terms of the Evian accord were made public, Brissaud exploded in predictable outrage. The noble dream of French Algeria which would have guaranteed "the salvation of the French population and the fraternity of the two communities through their shared membership in the French nation," had been destroyed.[14] For Roland Laudenbach, the accord testified to the utter bankruptcy of France's liberal and left-wing thinkers, a bankruptcy for which Christians as well as Socialists must be held responsible. Socialists in the metropolis were particularly blameworthy he wrote, because they had abandoned the humble folk of Algiers and Oran who had invested as much faith in SFIO as had the party's supporters in France.[15]

The negotiations at Evian were inevitably brought before the National Assembly. On 20 March, following a presentation of the government position by Prime Minister Debré, Francis Leenhardt, while supporting the signing of the cease-fire, took the opportunity to justify what he presented as the consistently progressive Socialist policy on Algeria. He went on to condemn:

> The long-term blindness of those who, beginning with the Blum-Viollette project of integration, through the non-implementation of the 1947 statute and the rejection of the single college as well as the first *loi-cadre*, kept the lid closed on the pot until it exploded, thereby stubbornly obstructing all those social and political reforms which, had they been enacted in time, would have allowed a pacific evolution of the two communities.[16]

The power of intimidation exercised by the OAS over the settler community had left the impression among many French liberals that all *pieds-noirs* were spontaneous supporters of the Secret Army and its cause. In an effort to combat this negative image, and the widespread prejudice against all settlers which it had generated, Marc Lazerges published an open letter in the February/March issue of *Le Semeur*. It was important, he argued, that the French population at large understand that their European cousins in Algeria were an integral part of the same family. Their adaptation to the radical changes going on in Algeria should be encouraged but their prospects for a reasonable life in an independent Algeria were seriously jeopardized when they were denounced as supporters of the OAS, nor was the cause of future Franco-Algerian cooperation made easier by such irresponsible comments.

The truth of the matter, the correspondent of *Le Semeur* said, was that most settlers, whose situation was already desperate, had become victims of the OAS rather than its partisans. The present tragedy was not simply the result of errors committed by wicked *colons*. The responsibility for this unhappy state of affairs must be shared by those living in France: "We are all guilty of the sin of botched decolonization, all guilty of the excesses which have been committed, the racism, the blindness to reality, the sheer stupidity.... The OAS is thus our responsibility."[17]

In the same issue of the French student newspaper, Françoise Koehler made an equally impassioned plea on behalf of the *colons*. Citing Camus, she pointed to the genuine passion for the land which the settlers had developed over the generations, something far transcending the greed or lust of simple-minded colonizers.[18]

The intimidation of the settler community by the OAS was at this stage clearly taking its toll of those working for CIMADE. By the end of March, Philippe Jordan was experiencing an increasing sense of helplessness, if not hopelessness. The theologically trained layman still dreamt of an "idyllic peace" but was convinced that, if and when such an end to hostilities came, the Christian outreach to "the other," the surrounding Muslim masses, would be a long, hard process.[19]

To deal with the explosive situation in Algeria which would follow announcement of the cease-fire and to help prepare for the transfer of power, de Gaulle on 19 March chose as high commissioner for the territory Christian Fouchet. A liberal and long-time Gaullist, he had served as Mendès France's minister of Moroccan and Tunisian affairs and knew at first hand the kind of malaise the European minorities in the Maghreb would experience as France withdrew. Fouchet arrived in Algiers just a week after the signature of the Evian accord, bringing with him a team of progressive advisers. On 27 March, he set in place the Provisional Executive agreed upon at Evian over which

Abderrahmane Farès was to preside.

The OAS, meanwhile, had denounced the peace and proclaimed its determination to fight on in defense of French Algeria. In the face of what amounted to a declaration of war by Salan against those who accepted the peace terms, the French army and the FLN found themselves paradoxically allied. The worst, however, was still to come. On 23 March, elements of the OAS opened fire on a patrol of French soldiers in Bab-el-Oued, a European working-class suburb of Algiers and hotbed of Ultra opinion. Thus did they fulfill their grim pledge to condemn those wearing the uniform of the Republic as its enemies. General Ailleret retaliated swiftly, ordering the strafing of the suburb by French planes.

De Gaulle resolved at once to extinguish the Bab-el-Oued insurrection. The district was cordoned off and its inhabitants subjected to a severe curfew. Then, on 26 March, came the ultimate tragedy. The European population of Algiers, which had been forbidden to demonstrate, defied the order, insulting and threatening the soldiers sent to police their streets. Shots were fired, perhaps by an overly nervous conscript, leading to a volley from his comrades, some of them Muslim, leaving at least forty-six civilians dead.

On 26 March, in a final burst of rage at the impending death of French Algeria, ex-general Salan urged the *pied-noir* population of Algiers into the streets. The OAS leader hoped that the sight of a crowd of Europeans marching on the besieged Bab el-Oued district would convert French soldiers to the Secret Army's cause. Instead, when the crowd reached the city's central post office on the rue d'Isly, nervous Muslim partisans, who would have been overwhelmed by the mob, opened fire. Forty-six Europeans were killed and some 200 wounded. Not surprisingly, this bloody encounter turned an already nervous exodus of settlers into a panic.

Terror struck from all directions during the spring of 1962. Late in April, J.-P. Haas, the pastor of the Reformed church in Oran, wrote to CIMADE headquarters in Paris that the OAS repression had turned into an indiscriminate attack on the whole *pied-noir* community. His church had been transformed into a dormitory for Europeans who no longer felt secure in their homes after an assault on the settler district by soldiers in tanks or wielding machine-guns. While soldiers stood guard outside, the CRS (special security police) had searched each house for evidence of complicity with the OAS, terrorizing whole families and destroying furniture and other property in their zeal. Although no violence had been visited upon his person, the pastor and his family had been treated roughly.

If genocide consists in an attempt to wipe out a whole people, Haas went on, France was now proceeding to commit an act of genocide against the entire *pied-noir* population. The church should be made aware of this. The pastor added:

> I am not myself a *pied-noir*. These people did not have my sympathy until these recent events. However, I took a vow during my consecration to devote myself to children, to those who are suffering and to the distressed, whatever the nature of their suffering.[20]

Haas went on to note that the rest of the world had condemned the whole German people for having consented to the use of torture and concentration camps even in cases when the Germans were not aware of their existence. France was now engaged in committing the same crimes, and this against her own children. Should we act now, Haas asked, or wait for the judgment of history on these atrocities.

The indiscriminate assault on the *pieds-noirs* which Pastor Haas reported to CIMADE was matched in purpose if not in intensity by an OAS attack on CIMADE headquarters in Algiers in May. At the end of the month, Philippe Jordan sent an alarming letter to Paris about an invasion by four adolescents who threatened those inside with grave consequences if they did not vacate the premises within twenty-four hours.[21] The pretext for this insolent demand was that CIMADE team-workers had been seen distributing food and other supplies in the Casbah.

Jordan then broached the question of how the Protestant relief organization was to function in the longer term. June or July seemed appropriate months in which to consider evacuating the more exposed sites. Belkitane, where Jean Carbonare was in charge, seemed calm, ready to live through and beyond the achievement of independence. In the meantime, because of the extreme danger in which most team-workers were living, it would be appreciated if their friends and relatives were kept in the dark about their situation.

The arrest of the OAS leaders in the spring of 1962 (most notably, the apprehension of Raoul Salan on 20 April) posed no problem for Protestant commentators. There were, however, differences of opinion about the sentences meted out—Salan was condemned to prison, not death, on 23 May. Albert Finet doubted whether the general was in fact the real leader of the OAS but approved of his incarceration because his aim had clearly been to overthrow the regime.[22] René Courtin, noting that de Gaulle had pardoned Ben Bella, felt that granting equivalent commutation to the French general might have been more appropriate (and more Christian) than imprisonment.[23]

In response, Finet defended the judgment arguing that, if anything less severe had been decided, France might have compromised her future stability. Perhaps an unconditional condemnation followed by a presidential pardon would have had the desired effect?[24]

André Philip linked the trial and condemnation of Salan to the long series of assaults on republican integrity by the military, noting that some of those who supported the OAS leader had been implicated in plots to overthrow the Fourth Republic. There was also, in the zealous leftist's view, a historic link between Salan's treachery and the anti-republican machinations within the military elite during the Dreyfus Affair. What was unpardonable in the current conspiracy was the number of crimes against innocent men and women of which French officers in Algeria were guilty.[25]

The terms reached at Evian and, most significantly, the right of Algerians to decide their own political future, were subject to two separate referenda, one in metropolitan France (on 8 April) and one in Algeria (1 July).

As the French referendum approached, *Réforme* opened its pages to a variety of opinions. Francis Leenhardt relayed the news that the SFIO had overwhelmingly endorsed the "yes" position (2,982 to 4 for the "no" option and 9 abstentions). The delegates had roundly condemned the OAS for attempting a *congolisation* of the Algerian conflict as well as the installation of a dictatorship in France itself. A massive "yes" vote, according to Leenhardt, would be the best means of stopping the OAS and the threat of fascism. The negotiations at Evian were consonant with France's obligation to lead the peoples it had colonized towards independence, something that had been made manifest in the *loi Defferre*.[26]

Responding to Leenhardt, René Courtin argued the case for the "no" side, not (as he put it) out of support for the far Right (which had destroyed itself in the insurrection of January 1961) but because Charles de Gaulle had taken advantage of the crisis in Algiers to create a regime of personal power backed by arbitrary courts-martial. Further, he was at the same time subverting the movement towards European unity as well as NATO. The recently signed Evian accords, meanwhile, offered no real guarantee to Algeria's Europeans or to the Muslims who had linked their fate to France. Some form of international guarantee would have given these two groups a degree of security but de Gaulle had turned his back on all trans-national bodies which limited France's absolute sovereignty.[27]

Jacques Beaumont, reflecting in advance on the prospect of peace and hope which might develop following a triumph of the "yes" side, urged reconciliation and rapprochement with the new Algeria. France had remained ignorant of the Muslim masses there; she must now be prepared to welcome the aspirations of the soon-to-be-born nation and help in its construction. Beaumont had encountered deep-seated animosity towards France among Muslim detainees in French prisons during the conflict. Paradoxically, however, he pointed out, the war had also created a number of bonds between Christians and Muslims. It was now time to show compassion both for *pieds-noirs* who were fleeing Algeria and for Muslims who wished to remain in France.[28]

One of the most challenging moments of Jacques Beaumont's career as secretary-general of CIMADE came towards the end of the conflict when he made a final visit to Larzac, the largest of the internment camps in France for FLN members and sympathizers. Beaumont's mission was to hand over to the prisoners before their release the 75,000,000 francs which the French Federation of the Front had collected to sustain them during their return to Algeria.

The secretary-general, whose reputation with French police authorities put him in some jeopardy, was accompanied to and from Larzac by two burly escorts furnished by the FLN as well as an interpreter (who a few years later became the Algerian ambassador to Japan). In the end, Beaumont was able to ensure that each prisoner, upon release, would be given not just 15,000 francs but decent clothing as well. Not long after the secretary-general's visit, the Muslim prisoners emerged from Larzac and five other detention centres, properly dressed and adequately supplied with funds, ready to make their way to Marseilles and then in ships to Bône. To make sure they were properly dealt with on arrival, Beaumont phoned ahead to the indispensable Robert Poujol who had become prefect of the Bône department.

In the end, 90.71 percent of those French citizens who voted endorsed the Evian accords. The editorial board of *Réforme* interpreted the overwhelming victory of the "yes" side as guaranteeing FLN support for the Evian accords while rendering a putsch by the OAS as inconceivable. The only drawback to the victory was the plebiscitary aspect of the vote which amounted to consecration of de Gaulle's personal power.[29]

Meanwhile, the OAS intensified its terrorist attacks and other right-wing groups revived the idea of establishing a series of European mini-states along the coast. These events led even the boldest spirits among the *pieds-noirs* to plan departures for metropolitan France, going so far as to defy death threats for such "desertion." Early in April, writing in *Cité nouvelle*, Marc Stéphane described the plight of "poor whites" who, unlike the rich *colons* who had already left Algeria, were unable to flee and felt quite despondent. In the end, Stéphane suggested, sheer necessity would force their hand and, whatever their choice, raw courage alone would enable them to survive on whichever side of the Mediterranean they found themselves.[30]

On 17 June, the war formally ended and the European exodus began in deadly earnest. Within the next three months some 900,000 *pieds-noirs* took flight. In the midst of this frantic emigration, on 1 July, Algerians voted by 91.23 percent (almost 9,000,000 to 16,000) in favour of founding their own sovereign nation. Two days later, de Gaulle recognized Algeria's independence.

Tania Metzel made her last trip to Algeria just before the independence proclamation. Her aim was to visit all the prisons in the territory and to arrange for the transport to France of as many inmates as wished to make the trip.[31] In many cases she talked to men who had not received a single visitor since their incarceration.

Although her visit was endorsed, even welcomed, by French prison authorities, Mlle Metzel was given a cool welcome by the European minority. The wife of one pastor made her anger about the mission known to the visitor, a sentiment no doubt easy to understand given the utter panic sweeping through the settler community at this point and the feeling that rescuing prison inmates from whatever fate awaited them under the new regime was not a high priority.

During her visit to the Constantinois area, Mlle Metzel ran across a Protestant seminarian who was serving as a second-lieutenant in the army. He talked to her at length about seeing the methods of psychological warfare waged by the Fifth Bureau. This of course simply confirmed what Mlle Metzel had known from François Hauchecorne and Maurice Causse three years earlier. After her return to France, she reported on these conversations about the Fifth Bureau's tactics to Jacques Ellul. The professor was appalled at the thought that his own courses on propaganda might have been perversely put to use by his own compatriots. "C'est donc à ça qu'a servi mes cours!" he exclaimed in horror.

Following the coming of peace, as a French army unit in the Constantinois area was moving back towards the coast preparing to evacuate, a small 2CV Renault chugged past them moving in the opposite direction. It was heading south towards Belkitane where Jean Carbonare had launched his reforestation programme the previous year.[32] One of the French soldiers shouted to the CIMADE volunteers cramped together inside the tiny vehicle: "Mais vous êtes tous un peu fous!" ("Are you people out of your mind?"). One symbol of France in Algeria had crossed another. Force had failed to stop the impulse towards Algerian independence but for the tiny band of French Protestants driving south at least, there was still a chance for reconciliation between Christians and Muslims, Europeans and Arabs.

The spring of 1962 brought panic to the community in Blida to which Pastor Elisabeth Schmidt had been ministering. A mass exodus began in fearful anticipation of the future and the OAS then instituted a ruthless campaign of intimidation to prevent these departures.[33] When, following the Evian accords on 19 March, the OAS ordered a general strike, Pastor Schmidt defied the call, keeping the church open, even venturing out into the street on her own.

At Blida, as elsewhere, things went from worse to worse. A Protestant nurse whom Pastor Schmidt had befriended refused to take on any more Muslim patients given the harm "they" had done to "us."

On 1 July, as the newly emancipated Algerian masses celebrated their independence, crying "Algérie yahia!" in place of the strident "Algérie française!" she had heard for so many months, Pastor Schmidt felt a sudden, quite spontaneous, surge of sympathy. The enthusiasm of the almost exclusively Muslim crowd reminded her of the exultant Paris parade down the Champs-Elysées she had witnessed as a child on 14 July 1919. The long ordeal, she told herself, was over: the Algerian people had found their freedom. Beyond this joyous moment, she hoped, they would discover their happiness.

Grave concern was expressed by a number of Protestants about the treatment meted out in the newly independent Algeria to those *pieds-noirs* left behind. Soustelle, whose fury at de Gaulle's "betrayal" of French Algeria reached a new intensity in 1962, spoke about the "disappearance" of 5,000 Europeans in the weeks following Evian. The reality was grim enough: perhaps as many as 400 *colons* were killed by FLN partisans during June and July 1962.[34]

As serious a problem of conscience for France was the fate of the *harkis* at the hands of the FLN. Under the terms of the Evian accord, the French were obliged to disarm these ancillary troops who had remained faithful to the tricolour in the face of grim warnings from the FLN. Soustelle talked of the slaughter of some 100,000 *harkis*; estimates of those murdered vary between 30,000 and 150,000.[35] Following such atrocity reports, the French administration acted, albeit tardily, bringing together as many *harkis* as it could find, placing them in special camps for their protection. In the end, thousands managed to get to France.

The fate of the *harkis* and of many *pieds-noirs* aroused indignation and horror among Protestants on both sides of the ideological spectrum. R. Goullet de Pugy in *Cité nouvelle* deplored the miserable conditions of the detention camp near Philippeville in Algeria where Muslim veterans were being held. His appeal for compassion brought an anonymous contributor to

Tant qu'il fait jour to remind his readers that France had opened its arms to earlier waves of refugees, including Hungarians in 1956. The response this time, it was said, should be overwhelming, given that it was a question of welcoming men and their families who had from the beginning opted for France.[36]

The fate of the *harkis* was made graphically clear to readers of *Réforme*. Perhaps as many as 80,000 of these Muslims had signed contracts to serve as auxiliary troops under French officers.[37] The Evian accords made no specific provision for these men, most of whom wanted to return to their homes after the signing of the cease-fire. Some had been murdered by the ALN soon after the war's end. In mid-May, 600 *harkis* were waiting at Mers-el-Kébir on the Mediterranean coast near Oran in hopes of being transported to safety in France. As Albert Finet saw it, France had a solemn obligation to defend and protect these men but was trying hard to avoid any direct responsibility for them. Surely, he wrote, the despatch of at least one ship to rescue those who had risked everything in a hopeless cause was the minimal way of discharging such a debt of honour?[38]

The *harkis*, together with other Muslims who had served in the regular French army during the war totalled some 120,000 in all, or perhaps as many as 270,000 if one includes their families. In May they formed an *Association des anciens des affaires algériennes* to defend their interests. Concerned French citizens on the Left as well as the Right asked whether these men and their families, who had risked everything to defend the cause of French Algeria, would be accorded the full integration into the national life which partisans of that cause had demanded? Were they, for that matter, to be welcome at all in a society divided and embittered by seven- and-a-half years of war and capable, potentially at least, of displaying the kind of racist sentiments which so many members of the settler minority had shown towards their co-religionists in Algeria.

Yvonne Trocmé, designated by CIMADE to help the integration into French life of those who were fleeing Algeria, the vast bulk of whom were European, was concerned about these Muslim refugees. No doubt too easily, Jacques Beaumont responded that the military authorities were accepting full responsibility for them. Muslim veterans and their families were to be housed at Larzac, the secretary-general of CIMADE pointed out, not pausing to note that this huge camp had been the object of his solicitous visits when it housed FLN leaders during the war. Beaumont added that these veterans would in time be trained to work in the forestry and mining sectors and that in the meantime any problems of adjustment they might be experiencing were transitory.[39]

In the end, however, CIMADE was anything but neglectful of the *harkis*. Four female team-workers greeted and did their best to accommodate these partisans of French Algeria where many of them had relocated, in the Gard department.

Late in October, J.-P. Lumire drew the attention of readers of *Réforme* to the continuing plight of the *harkis*, some of whom had just been forcibly returned to Algeria where thousands of their comrades had been crucified or burned alive. France, the editor remarked, seemed only to express a cowardly indifference to this grim settling of accounts.[40]

The editorial board of *Tant qu'il fait jour* issued a passionate plea in the summer of 1962 on behalf of those who were suffering most as the conflict ended. Outside the cities which had a substantial European minority, the victorious ALN was expropriating property, taxing by force and abducting *colons*, killing or mutilating those Muslims who remained loyal to France. The atmosphere was one of xenophobic frenzy; extremists on both sides of the ethnic divide were plunging the territory into chaos. In this grim aftermath of the war, France had the greatest debt of conscience to the Muslims for whom flight was now the only recourse; these men and women should be offered housing, jobs and financial aid; precise addresses in France should be made known to *harkis*.[41]

The final issue of *Tant qu'il fait jour* which appeared in November 1962 came after the newspaper's financial problems were beginning to prove unmanageable. Brissaud's last salvo in defence of the lost cause of French Algeria came in a review of *Mon pays, la France* by Said Boualam. As a commander of the Legion d'honneur, captain in the French army, and former deputy from Orléansville as well as vice-president of the National Assembly, this author could be seen as the perfect incarnation of the failed principle of integration. The text was a moving tribute to France by a man who had loyally served her and by whom he had in the end every reason to feel betrayed. As Brissaud put it: "The entire text reveals the same feeling of truth, simplicity, nobility and an infinite (although never bitter) sadness."[42]

The resettlement in France of hundreds of thousands of *pieds-noirs* as well as of many Muslims posed a moral as well as material challenge to the nation's Protestants. Late in 1961 and throughout 1962, the French Protestant community mobilized itself at every level to deal with the massive influx of *pieds-noirs*, often misleadingly referred to as *rapatriés*. Very few had ever visited France and were thus more accurately identified as *repliés* (literally those who "fell back" on France).

A circular notice inviting the Reformed community to provide a welcome for the refugees issued in October 1961 was largely ignored.

Accordingly, the national council of the ERF on 5 February 1962 exhorted presidents of the regional synods to move on the issue by identifying potential hosts for newly arriving *repliés*. Settlers who showed up, the authors cautioned, should be addressed not as *rapatriés* but as refugees. While the new arrivals might not be any worse off than many others in the world, they saw themselves as victims and should be treated as "friends who feel hurt" ("*amis blessés*"). The new arrivals were by no means all wealthy, it was stressed; their background and skills varied widely and should be taken into account in any effort to integrate them into the nation's economy.[43]

On 3 March, largely as a result of an initiative coming from CIMADE, the French Protestant Federation created a *Commission nationale d'accueil aux repliés d'Algérie*. It was mandated to make the appropriate arrangements to aid in the accommodation of the hundreds of thousands of men, women and children who had already begun to stream across the Mediterranean. Pastor Charles Westphal was named president and Yvonne Trocmé secretary. Thanks to cooperation with Catholic and Jewish agencies mobilized for the same purpose, a remarkable ecumenical exercise began.

To make the vast exodus and relocation process as tolerable as possible, Pastors Henri Capieu and Max-Alain Chevallier drew up guidelines for those suffering serious psychological and spiritual stress. Welcoming centres were set up at airports where the *repliés* landed. Not all new arrivals were guaranteed a helping hand, not surprisingly given the number. Bernard Roussel, having returned to France after two taxing years, remembers running across families wandering around totally at a loss in what was for them a quite alien world. He did what he could to find them food and shelter. In Paris, two CIMADE workers were assigned to greeting Muslims and finding them accommodation.[44]

At the end of July, there were incidents at Marseilles involving *pieds-noirs* who were denounced as "pillagers" as soon as they landed. In an attempt to explain the difficult psychological circumstances of these transplanted *colons*, Huguette Kauffmann reminded readers of *Réforme* that European settlers had been part of a "majoritary minority" in Algeria and that they needed to undergo a basic change of outlook which metropolitan French citizens should do their best to facilitate.[45]

While Protestant organizations did their best for the vast numbers of *repliés*, they were simultaneously anxious to maintain a spiritual presence, even a missionary vocation, in the new Algeria. In April 1962, Pastor Chevallier wrote Leslie Cooke of the World Council of Churches in Geneva asking for help in securing teachers of French in the new nation. The lycées and universities created by the French administration would in all likelihood be nationalized; some internationally based substitute seemed the best means of sustaining the cultural as well as the spiritual values imparted by the departing power.[46]

A week later, Chevallier wrote Cooke again, following a lengthy discussion with the missionary Alfred Rolland, the Methodist Hans Aurbakken, and Bernard Picinbono concerning the maintenance of a Christian presence in Algeria. All agreed that a direct link between Geneva and Algiers offered the best means of achieving that goal. (As the Catholics had not yet arrived at the ecumenical mood of Vatican II, "Christian presence" meant in fact Protestant.) Its best expression would not be in terms of charity (*bienfaisance*) which inevitably carried with it spiritual condescension but of *partage*, a shared participation in the religious and cultural life of the new nation.[47]

In the end, what emerged was the creation of a *Commission chrétienne de Service en Algérie* (CCSA) acting under the aegis of the World Council of Churches. It absorbed all previously separate Protestant entities including CIMADE. As Beaumont puts it, CIMADE disappeared as such in order to serve the new Algeria better. The protective umbrella provided by the Geneva-based organization was likely to shield French nationals who might be regarded with suspicion by Algeria's new rulers.

CIMADE, which remained committed to bringing relief to the afflicted in other parts of the world, asked for volunteers to serve the newly created CCSA. Men and women with specific qualifications in the fields of teaching, health, agriculture, medicine, industry and public works were needed. The commitment to this work would in the short term help guarantee the pluralistic nature of the new Algeria; in the longer term, it would allow the missionary perspective to be kept open.

In the trying circumstances of the interregnum between the withdrawal of the old regime and the consolidation of the new, a young Reformed pastor, Jacques Blanc, assumed direction of the CCSA.

As the war ended, the radical pastor Henri Roser returned once again to an old issue—the question of conscientious objection. President de Gaulle had used his power of pardon to free those who had spent five years or more in prison for refusing to bear arms. The 130 who remained in jail for their contravention of the law had gone on a hunger strike at the beginning of June. As a result, their penalty had been reduced from five to three years which meant that some twenty-five to thirty of their number would soon be released. Roser had joined those still on strike in the hope that their collective action would bring the president to liberate the rest.

Delegates to the national synod of the ERF meeting in Mulhouse at the beginning of May, expressed their gratitude that a Protestant conscientious objector, Michel Bourgeois, had been given no more than a six-month suspended sentence. The synod petitioned the ministry of the army to grant the soldier a reprieve which would allow him to avoid returning to duty, another refusal to serve militarily, and an inevitable new sentence. The best solution, as they saw it, would be to await the end of the current sentence and then to allow Bourgeois to perform civic service in lieu of military duty.[48]

A month later, the war being over, the government of Prime Minister Pompidou seemed well disposed to take up the whole issue of conscientious objection. The president of the national council of the ERF, Pierre Bourguet, wrote to the prime minister on 26 June welcoming the introduction of a bill concerning conscientious objectors, noting:

> Although the ERF as such does not support conscientious objection, it refuses to end its spiritual communion with those of its members who believe it to be their duty for purely religious reasons to adopt this approach; certain of these men were in fact among France's first conscientious objectors. By the same token, it is well known that the French Reformed were behind the idea of a statute of civic service. This suffices to indicate the interest which our church is showing in the adoption of such a measure, an adoption facilitated by the end of the war.[49]

Bourguet hoped passage of the proposed bill would be followed by the immediate release of those now in prison for conscientious objection who might then be assigned to various types of community service. (In the end, the projected legislation was not passed until much later—10 June 1971—when a statute governing conscientious objection became part of French law).

Like conscientious objection, the use of psychological warfare by the French army had been a source of concerned discussion by French Protestants and especially since the Battle of Algiers in 1957.

The Reformed church, meeting at Mulhouse in 1962, commissioned a group to study the question. What followed was a series of reflections at the regional level, a three-day colloquium early in September, and a brochure aimed at alerting the Reformed community to the perils both to society and to individual consciences which had been brought to light during the war.[50]

The battle for the mind was ultimately a spiritual conflict, the authors insisted. While the church should abstain from sanctioning one political option over another in such a conflict, it had a solemn obligation to make clear what was morally unacceptable. Among the more perverse effects of modern propaganda had been the demonization of one's adversary. The lesson from this must be learned: all intellectuals were not crypto-communists and all paratroopers were not torturers.

Another problem at once moral and political was the enormous accumulation of power in the hands of President de Gaulle during the Algerian conflict. Although metropolitan French Protestants gave de Gaulle's Algerian policy almost unconditional support between 1958 and 1962, many of those supporters, as well as all of those who opposed him, were bitterly critical of the way in which he took advantage of the conflict to reinforce his personal power and that of the executive branch. Jacques Soustelle had put the case with passion following his break with the general in 1960.

This criticism of excessive executive power intensified when, following a failed attempt on his life on 22 August, de Gaulle on 12 September appealed to the nation to modify the constitution through a referendum which would permit the direct election of the president of the Republic. In the aftermath of this appeal, politically sensitive Protestants resumed the constitutional debate which many of them had joined after 13 May 1958. Albert Finet hoped that a revival of parliamentary prestige and power would act as a check on what threatened otherwise to become an omnipotent presidency.[51] Much more exercised, André Philip charged that de Gaulle was violating the constitution through the referendum. He urged the Senate and National Assembly to propose a constitutional amendment eliminating the president's right to dissolve parliament. He also regretted the absence in France of a supreme court which might have ruled the referendum question out of order.

Roger Mehl acknowledged that, as a result of the crisis which had brought down the Fourth Republic, he and others had encouraged the evolution towards a presidential system of government; that development had produced a kind of political apathy in the national community. Like Philip, although far less passionately, he urged a reinforcement of parliament's powers to match the threatened increase in executive authority.

Notes

1   Jacques Soustelle, *L'espérance trahie* (Paris: Editions de l'Alma, 1962), p. 10.
2   Ibid., p. 255.
3   Ibid., p. 250.
4   REF, 27 January 1962.
5   TFJ, January 1962.

6   REF, Synod of the Paris region, 27 January 1962.
7   REF, 24 February 1962.
8   ACIM, Jacques Beaumont to Philippe Jourdan, 18 February 1962.
9   ACIM, Peter Dyck, "Report on Administrative Visit to Algeria," 27 February 1962.
10   REF, 24 March; 31 March 1962.
11   Ibid., 24 March 1962.
12   CN, 22 March 1962.
13   TFJ, February 1962.
14   TFJ, March 1962; April/May 1962.
15   Ibid.
16   JOC, 20 March 1962.
17   SEM, February/March 1962.
18   Ibid.
19   ACIM, Philippe Jourdan to Jacques Beaumont, 20 March 1962.
20   ACIM, Pastor J.-P. Haas to Jacques Beaumont, 29 April 1962.
21   ACIM, Philippe Jourdan to Jacques Beaumont, 20 March 1962.
22   REF, 21 April 1962.
23   REF, 5 May 1962.
24   REF, 2 June 1962.
25   REF, 9 June 1962.
26   REF, 31 March 1962.
27   REF, 7 April 1962.
28   Ibid.
29   REF, 14 April 1962.
30   CN, 5 April 1962.
31   This account of her visit to Algeria is based on a taped conversation with Pastor Metzel in Paris on 29 October 1994.
32   This anecdote derives from a taped interview with Jean Carbonare in New York on 2 October 1994.
33   Schmidt, *En ces temps de malheur*, p. 151.
34   Soustelle, *Vingt-huit ans de gaullisme*. p. 298.
35   A. Horne, *A Savage War of Peace. Algeria 1954-1962* (New York: Viking, 1977), p. 538.
36   TFJ, October 1962.
37   REF, 19 May 1962.
38   Ibid.
39   ACIM, Jacques Beaumont to Yvonne Trocmé, 18 June 1962.
40   REF, 20 October 1962.
41   TFJ, June-August 1962.
42   TFJ, November 1962.
43   REF, National Council, 5 February 1962.
44   This anecdotal information derives from a taped interview with Pastor (now Professor) Roussel in Paris on 2 June 1994.
45   REF, 28 July 1962.

46   ACIM, Pastor Max-Alain Chevallier to Dr. Leslie Cooke, 2 April 1962.
47   ACIM, Same to same, 7 April 1962.
48   ERF, National synod, Mulhouse, May 1962.
49   ERF, Letter of Pierre Bourguet to Premier Georges Pompidou, 26 June 1962.
50   *L'Église chrétienne et les problèmes posés par l'action psychologique et la guerre subversive. Plan d'étude*, (Paris: Conseil National de l'Église Réformée de France, 1962).
51   REF, 29 September 1962.

Professor Bernard Picinbono
(Courtesy Professor Picinbono)

CONCLUSION

Most of the Protestants who spoke, wrote, or committed themselves to action in response to the Algerian crisis were *pratiquants* or *croyants*, inspired by deep religious conviction. On the other hand, *protestants d'origine* who were no longer formal believers in (or observers of) the faith were motivated to become involved in the conflict by a keen awareness of what they owed to their Huguenot heritage. They regularly invoked the spiritual devotion which had inspired their Cévenol ancestors to fight for freedom of conscience against Louis XIV and, more recently, against Vichy and the Nazis.

As leader of the highly diverse French Protestant community, Pastor Marc Boegner had to deal with the ideological divisions of those within the French Protestant Federation who took differing positions during the war. As president of CIMADE, he managed to promote peace and reconciliation between Christians and Muslims. Meanwhile Jacques Beaumont, secretary-general of the relief organization, made sure this ecumenical outreach was expressed in deed as well as word, both in France and in Algeria. France's first female pastors, Elisabeth Schmidt and Tania Metzel, brought to Algeria and to its Muslim population a clear message of spiritual understanding as did two scholarly laymen of the Reformed faith living in Algiers, Maurice Causse and Bernard Hauchecorne. Bernard Picinbono, the son of well-to-do *colons*, became a leading champion of Franco-Algerian and Christian-Muslim reconciliation as the war intensified.

In France, the theologian and sociologist Jacques Ellul deplored the conflict as a product of nationalist fury on both sides of the Mediterranean and excoriated the use of propaganda to exacerbate old enmities. The philosopher Paul Ricoeur condemned the war from the beginning and joined protests designed to bring the conflict to an end.

Integral pacifists such as Henri Roser and André Trocmé were bound to express their outrage as the undeclared war began. They helped to mobilize the public and ultimately the government behind legislation to permit conscientious objection. Their colleague Etienne Mathiot became a symbol of ecumenical fraternity when he gave shelter to an FLN leader on the run.

André Philip, one of the few practising Christians in the upper ranks of the SFIO, became one of the most powerful critics of his party's complicity in the war. He was joined in this indictment by a Protestant from the next generation, Michel Rocard. Both men played key roles in preparing the moral and intellectual groundwork for a renovated Socialist Party.

At the opposite edge of the ideological spectrum were Protestants who came together to defend the cause of French Algeria in the pages of *Tant qu'il fait jour*. They were inspired by conviction that the Christian faith they proclaimed was at the very core of the western civilization they sought to defend. Pastor Georges Tartar and Professor Jean Bichon were equally committed to the view that Algeria's Muslims needed to accept Christ not only for their spiritual redemption but for the intellectual emancipation which would arm them for the modern age.

Finally, those who had drifted away from their childhood faith, men such as Jacques Soustelle and Charles-André Julien, were imbued throughout their lives with a deep sense of what they owed to their huguenot inheritance. If Soustelle ended up as a man of the Right, he remained convinced that the policies he defended in Algeria were those of the Jacobin tradition. That included the freeing of consciences from the kind of theocratic tyranny Protestants had endured under Louis XIV and which he rightly guessed Muslims would face following independence. Julien, on the other hand, saw Algeria's national emancipation as an inevitable and desirable development as a result of which Muslims would come to enjoy the spiritual and intellectual freedom for which France's Protestants had consistently fought.

Eleven years after the Evian accords, Charles-André Julien deplored the blindness to reality which had delayed what he saw to be the inevitable coming of Algerian independence. He praised de Gaulle for his willingness after 1958 to abandon his attitude as a *colonial intégral* in favour of a realistic accommodation to Algerian nationalism.[1]

Jacques Soustelle was unanimously praised by liberal and left-wing Protestants during the first half of his mandate. Then he was all but unanimously denounced by these same observers when he shifted tactics in late August 1955. Yet he was able to win the abiding respect of a number of moderates including Louis Joxe who observed, long after the war, that the governor-general had been one of the few French administrators who had understood the Algerian dilemma and the enormous difficulties facing anyone who tried to resolve it.

> As a champion of integration, Jacques Soustelle defined the problem clearly when he discerned the fatal tendency of the *colons* to try to exercise total political and social control over successive ministries and when he pointed out how at the same time administrators sent out by the metropolitan government learned to shut their eyes to Algerian realities.[2]

After an eight-year exile Jacques Soustelle returned to France in 1969 to resume his academic career at the *École des hautes études*. He was elected deputy for the Rhône department in 1973 and chosen a member of the Académie française in 1983. Ten years after the peace, he offered his own scathing indictment of France's post-1958 Algerian policy; he described it as "the most complete fiasco, the most humiliating failure in our country's history." Algeria's independence, the ex-governor noted, had been followed in the short term by the massacre of Muslims as well as Europeans.

What a contrast to the Algeria of the 1950s which had long since passed through the colonial phase of its history and had in the explosion of fraternization on 16 May 1958 testified to its eagerness to move forward to an ethnically diverse and prosperous future. Instead, Soustelle noted bitterly, those who had sold out French Algeria in Paris or subverted it through the FLN had produced a monstrous tragedy:

> Two peoples had once lived together in harmony—Muslims of Arab or Berber ancestry, Christians and Jews of French background. The latter have now disappeared, dispersed to the four winds, living in exile, deprived of everything, regarded with suspicion, treated with parsimony, still bearing the special scars of their condition ten years later; while Arabs and Berbers, handed over to the arbitrary whim of a police state, were eking out a bare existence or had sought out a better life elsewhere.[3]

When Jacques Soustelle died on 7 August 1990, *Le Monde* published a substantial obituary, including a review of the one-time leftist's experience as governor of Algeria. In this capsule biography, the terrible massacres of 20 August 1955 were seen as a turning-point in the psychological as well as political evolution of a man described as "a cold and reserved Cévenol."[4]

The sober and detached evaluation offered in *Le Monde* was followed by a dithyrambic tribute from the Protestant sociologist Roger Mehl in the pages of *Réforme*. In this "Hommage à Jacques Soustelle," subscribers to the leading Protestant newspaper were reminded that, although the ex-governor had been treated as a traitor by leftists for having helped de Gaulle's *Rassemblement du peuple français*, he had been part of a genuinely left-wing group inside the RPF. The integrationist programme that Soustelle had tried to apply in Algeria had been both bold and generous. His only error had been not to abandon that programme when it had become apparent that efforts to implement it would lead inexorably to the classical cycle of rebellion, massacre and repression.

Finally, Mehl pointed out, it should be remembered that de Gaulle, having returned to power in 1958 pledging support to French Algeria, had then betrayed the ex-governor's trust by arranging independence for the territory through a mixture of duplicity and hypocrisy. In Mehl's view, Soustelle's subsequent decision to break with de Gaulle had brought him honour. It was no doubt deplorable that the one-time partisan of the RPF had flirted with the OAS, but Soustelle had stayed true to his convictions, never accepting the double game which lay behind de Gaulle's attempt at high politics. Finally, and most provocatively, Mehl saluted the Protestant in Soustelle and indirectly damned the Catholic in de Gaulle:

> Would it be exaggerated to argue that, between de Gaulle who turned out to be right and Soustelle who was wrong, there is a wide gulf: the gulf which separates a student of schools run by priests and educated in an atmosphere tinged with Maurrassianism and a Huguenot of Cévenol background?

This invocation of Cévenol inheritance was bound to elicit an angry response. The retort came in the pages of *Réforme* from Michel Rodet, a Protestant Gaullist who had once venerated Soustelle. The claim that the ex-governor of Algeria was a model of fidelity was outrageous, Rodet wrote. He pointed out that Soustelle had initiated a campaign of denigration against de Gaulle as early as 1956, long before their rupture. And, if the Huguenot had swerved away from his leftist convictions on 20 August 1955, it had been as much because the territory's *gros manitous* (wealthy settlers) had seduced him as because of an instant on-the-scene revulsion.

Rodet's summation was devastating:

> To present as "cévenol" or "huguenot" a stubborn conviction which is in the end no more than frustrated ambition, bitterness, deeply felt hatred and violent fantasies seems to me wildly off the mark.... Offer homage to Soustelle because he is a "huguenot?" In this sense, then, Eugene Terreblanche, the führer of the South African Nazi party, is also no doubt a huguenot![5]

Pierre Cochet, who had defended the cause of French Algeria and befriended its chief advocate in the years that followed, officiated at Soustelle's civil and religious funeral in the *Temple de l'Oratoire* in Paris.[6] He reminded the audience which included representatives of France's political and cultural establishment, that the man they were all there to mourn had been working on a definition of the word "Consistoire" for the French Academy at the time of his death, a sure sign of his continuing attachment to the tradition of his ancestors.

While Protestants, as devout republicans, were concerned about the challenges posed to the regime by the presence of millions of Algerian Muslims within the nation, they were also troubled by the dangers posed to the parliamentary system by a prolonged but undeclared state of war. This concern was particularly evident within the ranks of the SFIO following the victory of the Republican Front and the intensification of the conflict by the Socialist premier Guy Mollet. Attacks on Mollet's Algeria policy by Charles-André Julien, André Philip and Michel Rocard (among others) helped set the stage for a schism within Socialist ranks and, ultimately the emergence of a new Socialist formation, the *Parti Socialiste unifié*.

Political strategy apart, doubts about the justice of waging war against Muslim insurgents were voiced by some Protestants from the beginning of the conflict. Such doubts, however, were often balanced by condemnation of the methods used by the *fellagha*. Revelations by Protestant witnesses of techniques used by paratroopers during the Battle of Algiers, together with the testimony of Maurice Causse and Tania Metzel, helped educate the public to the indiscriminate violence with which the army was waging battle.

Increasing awareness of the brutal methods sanctioned by France's army leaders, together with disgust among recruits about the mentality of the European settlers whose interests they were asked to defend, intensified resistance among many youths called up to join the fighting in Algeria. Some deserted while others stated their conscientious objection to the war and suffered the consequences. Protestant officialdom meanwhile refused to endorse *insoumission*. The grounds for such a refusal was that, however grim the war, the French state had not fully corrupted its mandate by prosecuting it, nor would the highest bodies of the Protestant churches officially sanction the recourse to conscientious objection. However, both the ERF and the FPF offered spiritual comfort to individual Protestants who felt conscience-bound not to serve and both bodies pressed successive governments to enact legislation allowing for a form of civic service for those who refused to bear arms. This pressure was largely responsible for putting conscientious objection on the national agenda and for the passage in 1971 of a statute guaranteeing the right to opt for the performance of non-violent civic activity in lieu of serving in the armed forces.

Two moral dilemmas which would not have been foreseen in 1954 faced Protestant observers as the conflict wound down. The plight of the *pieds-noirs* and, even more dramatic, the situation after 1962 of the *harkis* and other francophile Muslims, received compassionate attention from concerned

Protestants with the coming of peace. Originally categorized as *Français musulmans rapatriés* (FMR), the *harkis* were then renamed *Rapatriés d'origine nord-africaine* (RONA). The *harkis* were perfect exemplars of the desire for fraternization and, ultimately, integration which Soustelle and the partisans of French Algeria had always promoted. The first formal gesture of atonement for France's negligence of these people came a full generation after Evian in a speech by Premier Michel Rocard on 4 December 1990. The Protestant prime minister who had helped lead the campaign against the Algerian policy of the SFIO in the middle of the war, saluted the *harkis* during this speech and offered belated recognition of their valour. The premier added that the government would ensure proper housing and job training for these men so that they might at last be truly integrated into the nation which they had chosen to defend.[7]

Notes

1   C.-A. Julien, "Algérie: une histoire au passé," *Jeune Afrique*, 8 June 1974, p. 249.
2   Louis Joxe, "Les raisons de la France," *Historia*, April 1971, p. 61.
3   Soustelle, *Lettre ouverte aux victimes de la décolonisation* (Paris: A. Michel, 1973), p. 158.
4   *Le Monde*, 8 August 1990.
5   REF, 11 August 1990.
6   This information derives from a taped conversation with Pastor Cochet in Passy on 28 October 1994.
7   Cited in Abed-el-Aziz Meliani, *La France honteuse* (Paris: Perrin, 1993), pp. 262-263.

EPILOGUE

The sense of responsibility and commitment which had led so many Protestants to become involved in the Algerian war was sustained in a variety of ways following the coming of peace.

Jacques Beaumont continued to serve as secretary-general of CIMADE until March 1968, urging the Protestant relief organization towards new commitments throughout the developing world as well as towards a fuller expression of its ecumenical potential. At the executive meeting which accepted Beaumont's resignation, Pastor Marc Boegner paid special tribute to qualities of intellectual daring and faith which had brought the secretary-general to take risks which others would not have considered. In his response, Beaumont pointed with pride to the example given by CIMADE of a *service sans frontières*, an initiative that had served as a model to other ecumenical minded relief organizations such as *Médecins sans frontières*.[1] A few years after leaving CIMADE, Beaumont quit France for New York where in the mid 1990s he acted as lobbyist at the UN and in American academic circles on behalf both of the developing nations and of the world's homeless.

Several of Beaumont's collaborators during the Algerian crisis stayed on in the newly independent country after the war. Mireille Desrez, who had spent two years in Médéa, was reminded by Prefect Poujol towards the end of her stay that the Constantine Plan of 1959 had included a solemn French pledge to establish a nursing school in Algeria. Eager to take up the hint, she went back to France to complete her own professional training, then returned to Algeria after independence to accept the direction of the nation's first *Centre d'Enseignement médical* at Constantine. Over the next six years, until replaced by an Algerian, Mlle Desrez supervised the training of 350 nurses.

Like Mireille Desrez, Jean Carbonare committed himself after the war to preserving, even enlarging, the personal as well as social bonds established with Algeria's Muslim community. On 1 April, 1962, Robert Buron wrote to convey his own and the government's gratitude to the former CIMADE worker who was "among those who have created bonds between the two communities as well as between French and Algerian leaders and who have never hesitated to reforge these bonds whenever one party or the other has broken them."[2]

Carbonare's commitment to the new Algeria included fourteen years service as director of the *Chantiers populaires de reboisement*, a radically expanded version of the reforestation project he had launched from Constantine in 1961. Early in 1963, Premier Ben Bella wrote to express thanks on behalf of the new republic for the substantial contribution Carbonare was making not only to the nation's economic development but to the maintenance of the fraternal relations between the peoples of France and Algeria.[3]

As a student leader during the war Pastor Jacques Maury protested against the government's Algeria policy and the army's methods there. Later he served as president of both the ERF and the FPF and in the mid-1990s headed the CIMADE executive. Madeleine Barot after devoting a great deal of her time and energy to the cause of women's emancipation, died in 1995.

Pastor Tania Metzel, although severely handicapped, remained committed to the dispossessed until her death in 1997. Mme Marjolaine Chevallier, widow of the last president of the Algerian synod, is a professor in the Faculty of Theology at the University of Strasbourg. Bernard Roussel, no longer a pastor, is a professor of religious studies at the Sorbonne.

A tiny band of French academics, including Bernard Picinbono and Jean Bichon, remained on the faculty of the University of Algiers until tensions inside as well as outside the campus meant the end of academic freedom and of civilized social relationships. As of the mid 1990s, Picinbono is professor of physics at the University of Paris—d'Orsay. Maurice Causse, after many years teaching in Algiers, lives in Saintes north of Bordeaux, pursuing a number of research projects, still deeply troubled by what he learned during the war, and still battling against what he considers to be philistines in the French Protestant establishment.

Elisabeth Schmidt stayed on in Algeria into 1963. Then, despite pleas from local Muslims including her *fatma* who assured her that "there will be no Saint Bartha's (St. Bartholomew's Day, a reference to the massacre of Huguenots by Catholic mobs in 1572) in the new Algeria" she left to take up a post as pastor in Nancy.[4] She died, after publishing an account of her Algerian experience, at Castres, in 1986.

Pierre Cochet, after serving in various diplomatic posts in Africa following the end of the Algerian war, returned to the pastorate and as of 1995 was in charge of the upper-class Reformed parish in Passy. An unabashed conservative, nostalgic for the monarchy, he deplores the present state of French public life for which, he feels, the Gaullist constitution of the Fifth Republic is largely responsible.

For those Protestants whose conscience had been aroused during the Algerian conflict, the Evian accords clearly brought no sense of complacency. Algeria was for all of them a testing-ground on which they were ready to prove themselves as long as the battle lasted. But when it was over, there were other battles to fight and, so long as it was not accompanied by justice, the peace itself left consciences unappeased.

Notes

1   ACIM, "Message de Jacques Beaumont au Conseil de la CIMADE réuni le 25 mars 1968."
2   Personal papers of Jean Carbonare. Buron to Carbonare, 27 June 1960.
3   Premier Ben Bella to Carbonare, 19 June 1963, ibid.
4   Schmidt, *En ces temps de malheur*, p. 19.

BIBLIOGRAPHY

Primary Sources (Press and Parliament)

The following, here listed with their abbreviated form, are the newspapers, periodicals, party and parliamentary records consulted during my research:

ACIN   *Archives of the Comité Inter-Mouvements Auprès des Deportés et Evacués.* (CIMADE).

CN   *Cité nouvelle.*

JOC   *Journal officiel de la République française. Débats. Assemblée nationale.*

LAP   *L'Algérie protestante.*

OURS   *Office Universitaire de Recherche Socialiste.*

RCS   *Revue du Christianisme Social.*

REF   *Réforme.*

SEM   *Le Semeur.*

SFIO   Section Française de l'Internationale Ouvrière, typewritten minutes of Party meetings, 1954-1962.

TFJ   *Tant qu'il Fait Jour.*

Primary Sources (Monographs)

Abbas, F. *Autopsie d'une guerre.* Paris: Garnier frères, 1980.

Alleg, H. *La question.* Paris: Editions de Minuit, 1958.

Boegner, M. *L'exigence oecuménique. Souvenirs et perspectives.* Paris: Albin Michel, 1968

Chevallier, J. *Nous, Algériens.* Paris: Calmann-Lévy, 1958.

Coulet, Fr. *Vertu des temps difficiles.* Paris: Plon, 1967.

Couve de Murville, M. *Le monde en face. Entretiens avec Maurice Delarue.* Paris: Plon, 1989.

_____. *Une politique étrangère, 1958-1969.* Paris: Plon, 1971.

De Gaulle, Ch. *L'esprit de la Ve République. Mémoires d'espoir.* Paris: Plon, 1994.

Dresch, J. et al. *La question algérienne.* Paris: Editions de Minuit, 1958.

Galland, D. *L'espérance trahie. Chronique d'un homme du commun.* Paris: Le Centurion, 1979.

Hauchecorne, Fr. (pseud. B. Vollet), "Guerre psychologique en Algérie." *Réforme*, 26 July 1958.

Jeanson, C. and Fr. *L'Algérie hors-la-loi*. Paris: Editions du Seuil, 1955.

Julien, Ch.-A. *L'Afrique du Nord en marche. Nationalisme musulman et souveraineté française*. Paris: Julliard, 1972.

_____. *Une pensée anticoloniale. Positions, 1914-1979*. Paris: Sindbad, 1979.

Philip, A. *Le socialisme trahi*. Paris: Plon, 1957.

Rocard, M. *Le coeur à l'ouvrage*. Paris: Odile Jacob, 1987.

_____. "Le drame algérien. Rapport presenté par Henri Frenay (pseud. Rocard) au nom de la VIe Section de la Fédération S.F.I.O. de la Seine, mai 1957."

_____. "Sur l'évolution de la situation foncière en Algérie, avril 1959." Report of Michel Rocard to the *Inspection des Finances*. *Arch. Ministère des Finances*.

Schmidt, E. *En ces temps de malheur. J'étais pasteur en Algérie, 1958-1962*. Paris: Editions du Cerf, 1976.

Servan-Schreiber, J.-J. *Lieutenant en Algérie*. Paris: Plon, 1956.

Soustelle, J. *Algérie. Le chemin de la paix*. Paris: Centre d'information sur les problèmes de l'Algérie et du Sahara, 1960.

_____. *Après l'échec du sommet: l'Algérie et l'Ouest*. Paris: Imprimerie moderne de la Presse, 1960.

_____. *Le drame algérien et la décadence française. Réponse à Raymond Aron*. Paris: Plon, 1957.

_____. *L'espérance trahie, 1958-1961*. Paris: Editions de l'Alma, 1962.

_____. *Lettre ouverte aux victimes de la décolonisation*. Paris: Albin Michel, 1973.

_____. *Vingt-huit ans de gaullisme*. Paris: La Table Ronde, 1968.

Tillion, G. *L'Afrique bascule vers l'avenir. L'Algérie en 1957 et autres textes*. Paris: Editions de Minuit, 1960.

Tricot, B. *Les sentiers de la paix. Algérie 1958-1962*. Paris, Plon, 1972.

_____. *Mémoires*. Paris: Quai Voltaire, 1994.

Conversations with the following, all of whom were active participants in the Algerian drama, were an integral part of my research:

Pastor Jacques Beaumont; Jean Carbonare; Professor Maurice Causse;

Pastor Pierre Cochet; Mireille Desrez; Pastor Jacques Maury; Pastor Tania Metzel; Professor Bernard Picinbono; Professor Bernard Roussel; Eric Westphal.

Secondary Sources

Ageron, Ch.-R. *Histoire de l'Algérie contemporaine*. Vol. II: *De l'insurrection de 1871 au déclenchement de la guerre de libération*. Paris: Presses Universitaires de France, 1979.

Andréani, J.-L. *Le mystère Rocard*. Paris: Robert Laffont, 1993.

Auvray, M. *Objecteurs, insoumis, déserteurs. Histoire des réfractaires en France*. Paris: Stock 2, 1983.

Baubérot, J. *Le retour des huguenots. La vitalité protestante XIXe-XX siècle*. Paris and Geneva: Cerf and Labor et Fides, 1985.

Bolle, P. "Le protestantisme français et la guerre d'Algérie," in F. Bédarida and E. Fouilloux, *La guerre d'Algérie et les chrétiens*. Paris: Institut d'Histoire du Temps Présent, 1988, pp. 117-50.

Chenu, R. *Paul Delouvrier ou la passion d'agir*. Paris: Seuil, 1994.

Clark, M. K. *Algiers in Turmoil. A History of the Rebellion*. New York: Prager, 1959.

Courrière, Y. *La guerre d'Algérie*. 2 vols. Paris: Robert Laffont, 1990.

Droz, B. and E. Lever. *Histoire de la guerre d'Algérie, 1954-1962*. Paris: Seuil, 1982.

Encrevé, A. *Le protestantisme en France de 1800 à nos jours*. Paris: Stock, 1985.

Evans, M. *The Memory of Resistance: French Opposition to the Algerian War*. New York: Berg, 1997.

Etienne, B. *Les Européens d'Algérie et l'indépendance algérienne*. Paris: C.N.R.S., 1968.

Gevereau, L., J.-P. Rioux and B. Stora. *La France en guerre d'Algérie*. Paris: Bibliothèque de documentation internationale contemporaine, 1992.

Gordon, D. C. *The Passing of French Algeria*. London: Oxford University Press, 1966.

Hamon, H. and P. Rotman. *Les porteurs de valises. La résistance française à la guerre d'Algérie*. Paris: Albin Michel, 1979.

Heggoy, A. A. *Insurgency and Counterinsurgency in Algeria*. Bloomington: Indiana University Press, 1972.

Jacques, A. *Madeleine Barot*. Paris: Cerf, 1989.

Julien, Ch.-A. *Histoire de l'Algérie contemporaine*. Vol. I: *La conquête et les débuts de la colonisation, 1827-1871*. Paris: Presses Universitaires de France, 1964.

Kneubuhler, P. *Henri Roser, L'enjeu d'une terre nouvelle*. Paris: Les Bergers et les Mages, 1992.

Lacouture, J. *1962. La mémoire du siècle. Algérie, la guerre est finie*. Paris: Editions complexe, 1985.

Le Goyet, P. *La guerre d'Algérie*. Paris: Perrin, 1969.

Le Sueur, J.D. "French Intellectuals and the Algerian War." Doctoral dissertation, University of Chicago, 1996.

Maquin, E. *Le parti Socialiste et la guerre d'Algérie, 1954-1958*. Paris: L'Harmattan, 1990.

Mehl, R. *Le pasteur Marc Boegner, 1881-1979. Une humble grandeur*. Paris: Plon, 1987.

Méliani, Abd-el-Aziz. *La France honteuse. Le drame des harkis*. Paris: Perrin, 1993.

Miquel, P. *La guerre d'Algérie*. Paris: Fayard, 1972.

Morin, G. "De l'opposition Socialiste à la guerre d'Algérie au Parti Socialiste autonome, 1954-1960. Un courant Socialiste de la SFIO au PSU" Unpublished doctoral thesis, Université de Paris I (Sorbonne), 1990-1991.

Nora, P. *Les Français d'Algérie*. Paris: Julliard, 1961.

Nouvel, C. "La présence protestante en Algérie au temps de la colonisation française." Typed M.A. thesis, Université d'Aix-Marseille, 1984-1985.

Nozière, A. *Algérie: Les chrétiens dans la guerre*. Paris: Editions Cana, 1979.

Philip, L. (ed.). *Politiques et chrétiens. André Philip*. Paris: Beauchesne, 1988.

Prochaska, D. *Making Algeria French. Colonialism in Bône, 1870-1920*. Cambridge, Mass.: Cambridge University Press, 1990.

Rioux, J.-P. *La guerre d'Algérie et les Français*. Paris: Fayard, 1990.

Rioux, J.-P. and J.-F. Sirinelli (eds.). *La guerre d'Algérie et les intellectuels français*. Paris: Editions complexe, 1991.

Rotman, P. *La guerre sans nom: Les appelés d'Algérie, 1954-1962*. Paris: Seuil, 1992.

Stora, B. *La gangrène de l'oubli: la mémoire de la guerre d'Algérie*. Paris: Editions La Découverte, 1991.

Talbott, J. E. *The War without a Name: France in Algeria, 1954-1962.*
New York: Knopf, 1980.
Vidal-Naquet, P. *L'Affaire Audin, 1957-1978.* Paris: Editions de Minuit,
1989.
Zorn, J.-Fr. *Le grand siècle d'une mission protestante. La Mission de
Paris de 1822 à 1914.* Paris: Les Bergers et les Mages, 1993.

INDEX

Series Published by Wilfrid Laurier University Press for the Canadian Corporation for Studies in Religion / Corporation Canadienne des Sciences Religieuses

Editions SR

1. *La langue de Ya'udi : description et classement de l'ancien parler de Zencircli dans le cadre des langues sémitiques du nord-ouest*
   Paul-Eugène Dion, O.P.
   1974 / viii + 511 p. / OUT OF PRINT
2. *The Conception of Punishment in Early Indian Literature*
   Terence P. Day
   1982 / iv + 328 pp.
3. *Traditions in Contact and Change: Selected Proceedings of the XIVth Congress of the International Association for the History of Religions*
   Edited by Peter Slater and Donald Wiebe with Maurice Boutin and Harold Coward
   1983 / x + 758 pp. / OUT OF PRINT
4. *Le messianisme de Louis Riel*
   Gilles Martel
   1984 / xviii + 483 p.
5. *Mythologies and Philosophies of Salvation in the Theistic Traditions of India*
   Klaus K. Klostermaier
   1984 / xvi + 549 pp. / OUT OF PRINT
6. *Averroes' Doctrine of Immortality: A Matter of Controversy*
   Ovey N. Mohammed
   1984 / vi + 202 pp. / OUT OF PRINT
7. *L'étude des religions dans les écoles : l'expérience américaine, anglaise et canadienne*
   Fernand Ouellet
   1985 / xvi + 666 p.
8. *Of God and Maxim Guns: Presbyterianism in Nigeria, 1846-1966*
   Geoffrey Johnston
   1988 / iv + 322 pp.
9. *A Victorian Missionary and Canadian Indian Policy: Cultural Synthesis vs Cultural Replacement*
   David A. Nock
   1988 / x + 194 pp. / OUT OF PRINT
10. *Prometheus Rebound: The Irony of Atheism*
    Joseph C. McLelland
    1988 / xvi + 366 pp.
11. *Competition in Religious Life*
    Jay Newman
    1989 / viii + 237 pp.
12. *The Huguenots and French Opinion, 1685-1787: The Enlightenment Debate on Toleration*
    Geoffrey Adams
    1991 / xiv + 335 pp.
13. *Religion in History: The Word, the Idea, the Reality / La religion dans l'histoire : le mot, l'idée, la réalité*
    Edited by/Sous la direction de Michel Despland and/et Gérard Vallée
    1992 / x + 252 pp.
14. *Sharing Without Reckoning: Imperfect Right and the Norms of Reciprocity*
    Millard Schumaker
    1992 / xiv + 112 pp.
15. *Love and the Soul: Psychological Interpretations of the Eros and Psyche Myth*
    James Gollnick
    1992 / viii + 174 pp.

Comparative Ethics Series / Collection d'Éthique Comparée

Dissertations SR

Studies in Christianity and Judaism / Études sur le christianisme et le judaïsme

3. *Society, the Sacred, and Scripture in Ancient Judaism: A Sociology of Knowledge*
Jack N. Lightstone
1988 / xiv + 126 pp.
4. *Law in Religious Communities in the Roman Period: The Debate Over*
Torah *and* **Nomos** *in Post-Biblical Judaism and Early Christianity*
Peter Richardson and Stephen Westerholm with A. I. Baumgarten,
Michael Pettem and Cecilia Wassén
1991 / x + 164 pp.
5. *Dangerous Food: 1 Corinthians 8-10 in Its Context*
Peter D. Gooch
1993 / xviii + 178 pp.
6. *The Rhetoric of the Babylonian Talmud, Its Social Meaning and Context*
Jack N. Lightstone
1994 / xiv + 317 pp.
7. *Whose Historical Jesus?*
Edited by William E. Arnal and Michel Desjardins
1997 / vi + 337 pp.

The Study of Religion in Canada /
Sciences Religieuses au Canada

1. *Religious Studies in Alberta: A State-of-the-Art Review*
Ronald W. Neufeldt
1983 / xiv + 145 pp.
2. *Les sciences religieuses au Québec depuis 1972*
Louis Rousseau et Michel Despland
1988 / 158 p.
3. *Religious Studies in Ontario: A State-of-the-Art Review*
Harold Remus, William Closson James and Daniel Fraikin
1992 / xviii + 422 pp.
4. *Religious Studies in Manitoba and Saskatchewan: A State-of-the-Art Review*
John M. Badertscher, Gordon Harland and Roland E. Miller
1993 / vi + 166 pp.
5. *The Study of Religion in British Columbia: A State-of-the-Art Review*
Brian J. Fraser
1995 / x + 127 pp.

Studies in Women and Religion /
Études sur les femmes et la religion

1. *Femmes et religions**
Sous la direction de Denise Veillette
1995 / xviii + 466 p.
* Only available from Les Presses de l'Université Laval
2. *The Work of Their Hands: Mennonite Women's Societies in Canada*
Gloria Neufeld Redekop
1996 / xvi + 172 pp.
3. *Profiles of Anabaptist Women: Sixteenth-Century Reforming Pioneers*
Edited by C. Arnold Snyder and Linda A. Huebert Hecht
1996 / xxii + 438 pp.
4. *Voices and Echoes: Canadian Women's Spirituality*
Edited by Jo-Anne Elder and Colin O'Connell
1997 / xxviii + 237 pp.

SR Supplements

1. *Footnotes to a Theology: The Karl Barth Colloquium of 1972*
Edited and Introduced by Martin Rumscheidt
1974 / viii + 151 pp. / OUT OF PRINT
2. *Martin Heidegger's Philosophy of Religion*
John R. Williams
1977 / x + 190 pp. / OUT OF PRINT

Available from:

WILFRID LAURIER UNIVERSITY PRESS

Waterloo, Ontario, Canada   N2L 3C5